# Somaliland

## with Addis Ababa & Eastern Ethiopia

## Philip Briggs

*With a foreword by Simon Reeve*

**edition**
**1**

www.bradtguides.com

Bradt Travel Guides Ltd, UK
The Globe Pequot Press Inc, USA

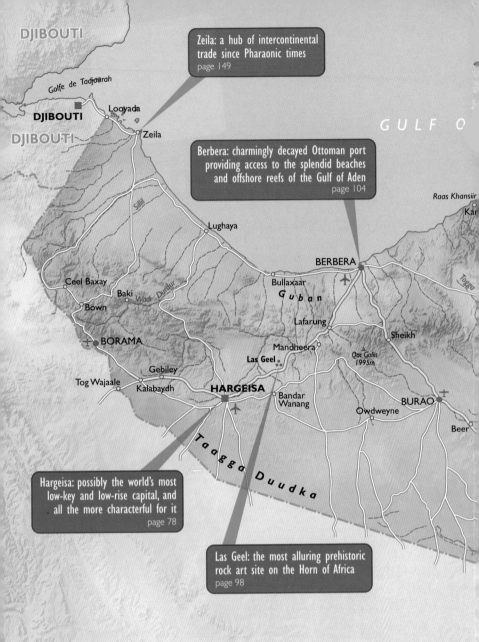

DJIBOUTI

Golfe de Tadjourah

DJIBOUTI

Looyada

DJIBOUTI

Zeila

**Zeila: a hub of intercontinental trade since Pharaonic times**
page 149

GULF O

**Berbera: charmingly decayed Ottoman port providing access to the splendid beaches and offshore reefs of the Gulf of Aden**
page 104

Raas Khansiir

Kar

Silīl

Lughaya

BERBERA

Togga

Bullaxaar

*G u b a n*

Ceel Baxay

Baki

*Wadi Durdur*

Bown

Lafarung

Sheikh

BORAMA

Mandheera

Las Geel

*Qar Goliis*
1995m

Gebiley

HARGEISA

Tog Wajaale

Kalabaydh

Bandar
Wanang

Owdweyne

BURAO

Beer

*T a a g g a*

*D u u d k a*

**Hargeisa: possibly the world's most low-key and low-rise capital, and all the more characterful for it**
page 78

**Las Geel: the most alluring prehistoric rock art site on the Horn of Africa**
page 98

ETHIOPIA

**KEY**

| | |
|---|---|
| Capital | ■ |
| Town | ● |
| Village | ○ |
| Airport/airstrip | ✈ |
| Major historical site | ⸪ |
| Mountain peak | ▲ |
| Main road | |
| Secondary road | |
| Seasonal river | – – – |

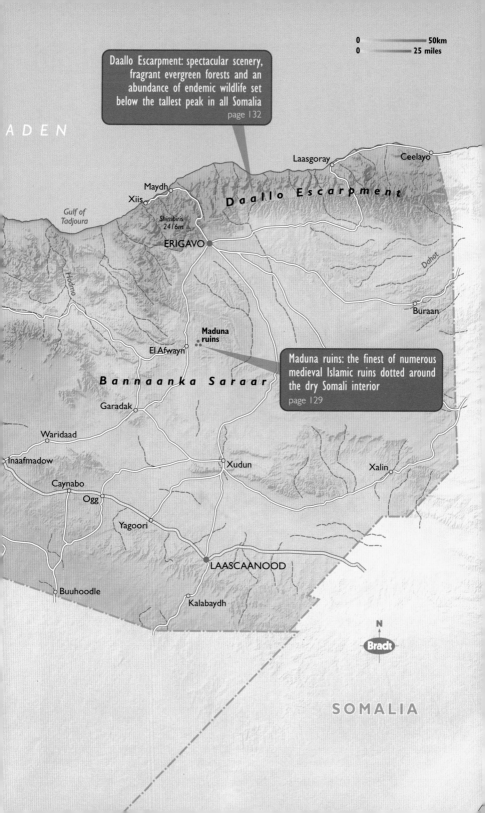

Daallo Escarpment: spectacular scenery, fragrant evergreen forests and an abundance of endemic wildlife set below the tallest peak in all Somalia
page 132

Maduna ruins: the finest of numerous medieval Islamic ruins dotted around the dry Somali interior
page 129

ADEN

Gulf of Tadjoura

Laasgoray

Ceelayo

Maydh

Xiis

Daallo Escarpment

Shimbiris 2416m

ERIGAVO

Dahot

Hodmo

Buraan

Maduna ruins

El Afwayn

Bannaanka Saraar

Garadak

Waridaad

Inaafmadow

Xudun

Xalin

Caynabo

Ogg

Yagoori

LAASCAANOOD

Buuhoodle

Kalabaydh

N

Bradt

SOMALIA

0      50km
0      25 miles

# Somaliland
# Don't
# miss...

### Berbera old Ottoman city
Mosques and Ottoman architectural relicts line the old town streets of this ancient maritime centre
(AVZ) page 104

### Hargeisa Camel Market
Teeming with camels, goats and 'fat-tailed' sheep, Hargeisa's bustling Camel Market is a must-see in Somaliland's capital
(AVZ) page 95

**Las Geel rock art**
Estimated to be at least 5,000 years old, the superb rock art at Las Geel ranks among the oldest and best preserved of its type anywhere in Africa (AVZ) page 98

**Daallo Forest and Escarpment**
Somaliland's foremost natural attraction contains over 200 endemic plant species and the densest fauna of the Somali region (AVZ) page 132

**Beaches and reefs of the Gulf of Aden**
Whale sharks, dolphins and loggerhead turtles roam the wildlife-rich coral reefs of the Gulf of Aden (AVZ) page 44

*above*   Donkey carts jostle for road space on the dusty Hargeisa streets (AVZ) page 78

*left*    The Hargeisa Civil War Memorial, displaying an MiG fighter jet which crashed during an aerial bombardment of the town (AVZ) page 92

*below*   Overwhelmingly friendly and practically free of crime, Hargeisa feels more like an extension of the surrounding countryside than a proper urban conglomeration (AVZ) page 78

*above*    The small mountainside settlement of Maydh has been an active trade port for over 1,000 years (AVZ) page 132

*right*    Somali culture is strongly informed by Islam, which first arrived at coastal ports in the 7th century AD. Here, a mosque in central Burao (AVZ) page 119

*below*    Lying opposite Yemen on the Gulf of Aden, Berbera is Somaliland's main commercial seaport (JF/A/SS) page 104

above left    Tragically defaced in 2011, Dhagax Khoure remains an exceptional rock art site, comprising hundreds of individual bovid and human figures spread across six different panels (AVZ) page 141

above right    Borama is surrounded by numerous places of archaeological interest, including ruined stone cities, rock art sites and ancient graveyards (the latter pictured here) (AVZ) page 144

below    An old Ottoman fortification overlooks the ancient waterworks at the Dubar Springs (AVZ) page 104

# AUTHOR

**Philip Briggs** (e *philari@hixnet.co.za*) has been exploring the highways, byways and backwaters of Africa since 1986, when he spent several months backpacking on a shoestring from Nairobi to Cape Town. In 1991, he wrote the Bradt *Guide to South Africa*, the first such guidebook to be published internationally after the release of Nelson Mandela. Throughout the 1990s, Philip wrote a series of pioneering Bradt Guides to destinations that were then – and in some cases still are – otherwise practically uncharted by the travel publishing industry. These included the first dedicated guidebooks to Tanzania, Uganda, Ethiopia, Malawi, Mozambique, Ghana and Rwanda (co-authored with Janice Booth), all of which are now several editions old. Philip has visited more than two-dozen African countries in total and written about most of them for specialist travel and wildlife magazines including *Africa Birds & Birding*, *Africa Geographic*, *BBC Wildlife*, *Travel Africa* and *Wanderlust*. He still spends at least four months on the road every year, usually accompanied by his wife, travel photographer Ariadne Van Zandbergen, and spends the rest of his time battering away at a keyboard in the sleepy village of Bergville, in the uKhahlamba-Drakensberg region of South Africa.

## AUTHOR'S STORY

This guidebook has been a long while in gestation. Bradt first suggested the possibility to me five or six years ago, at which point I declined (a good call, as it transpired, since another author was commissioned to do it, but they struck too many bureaucratic obstacles to complete the research). Ever since, despite that setback, Somaliland has cropped up sporadically on our 'what's next' discussions, with both parties blowing hot and cold about the sales potential of a guidebook to a seldom-visited country that isn't merely unrecognised outside its own borders, but is also unfortunate enough to be legally part of war-torn Somalia.

Nevertheless, over those years of vacillation, I grew increasingly intrigued at the prospect of exploring this little-known breakaway state, and visiting the mysterious likes of Las Geel, Berbera and Daallo to see them for myself. When Bradt seriously revisited the idea of a Somaliland guidebook in 2010, I decided that if a first guidebook to this intriguing but unrecognised country was to be published, commercially viable or not, I wasn't going to pass up the opportunity to write it.

A year later, having visited Somaliland and written the guidebook, I'm truly glad I went for it. It's not that I harbour the delusion I've stumbled on the next big travel thing – hell no, it's *way* too unpolished and unpredictable for that – but that I had the opportunity to explore and document a country uncompromised by any semblance of a tourist industry. Somaliland – much like Uganda in the late 1980s, or Ethiopia in the early 1990s – is memorable not so much for any individual sightseeing opportunities, but for its capacity, by turns rewarding and frustrating, to make visitors experience it entirely on its own terms.

**PUBLISHER'S FOREWORD**    *Adrian Phillips, Publishing Director*

Rarely has a guidebook been so long in gestation – we've been discussing publishing a guide to Somaliland for nearly ten years! Simon Reeve must claim some credit for finally encouraging us to take the plunge. He regularly extolled its virtues to Hilary Bradt and me when our paths crossed at various travel fairs, and he's kindly provided a foreword to the book. And Philip Briggs is also now a Somaliland fan. The country is unlikely to become a tourist hotspot any time soon – and it has very few facilities – but it is peaceful and democratic. In short, even though the international community doesn't recognise its independence, Somaliland is not Somalia!

First published March 2012
Bradt Travel Guides Ltd
IDC House, The Vale, Chalfont St Peter, Bucks SL9 9RZ, England
www.bradtguides.com
Published in the USA by The Globe Pequot Press Inc,
PO Box 480, Guilford, Connecticut 06437-0480

Text copyright © 2012 Philip Briggs
Maps copyright © 2012 Bradt Travel Guides Ltd
Photographs copyright © 2012 Individual photographers
Project Manager: Elspeth Beidas

ISBN: 978 1 84162 371 9

British Library Cataloguing in Publication Data
A catalogue record for this book is available from the British Library

**Photographs**
Eric Lafforgue (EL), Jason Florio/Aurora/SpecialistStock (JF/A/SS), Ariadne Van Zandbergen (AVZ)
*Front cover* Camels in the desert in the Sanaag region (AVZ)
*Back cover* Somali girl in colourful dress (EL), Old Ottoman mosque, Berbera (AVZ)
*Title page* Somali girl in school uniform (AVZ), Rock art at Las Geel (AVZ), Northern red-billed hornbill (EL)
**Maps** David McCutcheon

Typeset from the author's disc by D&N Publishing, Wiltshire
Production managed by Jellyfish Print Solutions; printed in India

# Foreword By Simon Reeve (www.simonreeve.co.uk)

The Somaliland Minister for Tourism was delighted he finally had a rare foreign visitor he could take to see his country's national treasures.

'Don't worry!' said the enthusiastic government minister, as I reluctantly agreed to accompany him to some rock etchings discovered at Las Geel outside Hargeisa, the capital of Somaliland. 'The drawings are beautiful, and it will just be a small detour from the road!'

As we bumped along potholed dirt tracks through the parched African bush I started to think my scepticism was justified. But we crested a hill, dodged wiry bushes on a wide plain, and scrambled over vast boulders to find exquisite rock paintings dating back thousands of years. Even under the scorching sun, the paintings had strong, vibrant colours and stark outlines, showing the ancient inhabitants of the area worshipping cattle and venerating a pregnant cow. In a low cave further up the hill I found human figures dancing along the rock.

Las Geel is probably the most significant Neolithic rock-painting site in the whole of Africa, and for a brief moment I felt like an explorer finding hidden treasures, at a time when the entire world seems easy to reach on package holidays.

But there are still areas of the world off the beaten track that can excite and amaze. Somaliland is not on many tourist maps. In fact, it is not on any maps at all. According to the international community, Somaliland does not even exist.

Although there are almost 200 official countries in the world there are also dozens more unrecognised states like Somaliland which are determined to be separate and independent. These countries are home to millions of people, they have their own rulers, armies, police forces, and issue passports and even postage stamps, but they are not officially recognised as proper countries by the rest of the world.

Unlike neighbouring Somalia, which is still dogged by fighting and anarchy, Somaliland has a government, police, democracy and traffic lights, but no recognition, making it extremely difficult for Somaliland to attract aid, investment, or tourists.

Anyone brave enough to visit receives a humbling lesson in survival and self-determination. When I was last there, Hargeisa, where 50,000 died during the civil war with Somalia, bustled with activity and construction. A Somali MiG jet that bombed the city sits atop a poignant war memorial.

Outside Hargeisa there are ancient rock paintings and stunning journeys into the mountains and up to the port of Berbera, home to a runway once hired by NASA as an emergency landing strip for the space shuttle. Tracks run along the coast west from Berbera towards Djibouti, and there are mangroves, gorgeous islands and a coral reef. But Somaliland's main attraction is its determined and inspirational people. Largely ignored by the world, they are building a state from scratch and seem determined to keep their independence.

Perhaps one day Somaliland will have its own seat at the United Nations, and tourists will flock to its stunning beaches to swim at the mouth of the Red Sea. It is nothing less than Somalilanders deserve.

*Simon Reeve is a journalist who has been travelling around little-known regions of the world for a series of BBC television documentaries, including* Places That Don't Exist.

# Major Contributors

**Sean Connolly** taught English at the University of Hargeisa from autumn 2010 to spring 2011. When he's not discussing verb tenses, diplomatic recognition, or the merits of camel meat, you may find him riding in the back of a grain truck, sampling questionable local delicacies, or seeking out a country's funkiest records. Unusual destinations, specifically in Africa, have always absorbed Sean, and he hopes to bring life in these overlooked outposts just a little bit closer to home. Raised in Chicago and educated in New York, Sean is a full-time culture fiend (read: anthropology graduate) and stays on the move whenever possible (*www.sdc773.com*).

**Callan Cohen and Michael Mills**, who supplied supplementary details for many of the birding accounts in this guide, spend much of their year travelling across Africa in search of birds, and between them have written a number of books and scientific papers on birds and birding across the continent. From their base in Cape Town, they lead scheduled and customised birding tours to Somaliland, Ethiopia and elsewhere in Africa with Birding Africa (*www.birdingafrica.com*).

# Acknowledgements

My gratitude goes out to the following: Abdi Abdi, of the Oriental Hotel in Hargeisa, without whose support and encouragement this book might well not exist; Abdi Jama, whose input to several natural history sections, both before and after we travelled, was invaluable; Sada Mire, and her colleagues at the Department of Tourism & Archaeology, for heaps of useful advice about sites worth checking out; Callan Cohen and Michael Mills, of Birding Africa, for details of several birding sites around the country; Nik Borrow, of Birdquest, for allowing me access to his report of a 2010 birding tour to Somaliland; Mark Vanhalle, who we crossed paths with in Hargeisa, for generously forwarding me his detailed trip report from Zeila; Sean Connolly, for allowing me to cobble some of his excellent posts on www.somaliwhat.com for use in this guidebook; Michael Arkus, for forwarding me his trip report for Erigavo and Daallo as preparation for our own trip to the area; Katie Fahrland and Aubin Dupree for their feedback and input on several aspects of travel in Hargeisa; Josephine Heger, for providing the basis of the book's vocabulary section; Teresa Krug, a former Somaliland resident, for advice and feedback in the planning stages; Kim Wildman and Frank Rispin, updaters of the pending sixth edition of *Ethiopia: The Bradt Guide*, for last-minute checking of the relevant text and maps in the Ethiopia chapter; Ariadne Van Zandbergen, my wife and photographic collaborator, without whom a tough trip would have been a lot tougher; not least, Adrian Phillips and Hilary Bradt, for their persistence in getting me to write this book, and Elspeth Beidas for project managing it to fruition.

# Contents

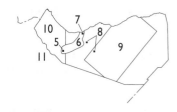

## NOTE ABOUT MAPS

Several maps use grid lines to allow easy location of sites. Map grid references are listed in square brackets after listings in the text, with page number followed by grid number, eg: [83 C3].

## LIST OF MAPS

# Introduction

Twenty years ago, on 18 May 1991, the Republic of Somaliland, practically unnoticed by the rest of the world, announced its secession from the rest of Somalia. In doing so, this former British protectorate, whose borders date back to the 1880s Berlin Conference, terminated a union it had entered into voluntarily as a newly independent state only three decades earlier, when it merged with its southern counterpart, a former Italian possession, to form the Somali Republic. This unilateral declaration of independence was neither frivolous nor premature. It was triggered by the January 1991 overthrow of President Mohamed Siad Barre, the Mogadishu-based military dictator who oversaw Somalia's gradual deterioration from crumbling democracy, to oppressive totalitarian state, to civil war, to – well, something not far short of anarchy. It followed a period of persecution that culminated three years earlier with the Mogadishu regime's bombardment of the former and future Somaliland capital Hargeisa, killing thousands of civilians and forcing the majority of survivors into exile.

The post-secession fortunes of the two parts of the Somali Republic are a study in contrasts. For the past 20 years, Somalia has been locked in an irresolvable civil conflict of almost unfathomable complexity – one that has claimed the lives of at least 300,000 civilians. Whereas Somaliland, despite a few early hiccups, has emerged as something approaching a beacon of peace, democracy, good governance, non-sectarianism and plain old common sense, in a corner of Africa where such qualities are often in short supply.

And yet, on 18 May 2011, when Somaliland celebrated its 20th anniversary of independence, it did so alone and unrecognised by the outside world.

It's true. Regardless of all it has achieved, and despite its compelling legal case for recognition (see box, *International recognition*, page 24), Somaliland is still treated as a mischievous breakaway state by the international community. Its sovereignty is recognised by neither the United Nations nor the African Union, by neither the IMF nor the World Bank, not by the Olympic Committee or by FIFA, not even by its former 'protector' Britain. To add insult to injury, it has the misfortune to remain legally bound to Somalia, a country widely regarded as the most dangerous and ungovernable in the world.

So, lest there be any confusion, this is not a guidebook to Somalia but to Somaliland – as far as we are concerned, a reasonably peaceful, self-governing territory whose relationship to Somalia is comparable to that of, say, Eritrea to Ethiopia, or the newly independent South Sudan to its northern namesake.

And what a unique, strange and intriguing place Somaliland is. Set along the northern shores of the Horn of Africa, lapped by the warm turquoise waters of the Gulf of Aden, its timeworn ports evoke an obscure history of maritime trade stretching back to Pharaonic times. Inland of this, the vast empty badlands of the Somali interior – populated as they are by a thin scattering of desert nomads, domestic camels and wild antelope – are studded with medieval Islamic ruins and shrines, mysterious stone tumuli dating to earlier times, and ancient rock art painted by one of the world's earliest cattle-herding societies.

It is one such site, the wondrous Las Geel, only an hour's drive north of the capital Hargeisa, that forms Somaliland's touristic *pièce de résistance*, with its richly multi-coloured panels depicting the pastoralist lifestyle of artists who trod these desert sands some 5,000 to 10,000 years ago. Other top attractions include the port of Berbera, with its characterful old town and superb offshore reefs, and the more remote and unexpectedly chilly Daallo Escarpment, where glades of aromatic junipers, otherworldly dragon's blood succulents, and frankincense-bearing *Boswellia* trees overlook a shimmering shoreline 2,000m below.

Make no mistake, Somaliland is not, as yet, a functional tourist destination in the normal sense of the word. Facilities fall somewhere between low key and non-existent, several main attractions are difficult to reach affordably, and assurances about safety are placed in perspective by the official (though, admittedly, often circumventable) requirement that all foreign travellers exploring outside the capital must be accompanied by a police guard. Then again, for open-minded and flexible travellers who are prepared to approach it with a spirit of adventure, Somaliland still offers the sort of unprescribed and unpredictable travel experience one might expect of a breakaway state that, at the time of writing, is not officially recognised outside its own borders.

## SOMALILAND UPDATES

Travel conditions tend to change quickly in Somaliland, and reliable printed and online resources are few and far between, for which reason the publication of this pioneering guidebook book will be accompanied by the simultaneous launch of an interactive website: http://updates.bradtguides.com/somaliland.

Administered by the author, Philip Briggs, the update website will supplement the printed Bradt guidebook, providing a forum whereby the latest travel news and views garnered from reader feedback can be disseminated online with immediate effect.

The update website is a free service for readers of Bradt's *Somaliland* – and for anybody else who cares to drop by and browse – but its success will depend greatly on the input of those selfsame readers, whose collective experience of Somaliland's tourist attractions and facilities will always be more broad, divergent (and, as time progresses, up to date) than those of any individual author.

So, if you have any comments, queries, grumbles, insights, news or other feedback, you're invited to post them directly on the website, or to email them to Philip at e philari@hixnet.co.za. Alternatively you can add a review of the book to www.bradtguides.com or Amazon.

# Part One

## GENERAL INFORMATION

**Location** The Republic of Somaliland comprises the most northwesterly part of Somalia. It extends for roughly 400km from west to east along the southern coast of the Gulf of Aden, and is nowhere more than about 150km long from north to south. It lies between latitudes 8° and 11°N and longitudes 43° and 49°E.

**Neighbouring countries** Djibouti to the west, Ethiopia to the southwest, and the autonomous but unrecognised Puntland State of Somalia to the east. Somaliland is still legally part of Somalia, which is bordered by Kenya to the southwest.

**Area** Approximately 137,600km$^2$. It is a rather small country by east African standards, comparable in area to Greece, Malawi, Bangladesh or the state of Arkansas.

**Climate** Most of the country is low lying, dry and hot, especially in summer when coastal temperatures soar to above 40°C.

**Status** Unrecognised constitutional presidential republic since 18 May 1991.

**President** Ahmed Mohamed Silanyo

**Vice-president** Abdirahman Saylici

**Population** 3–4 million (2011 estimate)

**Life expectancy** 50 (Somalia)

**Capital** Hargeisa

**Other main towns** Burao, Borama, Berbera, Erigavo

**Economy** Predominantly subsistence agriculture and pastoralism, as well as import and trade between the port of Berbera and neighbouring Ethiopia.

**GDP** US$600 per capita (Somalia)

**Languages** The official language of Somali is almost universally spoken. Arabic and English both have a semi-official status, with the former being a mandatory school subject, while the latter is often spoken to a very high standard by returned exiles.

**Religion** As good as 100% Islamic

**Currency** Somaliland shilling (Ssh). The US dollar can be used for almost all transactions. The Somali shilling (official currency of Somalia) is widely accepted in the east.

**Exchange rates** US$1 = Ssh 6,000

**National airline** none

**International telephone code** +252

**Time** GMT +3

**Electrical voltage** 220V, 50Hz

**Weights and measures** Metric

**Flag** Three horizontal bands: from top, green, white and red. There is a black star in the middle of the central white band.

**Public holidays** Somaliland has four fixed-date secular and four moveable Islamic public holidays (see page 61). Note the weekend is effectively Thursday and Friday.

# Background Information

## HISTORY

The history of Somaliland is patchily – and in some cases poorly – documented, and by comparison to the rest of eastern Africa the region has been somewhat neglected by archaeologists and other researchers. Paradoxically, however, it is a country of great historical interest, with coastal trade links to Ancient Egypt and the other great classical civilisations, and an interior scattered with intriguing rock art sites, mysterious cairns, and other monuments of a complex pastoral society that might date back 10,000 years. Over the pages that follow, we have outlined the ancient and more modern history of the Somali region in as much detail as possible within the constraints of a guidebook, drawing on a handful of intriguing ancient and medieval sources, which often pose more questions than they answer, as well as the few more modern histories that are in print. However, it is possible – indeed likely – that a few errors, omissions and misguided speculations have crept in, and we openly invite readers who notice anything of the sort to let us know and help improve the section for future editions.

**ANCIENT PREHISTORY** Little paleontological and archaeological research has been undertaken in post-independence Somalia, largely due to the ongoing political instability, for which reason its prehistory is poorly understood in comparison to other parts of Africa. Nevertheless, it can be assumed that hominines – the subfamily that comprises the entire human lineage since its divergence from chimpanzees about six million years ago – have inhabited the Somali region for practically as long as anywhere on earth. True, no significant hominine fossil has ever been unearthed in Somaliland, but equally true is that the world's most important known repository of early hominine fossils, the arid Afar region of the northern Ethiopian Rift Valley, lies only 500km from the Somali border.

The Afar region has yielded the world's oldest undisputed hominine remains, around 5.5 million years old and ascribed to the species *Ardipithecus kadabba*. In addition, several fossils of *A. ramidus*, a probable descendant of *A. kadabba* that lived at least 4.4 million years ago, have been located in the region. And it was also in Afar that the famous 3.2 million-year-old *Australopithecus afarensis* skeleton, named Lucy, was uncovered in 1972. In the late Miocene and early Pliocene era, when these ancient proto-humans lived, the lowland regions of the Horn of Africa were far moister and better wooded than they are today, and it seems more likely than not that any early hominine species that lived in Afar (which is particularly well suited to fossil recovery) would have ranged into similar habitats in what is now Somaliland.

Exactly when *Homo s. sapiens* – modern humans – first trod the sandy soils of Somaliland is an open question (as, for that matter, is the classification of and

3

relationship between the numerous *Homo* taxa that have lived within the past million years). However, a pair of human skulls uncovered alongside southern Ethiopia's Omo River in 1967, originally thought to be around 130,000 years old but re-dated as 195,000 years old in 2005, is now frequently cited as the oldest known fossil of anatomically modern humans, placing the Horn of Africa at centre stage not only of early hominine evolution, but also of more modern developments in the emergence of our species.

The oldest direct evidence of human habitation of Somaliland is Acheulean stone blades and flint tools discovered in the vicinity of Hargeisa and in caves along the Golis Escarpment. The sites where these tools were discovered have not, to the best of our knowledge, been subjected to modern dating techniques, but various sources place them at between 12,000 and 40,000 years old – relatively recent by comparison to similar finds in neighbouring countries. Almost nothing is known about these **Stone Age inhabitants** of Somaliland, beyond the fact that they were nomadic hunter-gatherers with few, if any, ethnic or linguistic links to the modern Somali people.

A more revealing relict of ancient human activity in Somaliland is a wealth of Neolithic rock art sites, preserved thanks to the dry climate. The most famous of these is Las Geel, 50km north of Hargeisa, but dozens of other rock painting and engraving sites are scattered around the country, and the likelihood is that others still await discovery. The paintings at Las Geel, and elsewhere in Somaliland, are placed in the so-called Ethiopian-Arabian school, examples of which occur at scattered localities across central Arabia and the Horn of Africa, as far west as Ethiopia's southern Rift Valley. Ethiopian-Arabian rock art has been divided into two different stages, with the later period widely represented in Somaliland, while the recently discovered Dhambalin site represents a rare example of the earlier period (otherwise restricted to southern Ethiopia). The age of these paintings remains conjectural, not least because the sensitive pigments cannot be tested without causing some damage, but the most recent panels are probably at least 5,000 years old and the oldest might be twice that age.

The Somali **rock art** includes many depictions of people and wild animals, but the dominant motif on most panels is stylised and often unnaturally colourful representations of domestic livestock. Most numerous by far are cattle, almost invariably painted in profile, showing only one front and one hind leg, with prominent udders, no necks or ears, and prominence given to the large arcing horns, which are depicted as if seen from above. Given their great antiquity, these paintings unambiguously demonstrate that Somaliland, like the rest of the Horn of Africa, supported one of the world's earliest pastoral (livestock-herding) societies, dating back some 6,000 to 9,000 years, several millennia before pastoralism was adopted in Europe or Asia. The art that adorns the rock shelters of Somaliland also appears to have a strong spiritual dimension, and – bearing in mind that any paintings made on a less durable or protected canvas would have vanished long ago – it probably represents a tiny surviving fragment relict of the region's sophisticated Neolithic artistic tradition.

## SOMALILAND AND THE LAND OF PUNT

A number of ancient Egyptian documents refer to a maritime trade with a distant country known as Punt or Ta Netjer ('Land of God'). The earliest such expedition took place c2480BC, during the 5th dynasty reign of Sahure, and other visits to Punt were recorded during the 6th, 11th and 12th dynasties. It seems all maritime trade fell victim to the general disarray that gripped Egypt c1775BC following the death of Queen Sobekneferu. But it was resumed under Queen Hatshepsut, who dispatched five ships to Punt c1525BC. Irregular trade continued for another four centuries, with one final large-scale expedition being dispatched during the reign of Rameses III, whose death in 1167BC initiated a long period of decline in Pharaonic Egypt. Subsequently, the memory of distant Punt was reduced, in the words of Egyptologist Joyce Tyldesley, to 'an unreal and fabulous land of myths and legends'.

The parochial nature of Egyptian trade records means they contain few clues as to the precise location of Punt. What is known for certain is that the Egyptian ships sailed to Punt via the Red Sea, then connected to the Nile by a navigable seasonal canal through the swampy Wadi Tumilat. Furthermore, seasonal factors – it would have been imperative to sail from Egypt to Punt between June and August, when the wind blew southwards, and to embark on the return leg in November – make it unlikely the relatively slow ships of the era sailed further afield than the eastern tip of the Horn of Africa. This places Punt somewhere along the Gulf of Aden and/or the Red Sea and, while minority academic opinion leans towards the Arabian shores of this oceanic divide, the greater consensus goes to the east coast of Africa. In other words, Punt most likely comprised some or all of the coastline of present-day Sudan, Eritrea, Djibouti, Somaliland and Puntland.

An African as opposed to Arabian location for Punt is strongly indicated by the selection of items traded with Egypt. This list includes gold, ebony and ivory, livestock, ostrich feathers and eggs, skins of wild animals such as giraffe and leopard, all of which originate in Africa, as well as a small number of Puntite slaves. To the Egyptians, however, the single most important trade item, still cultivated in Somaliland today, was aromatic resins such as frankincense and myrrh – indeed, in a failed attempt to initiate the domestic cultivation of these highly prized funerary items, 31 live myrrh trees were shipped home by the Hatshepsut expedition, and planted in the courtyard of the Deir el-Bahari, the queen's mortuary temple on the West Bank of Luxor.

A Somali location for Punt is supported by the remarkable set of reliefs that adorn the walls of Deir el-Bahari, the only such expedition records with something of a Puntite perspective. There is, for instance, a village scene that shows the natives of Punt living in stilted beehive huts, reachable by ladders, guarded by what appears to be a solitary dog, and set in a grove of date palms and myrrh trees where a long-tailed bird (consistent with the Nile Valley sunbird) is depicted in flight. Other scenes show typical African animals, such as giraffe, rhinoceros and baboon.

The most famous panels at Deir el-Bahari depict the ruler of Punt, named as Parehu, and his family. Parehu holds a staff in some pictures, and is dressed in a loincloth, with a small dagger in his belt, a decorative beaded collar around his neck, and an upward-curving beard suggestive of contemporary representations of the Egyptian gods and deceased Pharaohs. His wife Ati, dressed in a light skirt and adorned with bracelets, anklets and a beaded necklace, is strikingly obese, and her prominent buttocks have been the subject of considerable debate – some authorities cite their distended appearance as evidence that the queen was afflicted by elephantiasis, while others believe it reflects a Puntite ideal of feminine beauty that prevails in many traditional African societies to this day.

Egypt's maritime forays to Punt were probably too irregular to sustain organised trade outposts such as those evidently encountered by Hatshepsut's expedition (which took place after a 250-year lull in trade). In addition, not all of the items accumulated on these expeditions could be sourced along the Red Sea or the Gulf of Aden coastline. Gold, for instance, must have come from the African interior, while elephants, the sole source of ivory, are relatively uncommon along the arid coastal belt. Other exports, such as cinnamon bark, most likely came from Asia. It is clear from an Egyptian mural dating to the reign of Amenhotep that the people of Punt used dhow-like boats – propelled by a combination of triangular sails and oars – at least as early as the 15th century BC.

All of this points to the likelihood that the sporadic Egyptian forays to Punt form the only, and somewhat incidental, record of a substantial and well-organised (but otherwise undocumented) Afro-Arabian maritime trade that dates back at least 4,000 years. In all probability, this trade centred upon a string of ports along the coast of present-day Sudan, Eritrea and Somaliland, but it also extended deep into the African interior, to the Arabian shores of the Red Sea and Gulf of Aden – and possibly even further afield, to Madagascar and Asia.

**THE SABAEAN AND AXUMITE ERAS** The decline of maritime trade with Egypt evidently coincided with the rise to global importance of the Sabaean Kingdom, centred on the city of Ma'rib in the Saba'a region of present-day Yemen, on the southern Arabian Peninsula opposite Somaliland. The origin of the Sabaean Kingdom is obscure, but it was probably founded c1750BC. It became the dominant regional power, taking control of the overland spice trade routes to the Mediterranean and Asia, in Old Testament times (indeed, of the myriad speculations surrounding the identity of the Biblical Queen of Shaba, none is so plausible as the claim she was a Sabaean regent remembered locally by the name of Bilqis). Sabaean regional supremacy was cemented in the 9th century BC with the introduction of a written language (using south Arabian script, a variation on the ancient Phoenician prototype) and by the construction of a pioneering irrigation system that created 100km² of agricultural land around the Ma'rib Dam.

On the opposite side of the Red Sea, the 1st millennium BC witnessed the emergence of the Axumite Kingdom, encompassing what are now Eritrea, the Ethiopian province of Tigray and the northwest of Somaliland. The relationship between Axum and Saba'a is contentious: some historians regard the former to have been a Sabaean implant, founded and ruled over by settlers from southern Arabia, while others regard it to be an entirely African entity, rooted in an indigenous agricultural society which archaeological evidence dates back to 3,000BC. Either way, the Sabaean influences on Axumite culture range from the architecture of the 2,700-year-old Temple of Yeha (the oldest standing structure in Ethiopia) to the similarities between the Sabaean script and its Axumite counterpart Ge'ez, the progenitor of a unique script used in Ethiopia to this day.

Largely forgotten today, except by Ethiopians, the Axumite Kingdom was one of the most important and technologically advanced civilisations of its time, listed as one of the world's four great empires (along with Persia, China and Rome) by the 3rd century Persian writer Mani. The kingdom incorporated the Somali coast as far east as Berbera, and at its height it also extended inland to the Sudanese Nile and across the Red Sea to Yemen. The principal city Axum, still in existence today, boasts a wealth of ancient landmarks ranging from 2,500-year-old rock-hewn catacombs and ruined pre-Christian palaces to the spectacular field of sky-scraping stelae that overlook Ethiopia's oldest church, built in the 4th century BC after the Axumite king converted to Christianity. Axum's legendary wealth was based on a maritime trade network that extended from the principal port Adulis (in Eritrea, 50km south of Massawa), along with lesser ports such as Zeila and possibly Berbera, to the remote shores of the Mediterranean and Asia.

The 5th century BC writings of the Greek historian Herodotus contain one of the few ancient references to the people of the Horn of Africa. Herodotus refers to a race called the Macrobians, who lived to the south of Egypt, most likely in what is now Somali territory. The Macrobians, according to Herodotus, were known for their longevity, with elders frequently attaining an age of 120, which they attributed to their diet of meat and milk. They were also the 'tallest and handsomest of all men', the former an attribute that tallies with an extant oral tradition that the pre-Islamic cairns dotting Somaliland were constructed by a race of ancient giants.

The most detailed description of classical-era Somaliland is included in the *Periplus of the Erythraean Sea*, written CAD60 (see box, *Somaliland in the 1st Century*, page 8). The significance of this unique document is heightened by the absence of any other surviving description of the pre-Islamic Somali coast. Yet the Axumite Kingdom was very much in the ascendant at the time the *Periplus* was penned. A full 200 years would pass, for instance, before any of the great Axumite stelae were erected, or the first Axumite coins were minted. A century after that, King Ezana, the most powerful and influential of Axumite kings, converted to Christianity and made it the official religion of his realm. Another two centuries passed before the Alexandrian globetrotter Cosmos Indicopleustes, who visited Axum in AD525, found himself marvelling at the immense palace of King Kaleb, with its tame elephants and giraffes, and was on hand when the last of the great Axumite rulers amassed his troops at Adulis and crossed the Red Sea to win back Yemen from a Jewish usurper.

It can be assumed that most of the Somali ports described in the *Periplus* were still active in the 6th century, probably as part of the Axumite Kingdom, and that the 'Laurels of Acannae' were still producing the region's finest export-quality frankincense. But the dearth of historical records, and limited extent of archaeological excavation along the Somali coast, means we can only guess. What is clear, however, is that the Axumite Kingdom fell into decline shortly after the death of Kaleb's son and successor King Gebre Meskel, paving the way for the Islamic usurpation of its Red Sea trade routes in the early 7th century, and the increasing importance of the Swahili coast south of Mogadishu. By AD750, the once thriving port of Adulis was a ghost town and its inland cousin Axum had sunk into global obscurity. So it was, in the words of Gibbon, that the Ethiopians, 'encompassed on all sides by the enemies of their religion … slept near on a thousand years, forgetful of the world, by whom they were forgotten'.

**MEDIEVAL SOMALILAND** The 7th century AD witnessed two events pivotal to the formation of modern Somali culture. The first was the foundation of the **Islamic faith**, marked by the emigration of the Prophet Mohammed and his followers from Mecca to Medina in AD622, and its phenomenal expansion across the entire Arabian Peninsula over the subsequent decade. The other, more difficult to date with any precision, is the **migration** to the Somali Peninsula of the pastoral migrants whose Cushitic-speaking language evolved into the modern Somali tongue.

Arabic settlement in the ports of Somaliland, and elsewhere along the east African coast, certainly pre-dates the foundation of Islam. However, it appears to have gained impetus in the latter part of the 1st millennium AD, and with it came the spread of the Islamic religion, culture and architecture. The Masjid al-Qiblatayn in the Somali port of Zeila probably dates to the 7th century, indicating that the seeds of Islam were planted on the African side of the Gulf of Aden within decades of the prophet's lifetime. Further south, a ruined 9th-century mosque in the Lamu Archipelago demonstrates that Islam had by then reached present-day Kenya, and by the 10th century traders of Somali and Arab origin are known to have been active as far south as Sofala, near the Zambezi mouth in present-day Mozambique.

The *Periplus of the Erythraean Sea*, a partially first-hand Greek document that details trading opportunities along the Red Sea coast and further south, includes an unusually overt and detailed description of Somaliland cAD60. Chapter Four, for instance, refers explicitly to 'Adulis, a fair-sized village, from which there is a three-days' journey to Koloe, an inland town and the first market for ivory', and 'five days' journey more … to the city of the Axumites'. The *Periplus* then goes on to name several 'other Berber market towns, known as the "far-side" ports; lying at intervals one after the other, without harbours but having roadsteads where ships can anchor and lie in good weather'. It also asserts that 'these places … are governed by [the Axumite king] Zoscales; who is miserly in his ways and always striving for more, but otherwise upright and acquainted with Greek literature'.

Clearly, most of the Berber ports listed in the *Periplus* lay along the coast of present-day Somaliland, which was then part of, or a vassal to, the Axumite Kingdom. The ports named as Avalites and Malao probably tally with present-day Zeila and Berbera, the latter also preserving the ancient Greek name for the entire region. The more easterly Mundu and Mosyllum are frequently identified with present-day Maydh and Bosaso, although it could be argued convincingly that they actually lay between Berbera and Maydh. If that is the case, then the 'large laurel-grove called Acannae, where alone is produced the far-side frankincense, in great quantity and of the best grade' near 'a river, called Elephant … along the coast beyond Mosyllum', describes to a tee the forested base of the Daallo Escarpment, which lies a short distance inland of Maydh and still supplies it with copious quantities of high-grade frankincense. Either way, the 'Cape of Spices, an abrupt promontory, at the very end of the Berber coast toward the east' is unambiguously Cape Guardafui, the most easterly point in Africa, set in present-day Puntland.

The *Periplus* provides an interesting, albeit rather brief, description of Somali coastal trade 2,000 years ago. Popular import items ranged from 'undressed cloth [and] cloaks of poor quality dyed in colours' to glassware, Italian wine, olive oil and various metals – brass was 'used for ornament instead of coin', copper to make 'cooking utensils, and for bracelets and anklets for the women', and iron for 'spears used against the elephants and other wild beasts, and in their wars'. Export items included frankincense, myrrh, ivory, tortoiseshell and rhinoceros horn (the latter then, as now, used in Yemen and elsewhere in Arabia as the handle for a type of dagger called a *jambiya*). Slaves were also sometimes sold to passing ships, but this was rare.

Somali merchants played an important middleman role, as indicated in the *Periplus*, selling on a variety of goods that were transported to the region by Indian merchants. Among the items that were openly sold on in this manner were 'Indian iron, steel and cotton cloth … and a few muslins', and a scarlet insect-derived dye called lac. However, the writer of the *Periplus* clearly swallowed one myth perpetuated on the Mediterranean world by Somali and Arab traders for centuries. This was that cinnamon bark, used to make a highly valued spice, was produced locally, when in fact it was cultivated in the Far East, shipped on to the Red Sea region and then re-sold to Mediterranean traders at a whopping profit.

By the turn of the millennium, an elaborate gold trade linked southeast Africa to the Persian Gulf via the Somali region. The gold derived from alluvial sources in the highlands of present-day Zimbabwe, from where it was transported via the Zambezi Valley to Sofala, and then shipped northwards to Mogadishu through a chain of medieval city-states that lined the 'Swahili Coast' of Mozambique, Tanzania and Kenya. These self-governing trade ports, inhabited by a cosmopolitan mix of indigenous and foreign merchants, the latter mostly hailing from the Shiraz region of Persia, were united by their common adoption of Islam and the widespread use of Kiswahili (an indigenous African tongue strongly infused with Arabic words) as a *lingua franca*. Mogadishu remained the most important African trade emporium until the mid 13th century, after which improved navigational and shipbuilding techniques allowed the Arab merchants to sail further south in one season, and the focal point of trade relocated closer to the source of the gold, to Kilwa in present-day Tanzania.

The most important medieval port along the Somaliland coast was Zeila, which is mentioned by name in several Arab documents dating from the 9th century onwards (for further details, see *Zeila*, page 149). It appears that Zeila took over from Adulis as the main port serving the highlands of Ethiopia, indeed certain Arab reports suggest that for a period this 'emporium of Habesh' (Ethiopia) was an isolated Christian enclave on a coastline otherwise dominated by Islam. Half a century later, the inveterate traveller Ibn Buttata, whose first landfall on the African coast was Zeila, noted that its inhabitants were 'black in colour and the majority of them are Rafida' (literally 'deserters', a pejorative term used by Sunni Muslims to describe Shi'ites who reject early caliphs such as Abu Bakr).

Little is known for certain about the inhabitants of the Somali interior in early medieval times. Oral tradition and the limited archaeological evidence indicate that they were pastoralists, of similar stock perhaps to the ancestors of the Oromo of southeast Ethiopia, who emigrated from what is now the border region of Ethiopia and Kenya, and most likely found their way to the Horn of Africa in the 7th century AD. It is widely held that the modern Somali tongue derives from the Cushitic language spoken by these migrants and many other non-Islamic facets of Somali culture also probably arrived in the region with them. All the indications are that these Cushitic-speaking pastoralists still adhered to their imported religious beliefs for several centuries after their arrival. Indeed, it seems likely that they were responsible for some or all of the myriad pre-Islamic burial cairns and stelae that scatter the Somali interior, even though local traditions associate these mysterious monuments with the Galla (Oromo) rather than a proto-Somali people.

Oral traditions indicate that Islam took a strong foothold in the Somali interior between the 10th and 13th centuries. The existence of trade routes inland from ports such as Zeila and Berbera doubtless influenced this spread, but the main factor, it would seem, was the missionary efforts of several legendary sheikhs (a term meaning a religious teacher or revered elder) who originated in Arabia and settled in Somalia to found clans and subclans that are still integral to Somali society today. The epicentre of this Islamic infiltration into Somaliland (though not necessarily the rest of Somalia) was the port of Maydh, where the tomb of **Sheikh Isaq**, founder of the Isaq clan that dominates most of Somaliland, is still revered as a shrine by his descendants. Other influential leaders of this era were **Sheikh Issa**, also buried near Maydh, and founder of the Issa subclan that dominates Djibouti and the far west of Somaliland; and **Sheikh Ismail al-Jabarti**, founder of the Darod clan that dominates Puntland and the far east of Somaliland, whose tomb lies in the village of Haylaan in Sanaag.

**IFAT, ADAL, WARSANGALI AND ETHIOPIA** In the late 13th century, Zeila became the focal point of the **Ifat Sultanate**, an Islamic empire ruled by the Walashma Dynasty that extended across most of present-day western Somaliland, into Djibouti and parts of eastern Ethiopia. Founded by the Umar Walashma, Ifat supported an important trade network, with Zeila serving as the coastal terminus of an inland caravan route that followed a string of substantial Islamic settlements (see *Ruined towns around Borama*, page 147) to and from the inland emporium of Harar, in eastern Ethiopia.

In the early 1320s, **Haq ad-Din I**, the Sultan of Ifat and a grandson of Umar Walashma, launched a full-scale religious war on the Christian infidels of the Ethiopian Highlands. This campaign met with considerable success prior to the Ethiopian emperor **Amda Seyon** defeating Haq ad-Din in a battle that took place in 1328. After a few quiet decades, the Walashma *jihad* against Christian Ethiopia was resumed with renewed energy by **Sultan Sa'ad al Din**, who was killed by Emperor Dawit in 1403, on the offshore island near Zeila that still bears his name. The Ifat Sultanate fell into decline following Sa'ad al Din's death, which prompted most key members of the Walashma Dynasty to flee across the Gulf of Aden and take temporary refuge in Yemen.

The successor to Ifat, the more powerful and extensive Adal Sultanate, was established by **Sabr ad-Din**, the eldest son of Sa'ad ad-Din II, who built a new capital called Dakkar, east of Zeila, following his return from Yemen c1420. The most celebrated or notorious (depending on your viewpoint) Emir of Adal was **Ahmad ibn Ibrahim al-Ghazi**, a Zeila-born Somali better known as Ahmed Gurey or Ahmed Gragn (Somali and Amharic, respectively, for 'the left-handed'), Emir Ahmed seized power from his predecessor in the early 16th century, thereby ending a period of internal turmoil in Adal, and he proceeded to relocate his capital from the coast to Harar in 1528.

From Harar, Emir Ahmed led his army of Afar and Somali Muslims, supported by a battery of Turkish cannons, on a series of annual raids on the Ethiopian Empire, whose timing was designed to exploit the Christians' weakness during their Lent fast. The destructiveness of these campaigns are legendary in Ethiopia to this day: many of the country's famous rock-hewn churches still bear the scars of Emir Ahmed's attacks, while less permanent structures, such as the original 4th-century Church of Maryam Tsion in Axum, were razed entirely by the Muslims.

By 1535, most of Christian Ethiopia had been conquered by the Adal army, and the desperate Ethiopian emperor Lebna Dengal – who had hosted a pioneering Portuguese expedition in 1520 – was reduced to writing to the Portuguese monarchy for assistance. So it was that the Ethiopians, propped up by a heavily armed Portuguese contingent, killed Gragn and defeated his army in a battle near Lake Tana in 1543. After this decisive battle, the Islamic-Christian war didn't so much come to an abrupt end as peter out: the resources of both factions had been severely depleted over the long years of combat, to the benefit of the pagan Oromo or Galla, who expanded their core territory in the Rift Valley into several other parts of southern Ethiopia laid waste by fighting. By 1560, the Oromo expansion not only created a buffer zone between the exhausted Christians and Muslims, but it also posed a new threat to both parties.

The dominant late medieval entity in eastern Somaliland was the Warsangali Sultanate, an Islamic state founded in the 13th century. Named for the eponymous ruling branch of the Darod clan, Warsangali incorporated much of present-day Puntland as well as the Somaliland province of Sanaag. Despite the sultanate's great extent, it was evidently less expansionist than Ifat and Adal, and its leaders

Historical works tend to emphasise the medieval trade relationship between the east coast of Africa and Arabia, or to a lesser extent India, ignoring the region's similar relationship with China, whose ceramics have been unearthed at numerous sites. Possibly this is because it has long been thought that these Chinese exports were shipped to Africa indirectly, via India and Arabia. But this theory falters when you recognise that the earliest medieval description of the Somali region, and arguably the most detailed, was penned by the Chinese writer Tuan Ch'eng-sbib as early as the mid 9th century.

The port visited by Tuan Ch'eng-sbib's Chinese informants, named as Boboli (or Popoli), almost certainly lay somewhere along the coast of Somaliland, and may well be synonymous with Berbera. Tuan provided a detailed description of the land's inhabitants, including customs still practised to this day by certain East African pastoralist societies:

> They do not eat any of the five grains but eat only meat. They often stick a needle into the veins of cattle and draw blood which they drink raw, mixed with milk. They wear no clothes, but use goatskins to cover the parts below their waists … The country produces only ivory and ambergris … All, whether young or old, draw blood and swear an oath before they will trade their products. From olden times on they were not subject to any foreign country. In fighting they use elephant tusks and ribs or buffalo horns as lances, and wear cuirasses (shields), and bows and arrows. The Arabs make frequent raids upon them.

Tuan also asserts that a trade in female slaves operated out of Boboli, writing that, 'their women are clean and of proper behaviour; the inhabitants themselves kidnap them, and if they sell them to foreign merchants, they fetch several times their price'.

Another intriguing Chinese description of medieval Somaliland is included in Chou Ju-kua's two-volume *Chu-fan-chi* (literally, 'Description of the Barbarous Peoples'), which dates to around AD1225 and reproduces some information from a book written by the geographer Chou Ch'u-fei in 1178:

> The country … has four towns, and the rest are settled in villages that each try to gain supremacy over the others by violence … The country produces many camels and sheep, and camel meat and milk and baked cakes are their regular food. The country produces dragon's saliva [ambergris], elephant tusks and rhinoceros horns. Some tusks weigh more than 100 catty [about 60kg] and some rhinoceros horns more than 10 catty [about 6kg]. There is also much putchuk [a ginger-like root], liquid storax gum, myrrh, and extremely thick tortoise-shell which people from other countries all come to buy.

The *Chu-fan-chi* mentions that 'the people serve Heaven not the Buddha', which might be read as an obtuse way of saying they are Islamic, and are 'fond of hunting … with poisoned arrows'. It also describes some of the wildlife in the region: the giraffe ('in size like an ox … yellow in colour … its head high up and turned upwards'), the ostrich (which it calls a 'camel-crane' and claims can 'fly, but not to any height'), and what is presumably a zebra ('a mule with red, black, and white stripes wound like girdles around the body').

tended to focus on trade – in particular frankincense grown at the base of the Daallo escarpment – as opposed to the conquest of Ethiopia. Its ports included Maydh and Bosaso (in Puntland), and its capital was Las Khorey (or Laasgoray), a historic port now situated in the disputed Puntland-Somaliland border territory. Warsangali proved to be a political entity of unusual durability. Indeed, where Zeila and Berbera were captured by the Ottoman Empire in 1548, and remained under its nominal rule for 300 years, Warsangali remained a fully autonomous sultanate until the end of the 19th century.

**THE SCRAMBLE FOR SOMALI TERRITORY** In the mid 19th century, Somali pastoralists occupied a territory of some 1.5 million km$^2$, comprising practically the entire Horn of Africa east of the 41° longitude. They did not form a unified state as such, being divided into six distinct genealogical clans (see *Clans*, page 28) and numerous subclans. Nevertheless, the Somali as a whole shared strong cultural ties, then as they do today, as well as a common language and religion. By the century's end, the Somali-occupied territory in the Horn of Africa was arbitrarily divided between five different externally administered political entities: British Somaliland (present-day Somaliland), Italian Somaliland (Somalia), French Somaliland (Djibouti), British East Africa (Kenya) and the Kingdom of Ethiopia.

Britain's interest in Somaliland dates to 1839, when the **British East India Company (BEIC)** established a naval base at the Yemeni port of Aden. The main purpose of this naval base was to prevent pirate attacks on merchant ships travelling between three of its key possessions: Zanzibar, Bombay and Suez. But while Aden was well situated for military purposes, its hinterland was poorly stocked with food, and the BEIC came to rely upon the Somali ports of Zeila and Berbera, on the opposite shore of the Gulf of Aden, as its main source of fresh meat.

Zeila and Berbera were then, as they had been for 300 years, nominal vassals of the Ottoman Empire. However, it seems that the actual Turkish influence over the two Somali ports was minimal; both were effectively ruled by home-grown emirs who gladly entered into regular trade with the BEIC. The explorer Richard Burton, who visited Zeila and Berbera in 1855, describes both ports as supporting a lucrative maritime trade in goods sourced from the interior. They had quite different seasonal patterns, however, with Zeila supporting a relatively stable year-round trade, while Berbera's calendar centred upon the annual fair held over the 'winter' months of November to March.

In 1865, the Turks reasserted their dormant interest in the Horn of Africa by formally ceding the ill-defined province of Habesh, which included Eritrea and western Somaliland, to the **Khedive Ismail of Egypt**, which was then an autonomous tributary state of the Ottoman Empire. The Egyptian flag was raised at Berbera and Zeila in 1870, and Khedivate garrisons were stationed at both ports, as the first step in realising Ismail's ambition to control Ethiopia and the entire African hinterland between the Red Sea and the Sudanese Nile. This ambition was partly realised in 1875, when Egypt captured Harar, meaning it had full control over the most important trade route between the Ethiopian Highlands and the Somali coast. Two years later, Britain, anxious to ensure the supply of meat to Aden was not disrupted, signed a treaty that recognised Egyptian rule of the Somali coast in exchange for an undertaking that the region would never be ceded to another European power.

Egypt's interest in Ethiopia wavered following the retirement of Khedive Ismail in 1879, and when a more pressing military concern emerged in the early 1880s, in the form of the Mahdist Rebellion in Sudan (which was then under Egyptian rule), it was quick to withdraw its troops from the Horn of Africa. This paved the way for Britain to take control of the Somali coast, which it did by signing treaties of protectorateship with local clan leaders concerned at the prospect of Ethiopian expansion into their territory. In 1884, British vice-consuls were established at Zeila, Berbera and Bulhar. Three years later, the Somaliland Protectorate, comprising the northern Somali coastal strip, was formally proclaimed, initially as a dependency as Aden, but directly answerable to the Foreign Office as of 1898.

The colonial future of the Somali region took further shape over the remainder of the 1880s. In 1887, following the Egyptian evacuation, Harar was captured by **King Menelik of Showa**, who would go on to succeed Yohannes as the Emperor of Ethiopia in 1889. France, which had long had its eye on Zeila, and even contemplated a naval attack on the British-protected port in 1885, agreed to the colonial partition that forms the present-day border between Somaliland and Djibouti in 1888. And in 1889, the so-called **Ucciali Treaty** between Italy and Ethiopia recognised the former's claims to present-day Eritrea, while offering Emperor Menelik ample scope to extend his influence deep into Somali territory.

Between 1891 and 1894, a series of treaties between Italy and southern Somali clan leaders paved the way for the proclamation of Italian Somaliland, which incorporated the Indian Ocean coastline between present-day Somaliland and Kenya, with the ancient port of Mogadishu as its administrative capital. In 1896, Italy reneged on the Ucciali Treaty, launching a full-scale military invasion of Ethiopia, one repelled at the **Battle of Adwa**, a famous victory that guaranteed Ethiopia became the only African state to enter the 20th century uncolonised. In the aftermath of Adwa, Britain agreed to recognise Ethiopia's claim to present-day Harar and Jijiga, as well as to the Ogaden region (the vast swathe of badlands that now forms the core of Ethiopia's 279,252 km$^2$ Somali region), in exchange for the inclusion of the hinterland around Hargeisa in British Somaliland.

**THE EARLY COLONIAL ERA** British administration of Somaliland was a low-key affair with limited goals and ambitions – indeed, during the initial years of protectorateship, these amounted to little more than ensuring the continued supply of fresh meat to Aden. Prior to 1913, Berbera, the administrative capital, was the only municipality, and its Somali merchant classes thrived as ever on international trade, dominated by the export of 70,000 sheep across the Gulf of Aden annually. Development of the interior was limited, and Britain's hold on it tenuous due to the anti-colonial rebellion led by **Sayyid Muhammad Abdullah al-Hassan** over the first two decades of the 20th century.

Sayyid Muhammad – often referred to by his enemies as the 'Mad Mullah' – was a noble-born religious leader of the Dhulbahante clan (part of the larger Darod clan) whose exceptional Islamic scholarship led to him being made a sheikh at the youthful age of 19. After travelling to Ethiopia, Sudan, Italian Somaliland and Kenya as a teenager, he made an 1894 pilgrimage to Mecca, where he joined the Salihiya, a devout Islamic brotherhood that frowned upon the consumption of *khat* and tobacco. Returning to Somaliland in 1895, he settled in Berbera, where he came into conflict with the city's established Qadiriya religious leaders and its relatively decadent merchant class, while also growing concerned at the threat to Somali Islamic integrity posed by the region's Christian colonisers (not only the British, but also the Ethiopians and to a lesser extent the Italians and French). In 1898, the charismatic and devout leader returned home to Sanaag, where he recruited support among his Dhulbahante clansmen (who had never signed a formal treaty with the British). A year later, at an assembly in Burao attended by 5,000 of his supporters, dressed in their trademark white 'dervish' turbans, Sayyid Muhammad formally declared war on Britain and Ethiopia, motivated at least as much by scorn for their religion as by anti-colonial feelings.

Sayyid Muhammad's first military campaign took place in March 1900, when 6,000 of his followers stormed the Ethiopian town of Jijiga, ostensibly to recover livestock looted from the Dhulbahante. Three months later, he led a similar raid on an Isaq clan within the protectorate, making off with at least 2,000 camels. Over the next four years, the British administration launched four major punitive campaigns into Muhammad's stronghold in present-day Sanaag, depleting the rebel forces to the point where their leader was forced to retreat into Italian Somaliland, and negotiate a treaty with its administration. In 1908, however, Sayyid Muhammad was invited back into Somaliland by the leaders of the venerable **Warsangali Sultanate** (centred on present-day Erigavo and Maydh), which announced its dissatisfaction with the administration by firing on a British dhow that attempted to land in their territory.

Emboldened by Warsangali support, Sayyid Muhammad established a series of forts – the most important being on the slopes of Mount Shimbiris, and at his capital of Taleh, near the present-day border with Puntland – from which he launched a new series of attacks on Isaq settlements to the east. As a result of this renewed outbreak of inter-clan fighting, Britain made the understandable but ill-judged decision to abandon its limited policing of the interior. The result was an outbreak of internecine Somali warfare, and an associated famine in which as many as one-third of the protectorate's population of 300,000 died before the end of 1912.

Following this disaster, Britain reasserted its presence in the interior by establishing the **Somaliland Camel Constabulary** under the command of Colonel Richard Corfield, who was killed by Sayyid Muhammad's troops in August 1913, at the Battle of Dul Madoba. In early 1915, shortly after the outbreak of World War I, Britain captured Muhammad's fort on Mount Shimbiris and established a coastal arms blockade that kept the Dervishes at bay until the end of the war. Finally, in early 1920, a joint British aerial, naval and terrestrial attack on Taleh forced Muhammad to retreat to the Ogaden, in Ethiopia, where he initiated several further inter-clan clashes and refused to negotiate with the British right up until his sudden death – probably of influenza or malaria – on 21 December 1920, aged 54.

Hereafter, Britain exerted more complete control over the interior, which it divided into five administrative districts: Berbera, Hargeisa, Zeila, Burao and Erigavo. The pastoral economy was boosted by the establishment of extensive sorghum plantations in the vicinity of Hargeisa and Borama, which flourished despite being temporarily destroyed by a locust plague in 1928. Rather less progress was made in the field of secular education, a concept to which the fiercely Islamic Somali were inherently hostile. It didn't help that a scheme in 1920 to build primary schools in six major towns, along with one intermediate school, funded by a livestock tax, led to violent protests and rioting in which the District Commissioner of Burao was killed. However, a second attempt to introduce a secular education system in 1936 was greeted by violence on purely religious grounds, and eventually abandoned.

**WORLD WAR II AND THE BUILD-UP TO INDEPENDENCE** Between 1936 and 1950, the four main component territories of the Somali region, with the exception of tiny French Djibouti, all changed hands at least once. The first harbinger of this period of instability was the **Walwal Incident** of December 1934, wherein a remote Ethiopian military post on the disputed Italian Somaliland border region was attacked by Italian troops. In the aftermath of this incident, Italy made unreasonable demands for Ethiopian reparations, and these were ratified by the League of Nations, even though Italy rather than Ethiopia had initiated the skirmish.

As far as the Italian dictator **Mussolini** was concerned, the League of Nations's support over the Walwal Incident effectively gave him carte blanche to occupy Ethiopia, which his Blackshirts did in 1936, marching southwards from their Eritrean colony to Addis Ababa, and forcing **Emperor Haile Selassie** into European exile. Shortly afterwards, Ethiopia, Eritrea and Italian Somaliland were amalgamated to form Italian East Africa, with Addis Ababa as the capital. In August 1940, Italy further expanded its territory by capturing British Somaliland. Victory was short-lived, however, as the British Allies recaptured their former protectorate in early 1941 and then proceeded to liberate Ethiopia from fascist Italian rule, and also to seize control of Eritrea and Italian Somaliland.

After World War II, the **Bevan Plan for a Greater Somalia** (named after the British foreign secretary who formulated it) proposed that the former British, Italian and Ethiopian components of Somaliland be amalgamated into one territory under British stewardship. This plan was locally popular – so much so that it arguably sowed the seed for the subsequent post-independence unification of Somalia. It was vetoed by the UN, however, which returned the Ogaden to Ethiopia in 1946, along with the former Italian colony of Eritrea, which finally gave Haile Selassie and his formerly landlocked empire direct control over a seaport or three. Meanwhile, Britain held on to its original protectorate, while in 1950 Italy was awarded a controversial ten-year trusteeship over Somalia – following bitter riots in Mogadishu a year earlier, in which more than 50 Italian settlers had been killed.

Over the course of the 1950s, both the Italian and British portions of Somaliland started the countdown to **independence**. Italy, bound by the terms of its trusteeship, introduced a surprisingly progressive suite of preparatory policies: free primary education was introduced in 1952, and a School of Politics & Administration and a Higher Institute of Law were established, and within a few years several top administrative positions were held by graduates of these institutions. The 1954 municipal elections were followed two years later by the election of a Territorial Council, in which 60 of the 70 seats were voted for by an (all-male) Somali electorate, and only ten for Italian and other minorities. The oddly named **Somali Youth League (SYL)**, the country's oldest party, took 43 of the 60 available seats, and its co-founder Abdullahi Issa became the first Prime Minister of Somalia, which he steered peacefully through to full independence on 1 July 1960.

British Somaliland's path to independence was less regulated but the transition was just as smooth. Education was a high priority for the British administration, which built on progress made during the war years by establishing a trade school in Hargeisa and a vocational school in Borama in 1952 – although even by the mid 1950s the number of secondary school places available countrywide was fewer than 100. In 1957, the British administration openly expressed an ultimate goal of independence for the territory, as well as union with Somalia. Few would have expected Somaliland to beat its southwesterly neighbour to the first landmark, but it did so by a matter of five days. On 26 June 1960, Somaliland was granted full independence from Britain under the leadership of Prime Minister **Mohamed Haji Ibrahim Egal** of the **Somali National League (SNL)**. Five days later, Egal relinquished this role, in the process signing away Somaliland's sovereignty, when the two newly independent territories united to form the Somali Republic on 1 July 1960. A joint government was formed with the SYL leaders **Aden Abdullah Osman Daar** and **Abdirashid Ali Shermarke** serving as the first president and first prime minister, respectively, while Egal was appointed defence minister.

**THE SOMALI REPUBLIC** The union between Somaliland and Somalia was rooted in romance: the notion of a Greater Somali state had taken hold as a result of the territorial shifts associated with World War II, and was reflected in the star – whose five prongs represent the five nations incorporating Somali territory – that adorned the country's flag. But the integration of the two former colonies' administrations presented several practical difficulties. For one, in the absence of a then officially recognised Somali script, the two systems were **linguistically incompatible**, with English being the primary language of education and bureaucracy in the Northern Region (as British Somaliland was now known), while Italian served the same purpose in the Southern Regions. The two parts of the country also inherited contradictory legal systems, and their civil services operated on very different terms and salary scales. In addition, while English was obviously the language of the future in international terms, Italian was the tongue more familiar to the numerically and politically dominant southerners, as well as to the many Italians who stayed on to help guide the administration through post-independence teething problems.

Another obstacle to integration was the ancient **clan attachments** inherent to Somali culture. Parochial tribal concerns had been subdued by passionate patriotism during the build-up to independence, and they were also discouraged by the post-union government, but ultimately the notion of clan is far more deeply embedded in the Somali psyche than the more modern concept of national statehood. This tendency to clannishness was heightened by the numeric and political dominance of the south, which – being five times more populous than the north – was represented by 90 out of the 123 seats in the first National Assembly. Mogadishu, the former Italian capital and largest city in the republic, not only became capital of the newly merged state, but also dominated every facet of economic and political life. Most adversely affected by this imbalance was the Isaq clan, which had dominated the north prior to independence, but was now a relatively small player on the national scene. Bearing all of the above in mind, one might ask why it was that the northerners were so keen on union in the first place. The answer is probably that the allure of unity was primarily emotional, though it was also the case that the northerners – whose pastoral economy centred on the export of livestock from Berbera to Arabia – had hoped it might set a precedent for the incorporation into the Somali Republic of the vast grazing lands in the perennially disputed Ogaden region of eastern Ethiopia.

Northern unease at the union was reflected in the results of a constitutional referendum held in June 1961. The 90% 'yes' vote among the 1.6 million southern voters ensured the new constitution was ratified with overwhelming support, but of the mere 200,000 potential voters in the north, as many as half abstained, and of those who did cast a ballot, dissenters slightly outnumbered supporters. In December of the same year, a group of British-trained northern junior officers in favour of northern secession led an abortive coup against their southern senior officers. A presidential tour of the north in 1962 temporarily eased the growing dissatisfaction, but hikes in food and transport prices, caused by the introduction of a unitary tariff and customs system, led to widespread rioting in Hargeisa in May 1963. At around the same time, the SNL and several other mostly northern minority parties merged to form the **Somali National Congress (SNC)**, thereafter the country's second most important party after the SYL.

The integration of Somali parts of Ethiopia, Kenya and Djibouti into the Somali Republic was a high-profile concern throughout the early years of union. It was also one in which Somalia won little international sympathy. In 1962, the

British colonial authorities in Kenya held a referendum to determine whether the Somali-dominated **Northern Frontier District (NFD)** wanted to become part of Somalia at independence. The vote overwhelmingly favoured a merger, but in the end NFD remained part of Kenya, a decision that led to Somalia severing diplomatic ties with Britain in March 1963. The Somali government was even more bitter about the high level of international support accorded to Ethiopia's claim to the Ogaden, which it perceived to be based on highly spurious treaties contrived in the late 19th century 'scramble'. Low-scale wars broke out in both disputed border regions between 1963–64, though ultimately neither the NFD nor the Ogaden were ever merged into Somalia.

On the domestic front, the SYL took 69 seats and the SNC 22 seats in the second National Assembly election, held in March 1964. Shortly thereafter, SYL dominance was boosted by a series of inter-party defections that left them with 105 of the 123 seats. A subsequent intra-party power struggle led to the controversial appointment of **Abdirizak Haji Hussein** as prime minister. Even more rancorous were the 1967 presidential elections wherein the National Assembly awarded the presidency to (former prime minister) **Abdirashid Ali Shermarke**, and chose Mohamed Haji Ibrahim Egal, a northerner, as prime minister. Egal, already an unpopular choice in the south, was labelled a sell-out following his decision to restore diplomatic relations with Kenya, Ethiopia and Britain in the wake of an OAU Summit held in Mogadishu in September 1967. Although Egal led the SYL to another convincing victory in the 1968 National Assembly election, the national mood had by then turned to bitter disillusionment with a government that came across as corrupt, self-serving, arrogant and increasingly authoritarian. Things came to a head in October 1969, when President Abdirashid Ali Shermarke was assassinated, and Somalia's nine-year democracy was curtailed in a **military coup** led by the commander of the Army, **Mohamed Siad Barre**.

**SOMALIA UNDER SCIENTIFIC SOCIALISM** Almost immediately after the coup, Siad Barre stripped away all the accepted bastions of civilian rule. The Somali Constitution, the National Assembly, the Supreme Court and all political parties were abolished as the former commander installed himself as the leader of a **Supreme Revolutionary Council (SRC)** comprising 25 other army officers. Vowing to remove corruption and tribalism from public life, the SRC aligned itself with the Soviet Bloc, thereby consolidating a relationship initiated in November 1963, when the SYL had accepted a Russian military aid package worth £11 million in favour of a smaller Western-funded package.

On the first anniversary of the coup, Jaalle Siyaad ('Comrade Siad') announced a new national policy he dubbed '**Scientific Socialism**'. Thereafter, the self-styled Father of the Nation, given as he was to grand philosophical pronouncements and staged scenes of public adulation, made himself the focal point of a Maoist-style personality cult that extolled his humble lifestyle, and took every available opportunity to publicise his compassion for the dispossessed and orphaned children he referred to as the 'Flowers of the Revolution'.

The central paradox of the SRC, as with so many socialist governments of the era, was that it attempted to introduce a program of genuinely enlightened policies – the promotion of women's rights, adult literacy and education over tribalism and religious dogma – but using means of enforcement that might generously be called illiberal. Suspected or actual dissidents were arrested, subjected to a one-sided military trial, and dealt disproportionately harsh sentences ranging from long-term imprisonment to public execution. Furthermore, many SRC policies were incompatible with Islamic laws and/or traditional Somali customs, leading to a high level of tension between the state and religious leaders. In January 1975, for instance, ten sheikhs were publicly executed for preaching against a law that granted women equal inheritance rights to men. Meanwhile, Siad Barre's program of nationalism did nothing to improve the ailing economy, while bold educational policies summed up in the maxim 'if you know, teach; if you don't, learn' were almost impossible to implement in a nation of nomads, especially as the region was badly affected by drought and famine in the mid 1970s.

Undeterred by his manifest inability to manage the country he had taken by military coup, Siad Barre embarked on an overt agenda of **pan-Somaliism** in the mid to late 1970s. This was encouraged by the 1974 military coup against Emperor Haile Selassie, and the hard-won **independence of Djibouti** from France in 1977. However, when negotiations with the new socialist regime in Ethiopia broke down, the Somali army, assisted by dissident Ethiopian Somalis, invaded the Ogaden, precipitating a year-long border war in which both sides lost more than 10,000 troops prior to Siad Barre's effective concession of defeat in March 1978. This loss of pan-Somali face to Ethiopia precipitated a bloody attempted coup in April 1978, leading to further government repression. Moreover, the already strained Somali economy had to incorporate a sudden population growth of 20% as hundreds of thousands of Ethiopian Somalis, fearing reprisals from their government, fled across the border into a string of around 40 refugee camps.

The **Ogaden War** had a profound effect on international relations in the Horn of Africa. Russia and Cuba withdrew from the long-standing military and naval bases they had helped build in Somalia, and relocated to what was then the Red Sea coastline of Ethiopia (now Eritrea). As a result, Siad Barre switched allegiance to the West, making his first visit to the USA in 1982, prior to which he made the conciliatory gesture of releasing several prominent political prisoners, among them the former Prime Minister Mohamed Haji Ibrahim Egal, who had been jailed in the aftermath of the 1969 coup. But even this wasn't enough to save an economy in steep decline following long years of war and government mismanagement. Further stress was placed on the primarily agricultural and pastoral economy in 1983, when Siad Barre outlawed *khat* production, and the country's main trade partner, Saudi Arabia, placed a ban on all meat and livestock imports from Somalia on the grounds of alleged rinderpest. By the mid 1980s, domestic inflation rates approached the 100% mark.

In May/June 1986, Siad Barre, critically injured in a car accident, spent more than a month recuperating in a Saudi Arabian hospital, leading to increased speculation about his political longevity and eventual successor. Nevertheless, in December of that year, Siad Barre won another seven-year term as president, with 99.9% of the vote, a figure that reflected his status as sole candidate (nobody dared stand openly against him). By this time, however, popular support for the ageing dictator was rapidly waning. By 1990, his influence barely extended beyond the city limits of Mogadishu, and in January 1991 he was chased out of the capital by the **United Somali Congress (USC)**. Twice Siad Barre attempted, and twice he failed, to retake Mogadishu. He was eventually exiled to Nigeria, where he died of natural causes in 1995. Tragically, in the immediate aftermath of Siad Barre's forced exile from Mogadishu, an estimated 14,000 civilians were killed as the city of two million split along clan lines into northern and southern sectors, precipitating a brutal **civil war** that still wages on ferociously 20 years later.

The dying years of the Siad Barre regime were particularly hard on the Northern Region, as a special unit known as Duub Cas ('Red Berets') unleashed a campaign of terror against the Isaq and other clans perceived to threaten the government's grip on power. The worst of the killing took place in 1988, following the May occupation of Hargeisa and Burao, the two largest towns in northern Somalia, by the **Somali National Movement (SNM)**, a rebel Isaq movement dedicated to ridding the country of Siad Barre. The government reprised with aerial bombardments that not only forced the SNM to abandon both cities, but also literally razed them to the ground, a fate from which Berbera was partially but not wholly spared, thanks to its importance as a port. In addition, government troops victimised helpless rural Isaq communities by destroying their traditional wells and grazing grounds, and attacking and raping the women. Overall, during the course of 1988, the government killed an estimated 50,000 to 60,000 Isaq civilians, and up to 500,000 people decided to flee the bombed-out towns to take refuge across the border in Ethiopia or Kenya.

The collapse of the Siad Barre regime left the military, and most other Somali government institutions, even deeper in disarray than they had been before. It also left the door wide open for the SNM to liberate the northwesterly region that now comprises Somaliland (and for the affiliated Somali Salvation Democratic Front (SSDF) to do the same for the northeastern region we now know as Puntland). Indeed, within a couple of months of January 1991, Hargeisa, Burao, Berbera, Borama and Erigavo were all in the hands of the SNM, which then initiated wide-ranging consultations with local Dir, Darod and Isaq clan leaders in a series of peace conferences that helped restore the region to something approaching normality. So it was that on 18 May 1991, the SNM made a unilateral **declaration of independence**, severing the ill-fated 30-year-old union with Somalia, and restoring a state of sovereignty it formerly held for a mere five days in June 1960.

**SOMALILAND** The initial omens were inauspicious. In January 1992, less than a year after secession, fighting broke out between different Isaq subclans in Burao as a result of the caretaker President Abdurrahman Ali Tuur trying to reorganise the former rebel forces into a proper army. Further unrest occurred two months later at Berbera, following the fledgling government's attempt to impose customs and taxes on the country's most important port. More than 1,000 fatalities were recorded in the two incidents and the port at Berbera closed for six months as a result. Fortunately, however, the clan elders, tired of the ongoing killing, persuaded the government to attend the **Grand Conference of National Reconciliation** that opened in Borama on 24 January 1993, led by a committee of 150 elders from several different subclans.

One of the most truly remarkable events in Africa's recent political history, the Grand Conference was a think tank that endured for four months, and involved more than 1,000 participants. Foremost among its consensual achievements were the creation of a bicameral parliament wherein a non-elected House of Elders could keep check on the elected House of Representatives, and the formulation of a national charter that required the government to draft a proper constitution within two years. The Borama conference inspired a series of similar events elsewhere in Somaliland – most critically in the fractious Sanaag region – and it led to practically every last subclan being co-opted into the rebuilding process.

Crucial to the success of the Grand Conference was the appointment of Mohamed Haji Ibrahim Egal as President of Somaliland in its euphoric wake. Egal was a broadly popular choice for this post, thanks to a long and chequered political career that had already included a period as an anti-colonial firebrand in the 1950s, various ambassadorial and ministry posts including a five-day stint as

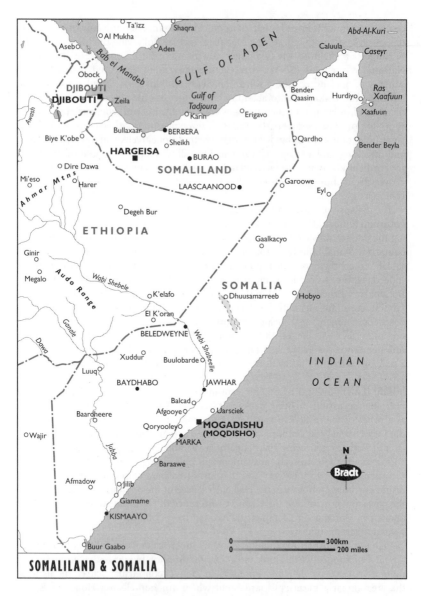

**SOMALILAND & SOMALIA**

Prime Minister of Somaliland prior to the 1960 merger, and two years as Prime Minister of the Somali Republic in the build-up to the 1969 coup – not to mention two periods of detention totalling 13 years under Siad Barre. And while Egal failed in one of his primary aims, the gaining of international recognition for Somaliland, his achievements were manifold. They included the disarmament of almost all rebel groups and the restoration of peace to the northwest; a trend of economic stabilisation, then growth, through the establishment of bilateral trade agreements with several countries; the introduction of organised customs and tax collection; the creation of reasonably effective government ministries, as well as a central bank, a civilian judiciary and a functional civil service; and the forging of a strong and disciplined police force from the region's various rebel groups. He also oversaw the institution of other trappings of normalisation, for instance the creation of a **national currency** and **national flag**.

Despite this, inter-clan violence claimed several thousand lives over the cusp of 1994–95 and it persuaded some 180,000 Somalilanders to flee back across the border to Ethiopia. The catalyst for this unrest was a dispute over control of revenue generated by Hargeisa airport, a national asset and justified source of central revenue that a local subclan *gad* long regarded as its own tribal possession. After the government took control of the airport in March 1995, the fighting spread to Burao, a hotspot between two powerful Isaq subclans, and this short but bloody civil war did immense damage to Somaliland's emerging administrative structures and recovering economy, as well as undermining its case for recognition as a sovereign state. However, differences between the government and other warring factions were eventually resolved in a national reconciliation conference held in Hargeisa between October 1996 and February 1997.

Delayed by the 1994–95 fighting, a temporary constitution was adopted in February 1997, when the National Communities Conference re-elected President Egal for a second term with a 70% majority. A full constitution was unveiled in May 2001, and went to a public referendum, which returned a 97% vote in its favour. President Egal died at a military hospital in South Africa on May 2002, aged 73, while still in office. His unfinished term was completed by the relatively youthful **Dahir Riyale Kahin**, who also won the country's first fully fledged presidential elections on 14 April 2003, representing the **United Democratic People's Party (UDUB)**. Held in September 2005, the first full election for the House of Representatives saw UDUB take 33 seats, while the rival **Peace, Unity, & Development Party (KULMIYE)** and **Justice & Welfare Party (UCID)** took 28 and 21 respectively.

Following the 2003 and 2005 elections, Somaliland, by any standards, could claim to be a fully fledged **democracy**, albeit it one still unrecognised by the rest of the world a full 15 years after secession. Subsequent years have seen the country's modest economy and low-key government flourish in the face of occasional adversity, much of it related to its relationship with the remainder of the former Somali Republic. Since the late 1990s, the eastern border area has been the subject of an ongoing dispute and occasional outbreaks of violence between Somaliland and self-governing Puntland (see box, *Puntland*, page 22). The most serious dispute to date occurred on 15 October 2007, when the Somaliland faction of the Dhulbahante clan attacked the inland city of Las Anod, deposing the ruling Puntland faction of the same clan, with an estimated death toll of 30 people. Further fighting occurred on 15 May 2010 when troops from Somaliland and Ethiopia wrested control of several villages in the Sool region prior to the election, leaving at least 13 people dead. And an isolated incidence of violence rocked the normally safe capital Hargeisa on 29 October 2008, when simultaneous **suicide bombings** of the Ethiopian consulate, the presidential palace, and a UNDP office killed at least 30 people. No group has ever taken responsibility for the bombings, but they are generally thought to have been the work of **Al-Shabaab**, a militant southern Somali insurgency group with links to al-Qaeda.

The presidential election of June 2010, held after two years of controversial delays, saw the incumbent President Kahin fall to **Ahmed Mohamed Silanyo** of KULMIYE, who took 49.6 % of the vote as opposed to his main rival's 33.3%. The outgoing Kahin immediately congratulated Silanyo, confirmed that he would stand down, and the transition was completed on 27 July at a swearing-in ceremony attended by officials from Djibouti, Ethiopia and Kenya. Whatever the

## PUNTLAND

Taking its name from the legendary land known to the ancient Egyptians as Punt, the autonomous state of Puntland comprises the far northeast of the country, including Cape Guardafui, the most easterly point in Africa. It came into existence in August 1998 as a result of the escalating clan warfare that had engulfed southern Somalia since the downfall of Siad Barre, and its constitution was hammered out at a three-month constitutional conference held in Garoowe – attended by the region's most prominent politicians, clan elders, businessmen and intellectuals. Its political structure is not dissimilar to that of Somaliland, with clan elders playing an important role in supporting the democratically elected president, but unlike its western neighbour it has never sought formal independence and its long-term goal is to be a federal state within greater Somalia.

The capital of Puntland, Garoowe, set along the main road between Hargeisa and Mogadishu on the unofficial border with Somaliland, is the seat of parliament and site of the presidential palace and government ministries. Despite its fast-growing population, currently estimated at 60,000, Garoowe is only the third-largest city in the territory, after the commercial capital and port of Bosaso, which supports a population of around 500,000, and the similarly sized inland city of Galkayo, which has a disputed location on the border of Somalia proper.

Although it is peaceful by comparison to southern Somalia, Puntland has endured considerable internal conflict, and sporadic fighting between Puntland and Somaliland has also occurred in the Sool and Sanaag regions – which are generally regarded to be part of Somaliland but are also claimed by claimed by Puntland on the basis of ethnicity. As a result, the eastern regions of Somaliland are relatively unstable and travel within them is restricted. Travel in Puntland itself is currently unsafe and emphatically not recommended.

Puntland is regarded to be the main base for the Somali pirates responsible for hundreds of attacks and hijackings of merchant ships and other seafaring vessels, in the Gulf of Aden and further afield, since 2005. Although the Puntland government has claimed to be taking steps to control the piracy, it has met with limited success. Indeed, by December 2010, it was estimated that at least four pirate bands were active in the region, collectively comprising 1,000 individuals, and holding at least 35 ships and more than 650 people hostage. In part, the inability to control the piracy is because it has a high level of local support. The pirate bands bring considerable wealth into an otherwise impoverished territory – their income from ransom was estimated at almost US$60 million in 2009 and more than US$200 million in 2010 – and the attacks are often justified as a legitimate response to the widespread illegal fishing and dumping of toxic waste by foreign ships along the Somali coast.

future for Somaliland might hold, with this peaceful presidential transition, in the aftermath of a multi-party election widely deemed to be 'free and fair', Somaliland has demonstrated a political maturity that has eluded many recognised African countries in the 50 years since independence. One senses that it can only bode well for the future of this young and unrecognised nation.

# GOVERNMENT AND POLITICS

Somaliland is a constitutional multi-party democracy headed up by a president, a vice-president and a cabinet. The president is elected directly in presidential elections held every five years, and no individual may serve for more than two five-year terms. The vice-president and cabinet are nominated by the president and must be approved by the bicameral parliament, which comprises two houses of 82 members each. The House of Elders (Guurti) is a council of Somali traditional leaders indirectly elected by local clans according to a prescribed proportionate formula for six-year terms. The members of the more conventional House of Representatives are elected directly for five-year terms. All laws must be passed by both houses before they can be enacted.

For Somaliland's first decade of independence, political parties were prohibited as divisive. The transition to a multi-party system took place in 2002. The constitution allows for a maximum of three political parties to stand for any election, and they are prohibited from being defined by religion or clan. The June 2010 presidential election was won for the ruling Peace, Unity & Development Party (usually referred to as KULMIYE) by Ahmed Mohamed Mohamed. The official opposition is the United Peoples' Democratic Party (Ururka Dimuqraadiga Ummadda Bahawday, or UDUB, in Somali), which ruled from 2002 until 2010 under President Dahir Riyale Kahin. The minority Justice & Development Party (Ururka Caddaalada iyo Daryeelka, or UCID, in Somali), won only 15.8 % of the vote in the most recent presidential elections.

# ECONOMY

Somaliland has a small, fragile economy that revolves around agriculture and pastoralism, both of which depend on good rainfall, an unreliable commodity in the Horn of Africa, which at the time of writing is suffering its worst drought since the early 1990s. Non-acceptance of Somaliland as a valid state is a huge hindrance to the economy, since it restricts the activity of international financiers and NGOs, and means the Somaliland shilling is unrecognised outside the country. Indeed, other than the Djiboutian Banque pour le Commerce et l'Industrie, which opened a branch in Hargeisa in 2009, no international banks are represented in Somaliland and most international transactions are handled by money transfer companies, the best known of which is Dahabshiil.

Somaliland's economic bulwark, today as it has been since the early 19th century, is the export of livestock to the Arabian Peninsula. The industry suffered greatly from a Saudi ban on Somali livestock (due to suspected rinderpest) in the 1980s, but that has since recovered to generate around US$25 million per annum. Other exports include meat, animal skins, myrrh and frankincense, and Berbera's modern Russian-built port is the oceanic terminal of a transport corridor to Ethiopia that has increased in importance since the closure of the Ethiopia–Eritrea border in 1998. The country also has some potential for grain agriculture, and as a tourism destination, though neither industry is fully functional at present. By far the biggest contributor to the Somaliland economy is those individual Somalis who live and work abroad, and are estimated to send a collective US$1 billion home annually.

# PEOPLE

Somaliland is populated almost entirely by the Somali, who form the dominant ethnic group in the Horn of Africa. The regional total of 15–16 million Somalis is divided between Somalia (whose total population of nine to ten million is divided more or less evenly between Somaliland, Puntland and Somali proper), eastern Ethiopia (home to 4.5 million Somalis), Kenya (home to almost one million Somalis) and Djibouti (350,000 Somalis). In addition, at least one million Somalis live outside of Africa, the majority of them in Yemen, but also in North America and Europe.

## INTERNATIONAL RECOGNITION · *Sean Connolly & Philip Briggs*

If any one cause unites just about every Somalilander, it is the quest for international recognition of their country. And the case for this status is exceptionally solid, as outlined below.

The international community has indicated repeatedly that recognition of Somaliland is to be determined by the African Union (AU). At the outset of Africa's modern era of independence, that same AU (then the OAU) set out guidelines agreeing that any re-negotiation of the continent's borders, despite their being arbitrary 19th-century colonial creations, would open up a Pandora's Box of tribal, ethnic and linguistic rivalries. As a result, the hastily drawn borders of the colonial era still define the political map of Africa today.

Somaliland clearly fits these guidelines, and its divorce from Somalia has many precedents in post-independence Africa. Somaliland was a British Protectorate, with boundaries approximating its present ones, for a full 75 years prior to gaining independence on 26 June 1960. It was also a sovereign state, albeit one of less than a week's standing, on 1 July 1960, when it voluntarily united with the former Italian Somaliland to form the Somali Republic. As such, it surely retains the right to dissolve that union, as it did by declaring unilateral independence on 18 May 1991.

The problem is that the AU doesn't take kindly to secession movements. This is, after all, an organisation that includes any number of states whose corrupt, greedy leadership has long exploited or ignored its own ethnic divisions, and who know that redrawing their own country's boundaries would diminish their power and wealth. In that context, certain parties view recognition of secessionist Somaliland as having the potential to launch the AU atop a slippery slope. Better by far to prop up the unelected status quo in Mogadishu, and pontificate about 'how to put Somalia back together', as if the cartographic integrity of a political entity that existed for a mere 30 years is inviolable.

The advantages of recognition barely need itemising. It would, for instance, grant the Somaliland government the legitimacy to borrow money from international institutions such as the IMF and World Bank, to enhance basic service delivery such as electricity, gas, water, telecoms and rubbish collection, and to fund state schools, universities and hospitals. It would also legitimise the territory's international boundaries, an essential starting point for policing border regions in this unstable corner of the world. And, given that Somaliland is still officially part of war-torn, piracy-riddled Somalia, the positive media exposure associated with international recognition would do wonders for its global image, attracting plenty of interest from potential tourists and investors.

**ORIGIN** According to legend, the common ancestor of most if not all Somali clans was Irir Samaale, a name which possibly derives from the phrase *soo maal* – literally, 'go and milk' – in reference to the almost exclusively pastoral lifestyle of his descendants. DNA studies suggest that the Somali share close ethnic links with the Oromo of southern Ethiopia and northern Kenya, and that the two groups share a mixed African and Middle Eastern ancestry going back perhaps 5,000 years, when

Though often downplayed or ignored, recognition has its possible downsides, too. Economically, as a legitimate inheritor state to the Somali Republic, Somaliland risks being burdened with a portion of the massive debt accrued under Siad Barre – effectively repaying money used to arm the very force it fought against prior to secession. And having accomplished so much without recourse to the aid money that forms a staggering percentage of many developing countries' budgets, one might question whether Somaliland's bare-bones efficiency would benefit from a budget swollen with international loans, grants and the like.

Recognition of Somaliland is bound to antagonise the rest of the former Somali Republic. For one, were it to be recognised in accordance with AU policy, that would mean resurrecting the old borders of the British protectorate, which includes areas currently controlled by Puntland, a self-governing state already embroiled in an ongoing border conflict with Somaliland. As for the insurgent Al-Shabaab, which controls much of southern Somalia, while it currently appears to view its breakaway neighbour as a secondary enemy (after the likes of Uganda, Burundi and the AU Mission in Somalia), global recognition of Somaliland might well make it a primary target for terrorist attacks.

More obtusely, one of the factors that has steered post-1991 Somaliland along the path of accountability is the desire to demonstrate its suitability for recognition by being 'better' than Somalia proper. Somalia has war? Somaliland has peace. They've got pirates? We have a coastguard. They've got foreign mercenaries? We have tourists. They have sectarianism and anarchy? We have multiple parties and free elections. So, what happens when the goal of recognition, with so many hopes, dreams and aspirations pinned to it, is finally attained? One need only cite Somalia in the 1960s – its long-awaited independence and unification giving way to the atrocities of the Siad Barre regime – as a reminder of what can happen when unifying causes give way to sectarian interests.

Lest there be any confusion on this point, international diplomatic recognition for Somaliland is a goal we fully support. Since the mid 1990s, shortly after it declared independence, this unheralded country has managed to get so much right, when so much around it has gone so terribly wrong. These efforts, made in adversity and obscurity, clearly deserve international acknowledgement and support. But recognition will bring risks as well as rewards, and it would be tragic for the accomplishments of the past two decades to be erased by the unforeseen consequences of the very thing Somaliland has so earnestly sought.

Simplistically, the Horn of Africa comprises two broad climatic zones: the fertile highlands that dominate central and western Ethiopia, and the drier lowlands that stretch east and southwards into the Somali region and northern Kenya. While the region as a whole is popularly associated with drought, the highlands of Ethiopia actually rank among the most well-watered of African breadbaskets. The Ethiopian capital Addis Ababa, for instance, receives an annual average rainfall of 1,200mm (almost double the figure for London or Johannesburg), while the city of Harar, near the Somaliland border, receives around 800mm, and the country as a whole supports a population of 80 million, at almost twice the average density of, say, South Africa, Madagascar or the DR Congo.

By contrast, the Somali region and low-lying parts of eastern Ethiopia mostly qualify as semi-arid or arid, with many areas receiving an average annual rainfall significantly below 50mm – too little to support any lifestyle other than nomadic pastoralism. Worse still, rainfall in these drier parts of the Horn of Africa is highly seasonal, and tends to be erratic, with some years being characterised by short but torrential downpours, and others by practically no rain at all. One occasional result of this unpredictable pattern is localised but destructive flash floods, such as the one that killed thousands of livestock at Tog Wajaale in April 2009. The other is the localised or widespread droughts that usually follow two or more years of successive rainfall failures.

But, while periodic drought is an unavoidable fact of life in the Horn of Africa, the famines associated with these rainfall failures often have human causes. For instance, while the Kefu Qan (Evil Days) of 1888–92, the most severe famine in Ethiopia's recorded history, was indeed preceded by widespread rainfall failures, its unique severity was down to an epidemic of rinderpest, introduced with Indian livestock imported by the Italians, that reduced the national cattle herd by 90%. Likewise, the notorious 1973 famine in the Ethiopian province of Wolo is largely attributable as much to the actions of Haile Selassie's ailing government, which initially refused to acknowledge the problem, actually going so far as to export food from Wolo to Addis Ababa to get better prices, and then – having retracted its initial denials – failed to respond with any action meaningful enough to prevent an estimated 200,000 deaths.

In 1984–85, three successive years of rainfall failure resulted in what BBC reporter Michael Buerk called 'a Biblical famine in the 20th century', transforming parts of the Horn of Africa into 'the closest thing to Hell on Earth'. Somalia was badly knocked (though no figures are available) and an estimated 250,000 lives were lost in Sudan, but it was Ethiopia that suffered most, with around eight million people affected by the famine, resulting in at least one million fatalities. Once again, while the famine was a result of drought, it is widely agreed that the tragic proportions it assumed were a result of political factors. The three worst-affected countries were all then ruled by socialist regimes whose impractical collectivist agricultural policies, excessive spending on a bloated military rather than on economic upliftment, and autocratic tendency to deny rather than deal with crises contributed greatly to the severity of the famine. In addition, many Western countries were ill disposed to send aid to socialist countries in the prevailing Cold War climate. And while charity efforts such as the bestselling singles *Do They Know it's Christmas?* and *We are the World*, along with the *Live Aid* concert, did raise considerable funds for famine alleviation, the local powers-that-be prevented aid from reaching those anti-government parts of the country where it was most urgently needed.

Tragically, as the first edition of this Somaliland guidebook goes into production, the same thing is threatening to happen all over again. A crippling drought, caused by rainfall failures in 2009 and 2010, is threatening the lives of more than 12 million people living in low-lying parts of Somalia, Ethiopia, northern Kenya and to a lesser extent Djibouti, Sudan and northeast Uganda. This time, however, the epicentre of the crisis is not Ethiopia but southern Somalia, in particular the provinces of Lower Shebelle and Bakool, which the UN declared a famine zone on 20 July 2011, following the lead of Somalia's President Sharif Sheikh Ahmed two days earlier. These provinces have experienced a 240% increase in staple prices in early 2011, tens of thousands of people have already died, and almost one million people have fled across the border into overcrowded and disease-ridden refugee camps in Ethiopia and Kenya.

Once again, the severity of the crisis, described by the British charity Oxfam as 'a preventable disaster', is largely rooted in politics. Oxfam has accused several European governments of 'wilful neglect' in not heeding 'warning signs [that] have been seen for months'. Despite this, the UN has thus far secured about half of the estimated US$1.6 billion required to feed the region, with the UK and Canada being the largest contributors, having respectively pledged total sums of more than £100 million and CA$70 million. The northern part of Somalia that comprises Somaliland has thus far experienced only limited effects of the drought, thanks to relatively high levels of internal stability and good governance. And there is reason to hope the crisis is still containable in affected parts of northern Kenya, eastern Ethiopia, Eritrea and Djibouti.

The situation in southern Somalia looks altogether more bleak. For one, there is the innate difficulty associated with providing humanitarian aid to remote parts of this highly unstable country. Particularly so when Al-Shabaab – a prominent Somali insurgency group with alleged ties to Al-Qaeda – has effectively forced organisations such as the United Nations World Food Programme out of the country, and its response to the UN pronouncement of 20 July 2011 was to deny the famine's existence and reiterate its threat to disrupt any aid operations managed by organisations of which it disapproves. It doesn't help either that the US has withheld all aid from the Somalia region, following reports that Al-Shabaab is taxing food convoys into the affected area, which contravenes a ruling preventing aid money from providing any material benefit to terrorist organisations, an 'overzealous approach' that has 'led to a damaging collapse in US humanitarian support to Somalia', according to Jeremy Konyndyk, policy director of the US Mercy Corps.

it is known that an element of trade existed between the Somali and Arabian coasts of the Red Sea and the Gulf of Aden.

**CLANS** While Somaliland – and the rest of Somalia, for that matter – ranks among the few truly homogenous African states in terms of ethnicity, religion and language, the clan and subclan allegiances inherent to Somali culture have often been responsible for problems and divisions similar to those associated with tribalism elsewhere. No two sources agree precisely on the number of clans in greater Somalia, or their precise relationship to each other, but broadly speaking there are three caste-like tiers. Clan membership plays an important role in Somali politics, and marriages between members of different subclans are probably more common than within the subclan, as they help cement ties or heal rifts between neighbouring families.

At the top of the Somali hierarchy are the four noble clans, all of which claim direct ancestry from the founder Irir Samaale. Ranked below them are the agro-pastoral Rahanwein clans, such as the **Digil** and **Mirifle**, whose homeland – between the Jubba and Shebelle rivers – lies outside present-day Somaliland. Even lower in status are the minority artisanal clans such as the **Tumal**, **Yibbir**, **Jaji** and **Yahar**, who traditionally live in their own settlements interspersed through the territories occupied by the various noble clans, where they perform specialist activities such as metalworking, tanning and hunting. They are regarded as unclean by the noble clans and are thus treated as outcasts who only marry among themselves.

Of the four noble clans, the most numerically significant is the **Hawiya**, which includes about 25% of Somalis, centred upon Mogadishu and southern Somalia, as well the border region of Ethiopia and Kenya, but is practically unrepresented in Somaliland. The main noble clan in Somaliland is the **Isaq**, whose territory incorporates Hargeisa, Berbera and Burao, and which comprises around 22% of all Somalis. The Isaq Somali are divided into several subclans, among them the Arap, Ayoup, Garhajis, Habar Awal, Habar Jeclo and Tol Jecle. The **Darod** clan is centred mainly upon present-day Puntland, but the historically significant **Warsangali** subclan also has a large presence in Somaliland, particularly around Erigavo and Maydh. The numerically less significant **Dir** clan is present in the far west of Somaliland, but its population main focus is Djibouti and bordering parts of Ethiopia, though the **Issa** subclan has strong historical links with Zeila and the Adal Sultanate.

**WOMEN** Traditional Somali and Islamic law both accord limited rights to females, and although improved property rights for women stand as one of the few positive legacies of the Siad Barre regime, Somaliland remains a strongly male-dominated society. Polygyny, the form of polygamy wherein men can take several wives simultaneously, but women are restricted to one husband at any given time, is still widely condoned and practised. Furthermore, marriages are frequently arranged indirectly between the groom and the family of the bride, without the latter's consent, and men have far more latitude than women when it comes to initiating a divorce.

According to a recent UNICEF report, the prevalence of female genital mutilation (FGM) in the Somali region stands at 95%. An extreme form of FGM is practised, involving the total removal of the clitoris and labia minora, and the suturing together of the labia majora to leave one small hole for urination and menstruation. FGM in Somaliland is mostly performed by untrained village midwives, using unsterilised instruments such as knives, razors or even broken glass, on unanaesthetised pre-pubescent girls, sometimes when they are only four years old. Many victims of this cruel, painful and unnecessary procedure suffer immediate medical problems, occasionally with fatal results. Long-term complications include genital malformation, recurrent urinary infections, increased vulnerability to HIV transmission, and obstetric complications that can result in the death of the woman and/or her unborn child.

## LANGUAGE

Somali is the home language of nearly all Somalilanders, making this one of the most linguistically homogenous countries in Africa. It is a Cushitic language, part of the same linguistic subgroup that includes Oromo and Afar, both of which are spoken in parts of Ethiopia. Prior to 1972, several different unofficial scripts were used to transcribe the Somali language. However, the official script throughout the region is now the same Romanic one used to write English and most other European languages, albeit with a few local variations (see page 176). Arabic has been widely spoken in Somaliland for centuries, particularly by the educated elite and coastal traders, and it still forms part of the school curriculum. English is not as commonly encountered, but the majority of returned emigrants who form a substantial part of the urban population speak it to a very high standard.

## RELIGION

Somali culture is strongly informed by Islam, which first arrived at coastal ports such as Zeila in the 7th century AD, possibly during the lifetime of the prophet Muhammad, and was widespread in the interior at least 800 years ago. Islam is the official state religion of Somaliland; indeed, the territory's constitution prohibits the promotion of any other faith, asserts that its laws must be grounded on Islamic principles, and is to discourage acts and behaviour considered immoral or reprehensible under them. As a result, Islamic law dictates most facets of day-to-day life: people generally dress in traditional Islamic robes, with women almost always donning a *hijab* veil in public; the consumption of pork is taboo; alcohol is not only illegal but more or less unobtainable; secular music and books are limited in availability; the Sabbath is taken on Friday; and the five daily prayer calls dictate the daily rhythms of life to an extent rare elsewhere in Islamic parts of sub-Saharan Africa.

Most Somalilanders belong to the **Shafi'i** school of the Sunni branch of Islam, but a minority adheres to the **Shi'ite** branch. The more mystical form of Islam known as **Sufism** also has a strong hold in Somaliland and it was strongly associated with the early 20th century Dervish movement led by Sayyid Muhammad. Koranic schools, called *duqsi*, have long been the most important medium of instruction in Somalia, and even today they form the only available educational opportunity for many Somalilanders, particularly among the rural nomads. Historically, Christianity has had an occasional presence in the region, first during periods of localised Ethiopian occupation and more recently during the British and Italian occupations of the north and south, but it has no significant presence here today.

## EDUCATION

During the colonial era, Somaliland lagged behind most British territories on the schooling front, not least because local Islamic leaders were strongly resistant to secular education, especially as overseen by a Christian authority. This changed somewhat after World War II, as independence loomed, and raising literacy levels was a high priority of the secular Siad Barre regime, which designated the first official Somali alphabet in 1972, and launched widespread adult literacy programmes in the mid 1970s. Nevertheless, then, as today, resistance to formal education remained high among nomadic Somali pastoralists, whose lifestyle is not conducive to regular school attendance and who question whether it has any direct benefit to the family income. Whatever progress was made in the 1970s was largely undone by the 1988–91 civil war, which left the education system – along with other amenities – in tatters.

Despite this, Somaliland has done much to build a proper educational system since it declared itself independent from Somalia in 1991. The construction of primary schools took priority for much of the 1990s, but 1999 saw the opening of Amoud University – the first post-war institution of higher learning – near Borama, to the west of the capital. Today, Somaliland boasts at least ten private and public universities, of which the most prominent are Amoud along with Hargeisa University and Burao University in the eponymous cities. In 2011, the Ministry of Education estimated that some 200,000 students – about 6% of the total population – are enrolled in government schools, and it also announced plans to recruit an additional 2,000 teachers and implement a system of free primary and intermediate education countrywide.

## ARTS AND MUSIC  *Sean Connolly*

For the outsider, the creative and performing arts scene in Somaliland can be a tough nut to crack. During the war and following two decades of recovery, cultural life suffered greatly as most Somalilanders were engaged primarily in meeting more basic needs. Accordingly, the number of people engaged in creative pursuits is very small, and venues in which to showcase their work are almost non-existent. There are no live music venues, museums, galleries or café exhibitions, and the national theatre in Hargeisa is only now being rebuilt, 20 years after it was bombed into the ground. As a result, the majority of live performances take place either in private homes (along with much of Somali socialising), or at weddings – one of the few occasions at which Somalis really let their hair down! However, unless you know someone who has offered to take you along, you're not likely to be invited in off the street to join the festivities, as Somalilanders tend to be somewhat reserved with outsiders until they get to know them well. Nevertheless, as life continues to improve in the present climate of stability, music and arts are bound to be an integral part of Somaliland's quest to define its nascent national identity. And for those with an interest, there is a rich heritage of creativity – it just takes a little digging to find it.

**VISUAL ARTS** The visual arts in Somaliland tend to exist almost exclusively for commercial purposes. Any shop or restaurant worth its salt will have a brightly painted mural out front replete with smiling fish (on a plate), larger-than-life medicine bottles, lopsided bananas, cheeseburgers (whether or not the menu actually features cheeseburgers is irrelevant), serene-looking camels, plates of pasta, floating forks, and whatever else they may or may not sell! These splashes of colour go a long way towards improving the sometimes lacking aesthetics of Somaliland cities.

The artists-for-hire behind these festive advertisements travel the city working for commissions, with some pursuing non-commercial art on the side. You'll see stalls around the city that act as the base for many artists and feel free to stop at any of these and see what kind of work they have in stock. A few do more tourist and souvenir-oriented fare (landscapes, camels, etc) in addition to their standard repertoire of sodas and *sambusas.*

If you see a business or restaurant that particularly catches your eye, give it a close inspection as nearly all the murals are signed with the artist's name and mobile number. It takes a little negotiation, and likely a Somali speaker to help arrange things on your behalf, but it's possible to arrange a commission of your own if you plan to spend more than a few days in town. Even the country's best artists work this way. Check out the MiG jet in downtown Hargeisa – there's a number on that too. Somaliland doesn't yield much in the way of souvenirs, but with a little effort you can go home with a one-of-a-kind piece of art, purchased directly from the artist.

**POETRY** 'The country teems with poets … every man has his recognised position in literature', said Sir Richard Burton in his 19th-century travelogue *First Footsteps in East Africa,* and this holds remarkably true in Somaliland today. Poetry has long been the most prized of Somali art forms, and as it requires nothing but ingenuity and the human voice, is perfectly suited to their traditionally nomadic lifestyle. Somali poets have enjoyed a societal role not unlike the griots of west Africa, acting as both keepers of historical lore and commentators on the vagaries of life, love, and of course, politics.

With poetry featuring so centrally in the cultural life of Somalis and Somalilanders, many poets are household names, enjoying the widespread recognition and esteem that would normally be reserved for pop stars in the West. Some of the most popular poets in Somaliland include **Hadraawi, Timacade** and **Gaariye** – Timacade passed away in the 1970s, but this has seemingly done little to dent his popularity. You're guaranteed a lively conversation any time these names are mentioned, and people are typically more than ready to defend and expound upon the skills and merits of their favourite.

Poetry recitation is typically performed either solo, or accompanied by an *oud.* This stringed instrument, widespread in the Middle East, helps set the tone for the poet according to the mood and subject of the performance. Cassette tapes of these performances are available, but the message is obviously lost to non-Somali speakers. Regardless, they still do make for an interesting listen, and any Somalilander friends you make will be more than happy to interpret for you. Poets are revered for their nuance and impeccable grasp of language, used to transport the listener into their story or convince them of a point of view. Prepare for some loss in translation.

**MUSIC** While poetry is without question the premier art form in Somaliland, there is also a music scene, albeit a small one. If you're arriving from elsewhere in Africa, the Somalilander approach to music is a drastic change. Gone are the maxed-out amplifiers and distorted speakers on every corner and in every car – in Somaliland you'll have ample opportunity to hear yourself think. This stems from Somaliland's deeply-held conservatism. Certain schools of Islamic thought prohibit music, and while it is by no means forbidden in Somaliland, music plays a much smaller role than in neighbouring countries. The music that you do hear, however, tends to be local. The ubiquitous Western pop so difficult to escape elsewhere is largely absent here – farewell 50 Cent and sayonara Snoop Dogg.

Today, due to music's frowned-upon status among Somaliland's more conservative elements, those in the business of selling boom-boxes have taken a clever step to prove their Islamic *bona fides* – keep your eyes out for 'Islamic Stereo' stores dotted around town. These places are fully stocked with the latest speakers and music players, ostensibly for the purpose of listening to Koranic recitations – with bass boost. Music is still very much enjoyed in Somaliland, only it is done so with a touch of discretion.

Given this relative absence of Western music, Somali and Somalilander music is widely listened to, and for the casual observer can be broken down into the following styles.

**Qaraami** Traditional Somali music, or **Qaraami**, usually involves a singer (or poet) backed by an *oud* and a drum (increasingly a keyboard-preset drum track.) The *oud* pushes the melody along, and the sometimes mournful, sometimes joyful trills of the singer sit gently on top. Always atmospheric and often hypnotic, it's the perfect soundtrack to get lost in the desert scenery as you bounce, bump and sweat your way down the Hargeisa–Berbera road. The late **Omar Dhuule** remains one of Somaliland's most cherished musicians, and a true master of the *Qaraami* style.

**Contemporary popular music** The popular music being produced in Somaliland today can be a mixed bag. Lifelong artists often find themselves competing with cheaply produced records made by relative unknowns. Casio keyboards are the instrument of choice, and songs typically build on a call-and-response theme. Thankfully, most of it remains far removed from the cookie-cutter Western-style pop found in much of the world. You will notice the Arab and Ethiopian influences, as Somaliland's geographic and cultural links continue to inform new music, creating a sound and flavour that is uniquely Somali. Check out Somaliland National Television (SLNTV) for whatever's topping the charts this week. There are no clubs and cars in these videos, just a green screen and some G-rated dance moves. The talented **Maryam Mursal** is the doyen of Somali pop singers today, and one of the few whose music has gone international. Other popular singers include **Ubax Fahmo** and **King Khalid**, while the Canada-based **K'naan** creates hip hop with an unmistakably Somali twist.

**Pre-war pop** Pre-war Somali pop can be a real treat. The 1980s saw several full bands gain popularity throughout Somalia, playing a distinct brand of funk and pop. These were true bands: driving horns, screaming organs, growling basslines, razor-sharp guitars and unstoppable drumming set the tone for male and female singers delivering their messages with swagger and panache – no reservations here. Many of their songs were furiously modern updates of traditional Somali songs, while others wrote equally funky originals. A handful of these recordings can be tracked down on repeatedly dubbed cassettes or on YouTube, but these bands are one of countless pieces of Somali cultural heritage lost during the war. **Iftin**, **Dur Dur** and **Sahra Dawo** are all names to look out for.

# 2

# Natural History

With its largely arid climate and recent history of civil conflict, Somaliland may not seem the most promising destination for wildlife enthusiasts. But while it is true it lacks the densely grazed savanna reserves characteristic of east Africa or the lush forests that swathe the Congo Basin, and that many large mammal species have been hunted close to extinction over the past century or so, Somaliland still supports a surprising amount of medium-sized mammals and other wildlife. It is also a highly rated destination for birders, thanks to the presence of several Somali endemics (that is, species found nowhere else in the world), and several near-endemics and other birds with limited distribution. Many of its more interesting mammals can be seen quite easily while driving through the scrubby badlands that separate its main urban settlements, but there are also a handful of more specialised wildlife destinations, the most alluring being the remote and scenic Daallo Forest Reserve on the escarpment between Erigavo and Maydh.

## LAY OF THE LAND

Somaliland lies on the so-called Horn of Africa, the most easterly part of the continent, comprising Ethiopia, Eritrea and Djibouti as well as the rest of Somalia. It is, with the notable exception of the moist Ethiopian Highlands, a predominantly low-lying and dry region, bounded by the Red Sea and Gulf of Aden to the northeast, and the more open waters of the Indian Ocean to the southeast. Geologically, the region is characterised mostly by relatively modern sedimentary rocks, dating from the Pleistocene to Oligocene eras (ie: the past 30 million years), but older Eocene limestone formations and quartzite basement outcrops are exposed along the main east-to-west escarpment running inland of the coast, while the Djibouti border area comprises volcanic rocks associated with the formation of the Rift Valley.

The Horn of Africa lies at the juncture of three tectonic plates. The Arabian Plate, which essentially comprises the Arabian Peninsula, is separated from mainland Africa by the Red Sea and Gulf of Aden, geologically recent creations that effectively form a northern extension of the Great Rift Valley. The Nubian Plate, which includes about 90% of the African mainland and lies to the north and west of the Rift Valley, which runs through central Ethiopia via the sweltering Afar Depression, to the coastline between Djibouti and Berbera. The bulk of Somaliland, however, is part of the Somali Plate, which comprises Africa south and east of the Rift Valley, an area that includes Hargeisa, the eastern Ethiopian Highlands around Harar, and the coastal belt of present-day Kenya, Tanzania and Mozambique. The gradual rifting of these three plates has been going on for around 20 million years, so the area is quite geologically stable in the short to medium term, but eventually – many millions of years from now – the Rift Valley as we know it will flood with seawater and those parts of present-day Somaliland that aren't submerged in the process will become part of a small new continent, reminiscent perhaps of Madagascar today.

Simplistically, Somaliland can be divided into three topographic regions: the narrow and low-lying coastal belt, the vast medium-altitude plateaux that run towards the Ethiopian border, and the high escarpment that divides them. The hottest part of the country, with temperatures regularly topping 40°C in summer, is the coastal belt, or Guban (literally 'scorched') which lies at altitudes of 300m or below, and is widest in the west, near the Djibouti border, graduating towards the east to be less than 10km wide near the unofficial border with Puntland. Generally it is sparsely vegetated, characterised in the east by loose sandy soils which form dunes up to 50m tall in some areas, and elsewhere by a patchy cover of low scrubland and grass that sometimes form meadows suitable for grazing in the rainy season.

Sometimes referred to as the Golis Range, the mountainous escarpment that runs the entire length of the country from west to east incorporates the 2,450m Mount Shimbiris, the highest peak in all of Somalia, as well as several other peaks that rise above the 2,000m contour. Receiving a relatively high rainfall supplemented in areas by water-bearing sea mists, the escarpment supports a reasonably lush flora, including patches of juniper forest and striking succulents such as the candelabra and Dragon's Blood Tree, as well as *Boswellia frereana*, whose resin is cultivated for export as frankincense. The escarpment incorporates three of Somaliland's best-known wildlife destinations, namely Daallo Forest, Ga'an Libah and Mount Wagar, but its dramatic contours are most accessible to casual visitors on the spectacular pass that divides Berbera from Sheikh.

Inland of the escarpment, the inclined Ogo Plateau comprises several vast plains that broadly decrease in altitude as they extend deeper into the interior. The likes of Sheikh, Hargeisa and Borama are set at above 1,000m, while the southeast border drops to below 300m before extending into the Somali-occupied part of Ethiopia, an immense arid plain known as the Haud. The climate also becomes drier further from the escarpment, where flat open plains support a sparse cover of acacia scrubs or seasonal grasslands. Vegetation and wildlife here depend greatly on soil types, which tend to be gypseous (dominated by a soft crystalline form of calcium sulphate dihydrate) in the Nogal Valley south and east of Burao, but more clayish on the plains southwest of Hargeisa. No permanent rivers traverse this plateau: there are a few seasonal watercourses (known locally as a *wadi*), among them the Togdheer (through Burao) and Wajaale (on the Ethiopian border west of Hargeisa), but a more important source of perennial water is the many scattered natural wells formed by limestone sinkholes, the presence of which is often indicated by a line of tall *Acacia tortilis* (umbrella thorn) trees.

## MAMMALS

Somaliland supports a relatively limited selection of large mammals, certainly when compared to the likes of Ethiopia or Kenya, and many safari icons – most notably perhaps elephant and rhino – became extinct during the course of the 20th century. Nevertheless, the national checklist includes several relatively localised species, many of which are seen quite easily on the open plains. What follows here is a country-specific supplement to any of the continental field guides recommended at the end of this book (see *Appendix 2, Further reading,* page 179), containing an overview of those mammals that are reasonably likely to be seen in Somaliland, with details of their local status and brief descriptions for identification purposes.

**PREDATORS** The largest predator most likely to be seen in Somaliland is the blotch-coated stoop-backed **spotted hyena** (*Crocuta crocuta*), which frequently scavenges on the outskirts of towns and is also sometimes encountered on the plains. From Ovid's *Metamorphoses* to Disney's *The Lion King*, popular culture has tended to portray this supposedly craven creature – which the ancients believed could change sex at will, a myth that stemmed from the false scrotum and penis covering the female's vagina – in an unfavourable light. In reality it is a fascinating animal which lives in loosely structured matriarchal clans of five to 25 animals who go though an elaborate dog-like greeting ritual whenever they meet. Also present but less common are the handsome striped hyena (*Hyaena hyaena*), whose coat is marked with dark vertical streaks and topped by a dark mane; and the insectivorous aardwolf (*Proteles cristatus*), which is closer in size to a jackal than to other hyenas.

Africa's three large feline species – **lion**, **leopard** and **cheetah** – were all quite common in Somaliland in the 19th century. Indeed, the area was once famed by hunters for its lion, the male of which, like its Ethiopian counterparts, sported an impressive black mane. Today, the lion (*Panthera leo*) and cheetah (*Acynonix jubatus*) are both very scarce in Somaliland, possibly even extinct. The leopard (*Panthera pardus*) remains quite numerous but very secretive, though spoor are sometimes seen in Daallo Forest and other well-wooded areas along the escarpment, where its favoured habitats of forest and rocky areas are well represented. Of the smaller cats, the most common is probably the spotted and streamlined **serval** (*Felis serval*), which might be seen on any rocky habitat or in open grassland. The lynx-like **caracal** (*Felis caracal*) and tabby-like **African wild cat** (*Felis silvestris*), the latter the wild progenitor of the domestic cat, are also present but very thinly distributed.

Far more common is the **golden jackal** (*Canis aureus*), a small and cryptically coloured wild dog often seen trotting singly or in pairs at dusk or dawn on the open plains of Somaliland. The less common **black-backed jackal** (*C. mesomelas*) is similar looking but with a prominent black saddle flecked by a varying amount of white or gold. The eerie call of the jackal is a characteristic sound of the African night.

Less common still is the **bat-eared fox** (*Otocyon megalotis*), an insectivorous long-eared dog with a uniform silver-grey coat, huge ears and black eye-mask. The uncommon **Ruppell's fox** (*Vulpes Ruepelli*), a bushy-tailed red and grey close relative of its European namesake, is confined to the coastal plain north of Berbera.

The most conspicuous small predators are the mongooses of the family *Herpestidae*, small and for the most part diurnal carnivores, characterised by a slender build, narrow muzzle, long tail, small eyes and ears, non-retractable claws used for digging, and uniformly coloured, grizzled coats. Of six species recorded, the most likely to be seen is the **banded mongoose** (*Mungos mungo*), a sociable, dark-brown creature, often found in groups of ten to 20, with 12 or so faint black stripes running across its back. The rarer **white-tailed mongoose** (*Ichneumia albicauda*), the largest species in the region, is a solitary nocturnal hunter whose slightly bushy white tail is diagnostic, though dark-tailed individuals do exist.

**PRIMATES** Primates are poorly represented in Somaliland, with even the vervet monkey, near-ubiquitous elsewhere in Africa, and the Sahel-associated patas monkey, being totally absent as far as we can ascertain. Possibly this is why the **Hamadryas baboon** (*Papio hamadryas*), Somaliland's only diurnal primate, is also the country's most common – or at least most visible – medium-to-large mammal species. Endemic to the Horn of Africa east of the Rift Valley, this ultra-sociable creature is also known as the sacred baboon – it played an important role in the religion of ancient Egyptians – and it is most notable visually for the grizzled grey coat and striking mane of the male, which is often twice as bulky as that of an adult female. Visitors to Somaliland are bound to see large troops of these agile terrestrial monkeys strolling or running along the plains, and their far-carrying bark is often heard in the hills and mountains of the escarpment area. The only other primate present in Somaliland is the bug-eyed **Somali bushbaby** (*Galago gallarum*), a vocal but seldom-seen nocturnal species that resembles a lemur more than a monkey.

**ANTELOPE** Several antelope species are present, some associated with the open plains and others with more wooded habitats, although many have become locally extinct since the 19th century, among them Swayne's hartebeest (now effectively endemic to Ethiopia) and the handsome rapier-horned Beisa oryx. Several of the surviving species belong to the gazelle family, a group of rather similar-looking-small-to-medium grazers associated with grasslands and other open habitats. Most gazelles have smallish horns, and a light chestnut-brown back with white underparts separated by a dark side stripe. Of all the antelope present here, however, the one of greatest interest to wildlife enthusiasts is the near-endemic **beira** (see box, page 103), a unique inhabitant of rocky slopes whose range is almost entirely confined to Somaliland.

The most conspicuous species is **Speke's gazelle** (*Gazella spekei*), which is regarded to be endemic to Somalia, although one record does exist for the Ogaden Plains in Ethiopia. The smallest of the gazelles is IUCN listed as 'Endangered', but is nevertheless quite common on the open plains between Burao and Erigavo, where small herds might be sighted several times daily. A remarkable, and indeed unique, feature of Speke's gazelle is the bridge of its nose. Its scrumpled-up appearance is down to a series of up to five folds of skin, which it inflates to become a large amplifying sac when it emits its loud honking alarm call.

**Soemmerring's gazelle** (*Gazella soemmeringi*), is a relatively large and long-legged species with no side stripe and a distinctive black face with white cheek stripes and relatively small, backward-facing horns. Also present is the much paler and smaller Somali race of **Dorcas gazelle** (*Gazella dorcas pelzelni*), a Saharan species whose range extends to the Horn of Africa. Both are largely confined to the western coastal belt.

An atypical and unmistakable relative of the gazelles, the **gerenuk** (*Litocranius walleri*) is a relatively large red-brown antelope, with a unique habit of feeding from acacia trees standing on its hind legs at full stretch, aided by its extraordinarily long neck. So striking is this neck that it is referred to not only in the name gerenuk, which derives from a Somali phrase meaning 'suckled from the giraffe' but also in the Swahili *swala twiga*, meaning 'gazelle giraffe'. The gerenuk is the most commonly seen medium-to-large antelope in the bush country around Hargeisa and is likely to be seen *en route* to Las Geel, Berbera or Borama.

Quite similar in appearance, the **dibatag** (*Ammodorcas clarkei*), IUCN listed as 'Vulnerable', is a localised antelope whose range has always been confined to a specific type of vegetation in Somalia and the Ogaden region of southeast Ethiopia. Its main range lies outside Somaliland but it is thinly distributed in the red sands east of Burao. The combination of a white eye-ring extending down the nose, elongated neck, and long black tail raised in flight (the name dibatag is Somali for 'erect tail') should be diagnostic.

The *Tragelaphus* antelopes, distinguished by their spiralled horns and striking markings, are represented in Somaliland by the **greater kudu** (*T. strepsiceros*) and

**lesser kudu** (*T. imberbis*). Arguably the most magnificent of African antelope, the greater kudu is second in stature only to the extralimital eland, standing up to 1.55m high at the shoulder, weighing up to 320kg, with a grey-brown coat and up to ten vertical white stripes on each side, but notable most of all for the statuesque male's double-spiralled horns, which can grow to be 1.4m long. The lesser kudu is not only smaller (shoulder height: 1m) but also has two white throat patches, a greater number of vertical stripes (at least 11), and less impressive horns. Both were once very widespread in Somaliland, occurring in any lightly wooded territory, but these days they are more or less confined to forests such as Wagar, Daallo and Ga'an Libah in the escarpment region.

Dik-diks are small, brown antelopes with tan legs and distinctive extended snouts. All dik-dik species are browsers that live independently of water and they are generally seen singly or in pairs in dry acacia scrub. Four species are recognised, two of which are found in Somaliland (with a third being present across the border in southern Somalia). **Salt's dik-dik** (*Madoqua saltiana*), a Horn of Africa endemic that is widespread in Somaliland, is frequently seen on the roadside around Hargeisa, often under the shade of a shrub. The less common and slightly larger **Guenther's dik-dik** (*Madoqua guentheri*) is mostly sighted east of Burao. Though very similar, with a grizzled grey upper coat, the two can be distinguished by the colour of their bellies: fawn in the case of Salt's dik-dik and white in the case of Guenther's.

The **klipspringer** (*Oreotragus oreotragus*) is a quirky small-to-medium antelope associated with rocky slopes and mountains, such as the Somaliland escarpment. Adaptations to this habitat include the unique capacity to walk on its hoof tips, coarse but hollow fur providing good insulation at high altitude, and binocular vision (more normally associated with carnivores) to better gauge jumping distances. Usually seen in pairs, which bond for life, it has a uniform grizzled grey-brown coat, short forward-curving horns and an arched back. Certain anatomical features suggest it represents an ancient lineage that evolved from the earliest African antelope stock in the Ethiopian Highlands some ten to 15 million years ago.

**OTHER MAMMALS** Several of the iconic large mammal species associated with other parts of east Africa, among them giraffe, Burchell's zebra and hippopotamus, have never occurred in Somaliland, mainly due to the limited supply of perennial water. Other species that were formerly resident, or regular seasonal visitors, are now extinct within Somaliland, or can be presumed to be so. This sorry list includes elephant, buffalo, black rhinoceros, Grevy's zebra and several varieties of large antelope.

The only species of swine found in Somaliland, the **desert warthog** (*Phacochoerus aethiopicus*) is a Horn of Africa endemic whose main range spans the northwest of Somalia/Somaliland and the dry plains of far eastern Ethiopia. To the casual visitor, this localised dry-country resident is probably all but indistinguishable from the more widespread common warthog associated with most other parts of sub-Saharan Africa. However, significant differences in dentition make it far more effective at masticating every last drop of nutrition from its food, and it has a shorter skull and more rounded forehead. Small family parties are frequently seen throughout most accessible parts of Somaliland, feeding by the road, or trotting off in a row with their tails held stiffly erect.

A contender for the oddest of all African mammals, the **aardvark** (*Orycteropus afer*), is the only living species of the ancient order Tubulidentata. An exclusive

## SOMALI WILD ASS

The Somali wild ass (*Equus africanus somaliensis*) is the only extant race of the African wild ass, the progenitor of all domestic donkeys (the nominate race *E. a. africanus*, commonly known as the Nubian wild ass, being an Egyptian endemic presumed extinct since the 1950s). It was once abundant on the dry eastern plains of the Horn of Africa, with a population of 10,000 estimated for Somaliland at the start of the 20th century. In his 1910 book *The Mammals of Somaliland*, Drake-Brogkman describes it as 'a magnificent beast, very much larger than the domestic donkey ... very inquisitive [but] difficult to approach after once being scared'. He also notes that it 'can travel very fast over stony ground' and that a 'sportsman would be lucky to get within four hundred yards'. He also noted that 'Somalis will not touch their flesh'.

Be that as it may, these once common equids are now IUCN-listed as 'Critically Endangered', with at most 200 individuals remaining in Ethiopia and no more than twice that in Eritrea. Its status in Somaliland is uncertain. The population was tentatively estimated at 200, centred on the Nogal Valley, in the late 1980s, but it had almost certainly declined significantly prior to the drought of 2005 in which several herds perished. The most recent sighting on record, according to Ahmed Ibrahim Awale, was a herd of no more than six in a village called Sha'ab in western Sanaag in 2006. All in all, it would be surprising if the global population of mature wild asses outside captivity were more than a few hundred, and some sources suggest it may even have dropped to a double figure. The captive population of 150 is concentrated at Zoo Basel in Switzerland, where a breeding programme has been under way since 1970.

If you are fortunate enough to see a wild ass in Somaliland – and it remains a possibility along the road to Erigavo or in the plains around Maydh – it will look much like a large domestic donkey, but should be readily distinguishable by the vertical black stripes on its legs, which are clearly visible even at a distance. In the interests of science, do your best to record the sighting photographically, and feel free to send us the results for our update website http://updates.bradtguides.com/somaliland.

---

insectivore that bears a superficial resemblance to the South American anteaters, the aardvark, as its Dutch-derived name (literally 'earth pig') indicates, also bears some similarity to the domestic pig in shape, size (up to 80kg) and its naked pinkish skin. It has a heavy almost kangaroo-like tail, long upright ears, and muscular long-nailed feet with which it burrows into termite mounds, snaffling up as many as 50,000 termites in one night by protruding and retracting its long sticky tongue into its elongated snout. The aardvark is a widespread inhabitant of arid savanna habitats, and can be quite common in areas with plentiful termite hills, but it is also very shy and forages late in the night, so sightings are rare.

Among the small mammals most likely to be seen in Somaliland are the **Ethiopian rock hyrax** (*Procavia capensis habessinica*) and **yellow-spotted bush hyrax** (*Heterohyrax brucei*). These superficially rodent-like creatures somewhat resemble an overgrown guinea pig, but are in fact dwarfish relicts of a near-ungulate order that dominated the African herbivore niche about 35 million years ago, when some species were as large as horses. A bizarre truism, much beloved of safari guides, is that the hyraxes' closest living relatives are elephants – a factoid that loses some of its 'golly gosh' value when you realise that the elephant/hyrax spilt dates back 40–50 million years. Common in rocky habitats (look out for them around Las Geel), it's difficult to tell the two species apart, though the yellow-spotted hyrax is significantly smaller than any rock hyrax and it has distinctive white eyebrows.

More than half the mammal species recorded in Somaliland are bats or rodents, most of which are rather nondescript and of little interest to non-specialist safari-goers. One regularly seen exception is the **unstriped ground squirrel** (*Xerus rutilus*), an endearing terrestrial dry country creature with a grey-brown coat, a prominent white eye-ring, a silvery black tail, and a habit of standing on its hind legs holding food in its forepaws. Another is the **springhare** (*Pedetes capensis*), a quirky nocturnal dry-country specialist that bounces along the plains like a miniature kangaroo. Finally, **Speke's Pectinator** (*Pectinator spekei*) is a peculiar endemic of the Horn of Africa that looks like an overgrown mouse with a rather squirrel-like tail that it flicks incessantly. It lives in vocal family groups in dry rocky habitats, and might well be seen at Las Geel or anywhere along the escarpment.

## REPTILES AND AMPHIBIANS

The predominantly hot and arid climate of Somaliland is arguably better suited to reptiles – cold-blooded creatures dependent on external heat sources to maintain their body temperature – than to perhaps any other vertebrate class. No figures are available for Somaliland specifically, but around 225 species have been recorded in Somalia as a whole, about 15% of which are endemic to the country. As might be expected, however, the country supports a rather low diversity of frogs and other amphibians, since the life cycle of most species is at least dependent on standing water. The total number of amphibian species recorded in Somalia stands at a mere 30, including three endemics, but it seems reasonable to assume that several of these are restricted to the two major perennial river systems that run through southern Somalia, and would be absent from Somaliland.

**SNAKES** A wide variety of snakes is found in Somaliland, although – fortunately, most would agree – they are typically very shy and unlikely to be seen unless actively sought. The largest snake present is the **African rock python** (*Python sebae*), which regularly grows to longer than 5m (longer than any other african reptile bar the extralimital Nile crocodile) and usually has gold-on-black mottled scaling. It is a non-venomous snake which strangles its prey, wrapping its muscular body around the victim until it cannot breathe, then swallowing it whole and dozing off for a couple of months while it digests. It feeds mainly on small antelope, large rodents, and the like, and is harmless to adult humans, but could conceivably kill a small child.

Most smaller snakes are non-venomous and harmless to any other living creature much larger than a rat. Several **cobra** species are present, however, and most have characteristic hoods that they raise when about to strike, although they are very seldom seen. Of the venomous snakes, the **Somali puff adder** (*Bitis arietans somalica*) is often considered to be the most dangerous, not because it is especially venomous or aggressive, but because it readily strikes when threatened and its notoriously sluggish disposition means it is more likely to be disturbed than other snakes. Growing up to about 1m long, the puff adder is a thickset and beautifully marked rodent-eater commonly associated with dry, rocky habitats, and the best way to avoid it is to look carefully where you place your feet (and, when scrambling, your hands) in such places.

**LIZARDS** All African lizards are harmless to humans, with the arguable exception of the giant **monitors**, which could in theory inflict a nasty bite if cornered. As far as we can ascertain, the Nile monitor, Africa's longest lizard, is absent from Somaliland, but the heavier **rock monitor** (*Varanus albigularis*), which grows up to 2m long, is present. It is occasionally seen in the vicinity of termite mounds, and will feed on anything from bird eggs to smaller reptiles and mammals, but will also eat carrion opportunistically.

Visitors to tropical Africa will soon become familiar with the **house geckos**, endearing bug-eyed, translucent white lizards that often inhabit houses and hotel rooms, where they make themselves useful by scampering up the walls and upside-down on the ceiling in pursuit of pesky insects attracted to the lights. Also very distinctive are the **agamas**, which can be distinguished from other common lizards by their relatively large size, habit of basking on rocks (you may well see them at Las Geel), and almost plastic-looking scaling – depending on the species, a combination of blue, purple, orange or red, with the flattened head generally a different colour from the torso. A species to look out for in Somaliland is the shield-tailed Agama (*Xenagama taylori*), a remarkable ground-dwelling lizard that can survive at temperatures of up to 50°C.

**TORTOISES, TERRAPINS AND TURTLES** These peculiar reptiles are unique in being protected by a prototypal suit of armour formed by their heavy exoskeleton. Most common is the **leopard tortoise** (*Stigmochelys pardalis*), named after its gold-and-black mottled shell, and known to live for more than 50 years in captivity. The form present in Somaliland is the giant leopard tortoise (often designated as the race *S. p. somalica*), which can weigh over 50kg and is particularly common seasonally along the roads running west from Hargeisa to Borama and Tog Wajaale, where it is regarded as a harbinger of rain. It is uncertain what, if any, species of **terrapin** – essentially the freshwater turtle equivalent – is resident in this dry country, but several species of endangered marine **turtles** have been recorded offshore (see page 45) .

# BIRDS

Somaliland doesn't compare to Africa's finest birding destinations in terms of avian diversity, thanks largely to its relative aridity and unvaried habitats. Nevertheless, most of the 720 bird species recorded in Somalia occur within Somaliland's confines, and because it remains relatively poorly known in ornithological terms, new species are frequently recorded by visiting birders. Somaliland is also of great interest for the presence of at least nine of the 12 birds regarded to be endemic to Somalia, along with a large number of near-endemics and other dry-country species with a limited distribution elsewhere. It is also worth noting that half of these Somali endemics would practically be Somaliland endemics were the country's sovereignty to be recognised.

Visiting birders are pointed to two fine books: the recently published *Helm Field Guide to the Birds of the Horn of Africa* and the out-of-print (but readily available online) *Birds of Somalia* (for more details, see *Appendix 2, Further reading*, page 179). In addition, an annotated overview of some key species follows, with Somali endemics indicated by a single asterisk (*) and Horn of Africa endemics and near-endemics (whose range might extend into Djibouti, Ethiopia, Eritrea, the far east of Sudan and/or northern Kenya) by a double asterisk (**).

** **Somali ostrich** (*Struthio molybdophanes*) Distinguished from the more widespread (and extralimital) common ostrich by its blue legs and by being a browser rather than a grazer.

Placed by some authorities in the same family as the closely related sparrows, the weavers of the family *Ploceidae* are a quintessential part of Africa's natural landscape, common and highly visible in virtually every habitat from rainforest to semi-desert. The name of the family derives from the intricate and elaborate nests – typically (but not always) a roughly oval ball of dried grass, reeds and twigs – that are built by the dextrous males of most species.

It can be fascinating to watch a male weaver at work. First, a nest site is chosen, usually at the end of a thin hanging branch or frond, which is immediately stripped of leaves to protect against snakes. The weaver then flies back and forth to the site, carrying the building material blade by blade in its heavy beak, first using a few thick strands to hang a skeletal nest from the end of a branch, and then gradually completing the structure by interweaving numerous thinner blades of grass into the main frame. Once completed, the nest is subjected to the attention of his chosen partner, who will tear it apart if the result is less than satisfactory, and so the process starts all over again.

**Socotra cormorant** (*Phalacrocorax nigrogularis*) IUCN listed as 'Vulnerable', this large, dark cormorant, endemic to the Persian Gulf and Arabian Peninsula, is occasionally seen at Maydh and other sites along the Somaliland coast.

\* **Archer's buzzard** (*Buteo [augur] archeri*) The Somali counterpart to the widespread augur buzzard, of which it is sometimes regarded as a sub-species or colour form, is a striking variable black, white and chestnut raptor whose range is confined to escarpment cliffs in Somaliland and Puntland. It is most likely to be seen in the vicinity of Daallo Forest.

**Barbary falcon** (*Falco pelegrinoides*) Northern Somaliland is probably the sole stronghold in sub-Saharan Africa for this dashing falcon, which reputedly breeds on the cliffs around Daallo (alongside the quite similar and more common **peregrine falcon**).

\*\* **Archer's francolin** (*Scleroptila lorti*) Recently 'split' from Orange River francolin, this smallish fowl is resident and likely to be seen in the Daallo Forest.

\*\* **Heuglin's bustard** (*Neotis heuglinii*) This large dry-country bustard, the male of which has a distinctive black head and bib, is widespread in Somaliland.

**Arabian bustard** (*Ardeotis arabs*) Another localised dry-country bustard, this looks rather like a smaller version of the gigantic **kori bustard** (which also occurs in Somaliland) but is restricted to the far northwest between Borama and Zeila.

\*\* **Buff-crested bustard** (*Lophotis gindiana*) This medium-sized bustard is probably the commonest member of the family in Somaliland, and the only one with an all black belly.

\*\* **Little brown bustard** (*Eupodotis humilis*) This small, pale bustard is common throughout Somaliland.

\*\* **Somali courser** (*Cursorius somaliensis*) Rather plover-like in appearance, this pale courser is a common and widespread ground-nester.

**Spotted sandgrouse** (*Pterocles senegallus*) Distinguished by its chestnut face, pale feathering and long tail, this Sahelian species reaches the southern extent of its range in northern Somalia.

\* **Somali rock pigeon** (*Columba oliviae*) This distinctive pigeon, which looks like a large grey dove with a chestnut nape, is very localised on rocky hills and escarpments along the northern coast of Somaliland and Puntland.

**Arabian scops owl** (*Otus pamelae*) The only putative African records for this species are from Daallo and Wagar, where it is most likely to be resident if present at all, which remains to be confirmed.

**Little owl** (*Athene noctua*) Quite often seen perching openly by day, this very pale Eurasian owl reaches the southern extent of its range in Somalia.

**Forbes-Watson's swift** (*Apus berliozi*) Cliff and cave-dwelling swift whose range is centred on the Somali and Yemeni coasts of the Gulf of Aden.

** **Somali bee-eater** (*Merops revoilii*) This small and unusually drab bee-eater is the most common of several species present in Somaliland.

** **Black-billed wood-hoopoe** (*Phoeniculus somaliensis*) This striking and noisy bird doesn't appear to be as common in Somaliland as the smaller but similar Abyssinian scimitar-bill, from which it can be distinguished at all ages by the white bars in the wing and tail.

**Lilac-breasted roller** (*Coracias caudatus lorti*) The lilac on the Horn of Africa race of this widespread safari favourite is restricted to the throat, and it is occasionally split as a distinct species (blue-breasted roller).

** **Hemprich's hornbill** (*Tockus hemprichii*) Large, striking, cliff-associated hornbill whose range centres on Ethiopia but extends along the Somaliland escarpment to the likes of Daallo, where it is quite common.

**Yellow-breasted barbet** (*Trachyphonus margaritatus*) Restricted to a narrow band along the Sahel, this striking, vocal and often quite confiding bird lacks the red cheeks of the similar red-and-yellow barbet.

* **Somali lark** (*Mirafra somalica*) The Horn of Africa is a rich centre of speciation among the larks, a family of mostly quite nondescript ground-dwelling birds, and several species are confined to the region. This Somali endemic, quite common in central Somaliland, is relatively large, very rufous, and has an unusually long bill.

** **Collared lark** (*Mirafra collaris*) An unusually distinctive lark with a bold black collar, this localised species reputedly hadn't been reliably recorded since the late 1980s prior to being observed on a 2010 expedition led by Nik Borrow. Its range is centred on the red sand country southeast of Burao.

* **Ash's lark** (*Mirafra ashi*) One of three Somali endemics whose known range lies entirely outside Somaliland (it is restricted to one area of grassy plains and dunes near Mogadishu).

* **Obbia lark** (*Spizocorys obbiensis*) Another Somali endemic that's unknown from Somaliland.

* **Archer's lark** (*Heteromirafra archeri*) Controversial species restricted to the clay plains around Tog Wajaale on the Ethiopian border near Hargeisa (see page 144).

** **Somali short-toed lark** (*Calandrella somalica*) This small and nondescript lark has a distribution centred on Somaliland, though a discrete population occurs in southern Ethiopia.

** **Blanford's lark** (*Calandrella blanfordi*) Confined to the eastern Horn of Africa and western Arabia, this common sparrow-like bird is the local equivalent of the widespread red-capped lark, and shares with it a distinct reddish cap. The race *C. b. daaroodensis* is more or less endemic to Somaliland.

**Greater hoopoe-lark** (*Alaemon alaudipes*) The far northwest of Somaliland is one of the best places to seek out this striking bird, which has a long, slightly curved bill and is patchily distributed through north Africa and Arabia.

* **Lesser hoopoe-lark** (*Alaemon hamertoni*) This Somali endemic is quite common all over Somaliland, which forms its core range.

** **Chestnut-headed sparrow-lark** (*Emeropterix signatus*) This regional endemic is one of three species of sparrow-lark – chunky and gregarious ground birds with boldly patterned males – recorded in Somaliland, and the only one with a white crown and chestnut on the back of the head.

** **Dwarf raven** (*Corvus edithae*) Recent, controversial split from larger *C. ruficollis*, range more or less confined to Somalia and the eastern half of Ethiopia.

** **White-rumped babbler** (*Turdoides leucopygia*) Common and conspicuous resident of wooded areas, noisy and easily distinguished from other babblers by its white rump.

** **Somali bulbul** (*Pycnonotus somaliensis*) Recent split from common bulbul, this cheerful garden bird has a very limited range within Djibouti, eastern Ethiopia and western Somaliland, where it is common in and around Hargeisa.

** **Dodson's bulbul** (*Pycnonotus dodsoni*) Another recent split from the common bulbul, this replaces the Somali bulbul in eastern Somaliland.

** **Somali wheatear** (*Oenanthe phillipsi*) A striking black, grey and white bird that tends to perch in the open. One of the most consistently conspicuous species in Somaliland.

** **Abyssinian black wheatear** (*Oenanthe lugubris vauriei*) The isolated Somali race of this pale-caped black wheatear has a white (as opposed to black) belly and is endemic to the Somaliland escarpment, where it is often seen along the road pass from Daallo to Maydh. It may well be a good species.

** **Sombre rock chat** (*Cercomela dubia*) Until recently, the only non-Ethiopian record for this nondescript and poorly known rock-dwelling bird came from the Wagar Forest in 1910. Exactly a century later, this old record was confirmed when an immature was photographed by Nik Borrow on the pass between Berbera and Sheikh.

* **Somali thrush** (*Turdus ludoviciae*) Recently split from the much paler olive thrush, this Somaliland endemic appears almost all black at a distance (indeed it is sometimes known as the Somali blackbird), but with a bright orange bill and eye-ring. It is common in the Daallo Forest but unlikely to be seen elsewhere.

**Clamorous reed warbler** (*Acrocephalus stentoreus*) The mangroves around Zeila form the most southerly African extent of this globally widespread species' range.

** **Ethiopian boubou** (*Laniarius aethiopicus*) Recently split from the widespread tropical boubou, this is a forest-associated black-and-white bird with a pinkish wash to the belly and a very distinctive duet that often alerts one to its presence. Its range in Somaliland is confined to the vicinity of Sheikh and Wagar.

* **Somali boubou** (*Laniarius erlangeri*) Another Somali endemic whose range lies entirely outside Somaliland, this is another recent split and similar to the Ethiopian boubou, though an all-black morph is common. The legendary Bulo Burti bush-shrike, described as a new species *L. liberatus* based on a live specimen captured and released in southern Somalia in 1991, is now assumed to be a yellow-washed morph of Somali boubou.

** **Red-naped bush-shrike** (*Laniarius ruficeps*) This is an odd and rather colourful boubou with a distinctive red cap and frog-like call. The nominate race is endemic to central Somaliland with a limited distribution centred on Mount Wagar, although recent reports suggest it is also common northeast of Burao.

** **Rosy-patched bush-shrike** (*Rhodophoneus cruentus*) One of the more characteristic and beautiful birds of bush country in Somaliland, this is also distinguished by its far-carrying whistling duets. The race *R. c hilgerti*, endemic to Somalia and eastern Ethiopia, has a distinctive black bib lacking in the nominate race.

- ** **Somali starling** (*Onychognathus blythii*) Associated with wooded and rocky ridges in Ethiopia and Somalia, this chestnut-winged starling with a long, tapering tail and (in the case of the female) grey head is common around Erigavo and Daallo.
- ** **Golden-breasted starling** (*Cosmopsarus regius*) This stunning and unmistakeable long-tailed bird is quite common in the bush country around Burao.
- ** **Shining sunbird** (*Cinnyrus hebessinica*) Brilliantly coloured sunbird common along the escarpment of Somaliland.
- ** **Ruppell's weaver** (*Ploceus galbula*) Restricted to the Horn of Africa and Yemen, this is a common and sociable resident of savanna and light woodland.
- ** **Brown-rumped seedeater (serin)** (*Serinus tristriatis*) Endemic to the Horn of Africa and common in Addis Ababa and other highland towns, where it seems to occupy a house sparrow-like niche.
- * **Somali golden-winged grosbeak** (*Rhynchostruthus louisae*) Listed as 'Vulnerable' by the IUCN with the global population estimated as a few thousand, this unmistakeable seedeater has a black head and bright yellow wings, and is endemic to the escarpment region of Somaliland, where it is most likely to be seen around Daallo.
- * **Warsangli linnet** (*Carduelis johannis*) IUCN listed as 'Endangered', with the global population estimated at below 1,000, this distinctive seedeater is more or less endemic to the escarpment around Daallo Forest, where it can be located most easily in the rainy season.

## MARINE WILDLIFE

Although Somaliland supports a rather small volume of large terrestrial animals, the offshore waters of the Gulf of Aden, and its protective fringe of coral reefs and islands, support a prodigious wealth of marine life. These areas remain undeveloped for tourism at the time of writing, but it is hoped that things will change following the recent creation of two new offshore marine parks with a combined area of 80km², together with the opening of a dive shop in Berbera. A brief overview of some of the marine wildlife associated with the Somali coast can be found below.

**MARINE MAMMALS** Ten species of cetacean (whales and dolphins) have been recorded along the Somali coast. These remarkable mammals have a similar body temperature to humans, and are as dependent on atmospheric oxygen as any terrestrial creature, yet they lead a totally aquatic existence, often in water so cold it would induce fatal hypothermia in most other mammals. Some species can spend up to an hour below water without surfacing, thanks to their large lungs, capacity to replenish 90% of their air supply in one breath, and the ability to store oxygen in their muscles, while a dense subcutaneous layer of insulating blubber protects them from the cold. Unfortunately, the commercial value of this blubber has also led to their persecution by the lucrative whaling industry, and most larger species of cetacean are now listed as 'Vulnerable' or 'Endangered' by the IUCN.

Cetaceans are divided into two distinct groups, based on their feeding anatomy. **Baleen whales**, named for the comb-like baleen plates that sieve plankton and tiny invertebrates from the water as they swim, are probably occasional visitors to Somali waters. However, odontocetic cetaceans – that is, **dolphins**, **porpoises** and toothed **whales** whose dental structure resembles that of terrestrial carnivores – are far better represented. The species most likely to be seen is the bottlenose dolphin (*Tursiops aduncus*), the world's most abundant and widespread cetacean, named for the elongated upper and lower jaws that create its characteristic smiling expression. It typically lives in pods of between three and 12 individuals, is known for its friendly character and curiosity about humans, and is often seen playing in the surf or swimming in the wake of a boat. Other species recorded include the spinner dolphin (*Stenella longirostrisis*) and common dolphin (*Delphinus delphis*), both of which frequently move in schools of several hundred, and five species of sperm and beaked whales.

The Somali coast is one of the last few strongholds for the **dugong** (*Dugong dugon*), a bulky (up to 1,000kg) marine mammal that feeds mainly on sea grass and is placed alongside the manatee of the Atlantic Ocean in the family Sirinia, whose closest terrestrial relatives are elephants and hyraxes. The name Sirinia, a reference to the sirens of Greek legend, has been given to this family of marine animals because they are considered the most likely source of the mermaid myth. Dugongs have suffered a drastic population decrease in the past few decades, probably because so many are trapped in fishing nets. IUCN listed as 'Vulnerable', the dugong is now threatened with extinction except in the seas around northern Australia and the Arabian Gulf.

**TURTLES** The Somali coastline is globally important to the survival of marine turtles – representatives of conservative reptilian lineage that first appeared in the fossil record more than 100 million years ago and evolved into distinctive modern genera some 60 million years back. Marine turtles remained common to abundant throughout their natural range until the late 19th century, when the combination of hunting (for food, skin, and 'tortoiseshell', the latter once an important item of trade off the Somali coast), accidental trapping, habitat destruction and pollution

## GIANTS OF THE OCEAN

Common in the waters off Somaliland, the whale shark (*Rhincodon typus*) is the largest living species of fish, measuring up to 12m long, weighing up to 35 tonnes, and with a life span comparable to a human or elephant. As one of only three filter-feeding shark species, this passive, slow-swimming giant is essentially harmless to humans (or anything else much larger than a goldfish), although there is a slight danger of snorkellers or divers who approach one too closely being swiped by its powerful tail fins. In common with whales, this gigantic shark feeds mainly on plankton and other microscopic organisms, which are imbibed together with water through its wide mouth, and trapped in a specially adapted gill apparatus when the water is expelled, although it will also occasionally eat small fish. Found throughout the tropical oceans, it is listed as 'Vulnerable' by the IUCN, with the main threat to its survival being commercial fishing.

Another common species, often associated with reefs, is the manta ray (*Manta birostris*), the world's largest ray, sometimes weighing two tonnes and boasting a wingspan of around 7.5m. Although manta rays have a flattened shape and long tails similar to stingrays, they cannot sting and are totally harmless to divers. Indeed, like whale sharks, they are filter feeders whose main diet is plankton and other tiny suspended organisms. An intriguing aspect of manta ray behaviour is the regular gathering of several individuals at cleaning stations, where wrasse and other reef fish feed on the parasites and dead tissue accumulated in their gills. They are also capable of breaching the surface and launching into the air – a rare but spectacular sight.

resulted in a serious decline in numbers. Indeed, of the seven recognised species, all but one is listed on the IUCN Red Data List, with eventual extinction being a distinct possibility for three 'Critically Endangered' species. At least four marine turtles are resident or regular visitors to the Somali coast, namely **green turtle** (*Chelonia mydas*), **hawksbill** (*Eretmochelys imbricata*), **loggerhead** (*Caretta caretta*) and **olive ridley** (*Lepidochelys olivacea*), and several breeding sites were uncovered in a marine survey of the coast east of Berbera in 1999.

The life cycle of marine turtles is unusual. Their full life span remains a matter of speculation, but most species reach sexual maturity in their 20s or later, and many individuals probably live for longer than a century. During breeding season male and female turtles converge offshore to mate. Once the eggs are ready, usually on a moonlit night, the female crawls onto the beach to dig a 50cm-deep hole, lays up to 120 eggs and covers them with sand, leaving them to hatch about two months later. Oddly, water temperature affects the sex of the hatchlings – a balance between male and female is to be expected at 28°C, but males will predominate in cooler waters, and females in warmer water.

**FISH** It is unknown how many fish species occur off the Somali coast, but a short survey in 1999 identified 135 reef-associated species in the vicinity of Berbera alone, and the likely figure exceeds 1,000. For visitors, the most interesting marine fish fall into three broad categories. Most prolific are a kaleidoscopic miscellany of colourful **reef fish**, several dozen of which might be encountered on a single snorkelling or diving session. Less numerous, but arguably more exciting, are cartilaginous marine giants such as **sharks** and **rays** (see box, *Giants of the ocean*, page 45), several species of which occur along the Somali coast. Finally, there are the game fish – **marlins**, **sailfish**, **barracuda** and such – that attract dedicated fisherman.

The coral reefs off the shore of Somaliland are spectacular multi-hued natural aquaria which form the focal point of most diving and snorkelling excursions. When exploring these reefs, one visual sweep of your surrounds might reveal a selection of a dozen or more species, whose memorable names reflect an extraordinary range of shapes and colours. There are the closely related **devil's firefish** and **red lionfish**, whose gaudy pattern and poisonous spines give them the appearance of psychedelic marine porcupines. Other memorable genera and species include the brilliantly colourful **sweet-lips**, **angelfishes**, **butterfly fishes** and **wrasses**, the predatory **honeycomb eel** and scalloped **hammerhead**, and the elongated **needlefish** and outsized **rock cods**. Snorkellers and divers may also encounter several of the region's species of **stingray**, most of which have a 'wingspan' of around 75cm to 1.5m and tend to swim close to the sandy ocean floor.

**OTHER MARINE CREATURES** The oceanic waters off Somaliland support a diversity of invertebrate species more remarkable even than its fish. For instance, **coral**, contrary to its rocklike appearance, is an organic entity comprising the limestone exoskeleton of colonial polyps that are related to sea anemones and feed mainly on photosynthetic algae, which thrive at a depth of up to 15m in warm aerated water along the continental shelf. One single reef might be composed of more than 50 different coral species, and as you examine the reefs closely, you see it is studded with sea anemones – spiky predatory polyps that often posses a nasty sting. There are also thousands of sea **molluscs**, **crustaceans** and other creatures with shells or exoskeletons, among them **crabs** and **crayfish**, and rock-loving invertebrates such as **mussels**, **oysters**, **barnacles** and **periwinkles**, which are often associated with intertidal rock pools.

# 3

# Practical Information

## WHEN TO VISIT

The most pleasant time to travel is over the northern hemisphere winter, from November to March, when it is relatively cool, with maximum temperatures of around 25°C typical on the plateau around Hargeisa, rising to around 30°C along the coast. By contrast, the summer months can be oppressively hot, especially along the coast, where temperatures in excess of 45°C are frequently recorded.

Winter is also the dry season, which is an advantage for those who plan to venture beyond the few asphalt roads – rainfall figures for Somaliland are low, but when the rain does come, seasonal watercourses and muddy depressions might double the travel times along routes such as Borama to Zeila and Burao to Erigavo, or worse still render them temporarily impassable.

There are, however, some advantages to travelling in the summer, among them that the countryside is much greener, and bird and mammal breeding activity reaches a peak.

## SUGGESTED ITINERARIES

The options are somewhat limited. Most visitors arrive in Hargeisa, whether by air or overland from Ethiopia, and the most popular excursions from here are a day trip to Las Geel or an overnight trip via Las Geel to the port of Berbera, which is the most interesting town in the country – as well as being the only one that is developed, albeit in a very low-key manner, for beach tourism, snorkelling and diving. You could easily see the best of what Berbera and Las Geel have to offer in a two or three-night excursion from Hargeisa.

Using public transport, it is usually possible to travel onwards from Berbera to Sheikh and Burao, a trip that might reasonably be characterised as travel for its own sake, and that would add a day or two to your itinerary. For those with private 4x4 transport, it is possible to divert from the Hargeisa–Berbera road to Ga'an Libah, or from the Berbera–Burao road to Mount Wagar, both of which are good destinations for wildlife and birds. Allow at least one additional night for either excursion.

More ambitiously, with a sturdy 4x4 you could continue on from Burao to Erigavo and the wildlife-rich Daallo Forest, from where a scenic mountain pass leads to the tiny port of Maydh. This excursion realistically requires at least two nights based in Erigavo, but having come this far we would strongly recommend you allocate four nights to exploring the region. At the time of writing, the part of Somaliland east of the track between Oog and Erigavo is disputed by Puntland and widely regarded as unsafe for travel.

Few people explore the far west of Somaliland beyond the main road to the Ethiopian or Djibouti border. However, the area boasts a selection of moderately

Somaliland generally has a hot, dry climate, and four main seasons are recognised. Jiilaal, from December to March, though technically winter, is hot and dry, with the main wind blowing from the northeast. Gu, from April to June, is the main rainy season, and hotter than the previous season, with occasional violent storms. The drier Xagaa, over July and August, is the hottest time of year, with a low chance of rain, characterised by winds blowing from the southeast. Dayr, from September to November, is cooler with occasional light rains. The climate charts below, for Hargeisa, Erigavo and Berbera, are respectively representative of conditions along the inner plateau, the high escarpment and the coast.

### Hargeisa

|             | J  | F  | M  | A  | M  | J  | J  | A  | S  | O  | N  | D  |
|-------------|----|----|----|----|----|----|----|----|----|----|----|----|
| Av max (°C) | 26 | 28 | 29 | 30 | 31 | 31 | 30 | 29 | 31 | 28 | 27 | 26 |
| Av min (°C) | 12 | 13 | 15 | 18 | 18 | 17 | 17 | 17 | 17 | 15 | 14 | 12 |
| Rain (mm)   | 2  | 10 | 25 | 80 | 65 | 35 | 40 | 55 | 65 | 30 | 10 | 2  |

### Erigavo

|             | J  | F  | M  | A  | M  | J  | J  | A  | S  | O  | N  | D  |
|-------------|----|----|----|----|----|----|----|----|----|----|----|----|
| Av max (°C) | 24 | 25 | 25 | 26 | 26 | 25 | 25 | 25 | 24 | 24 | 23 | 22 |
| Av min (°C) | 7  | 8  | 9  | 10 | 12 | 13 | 14 | 14 | 11 | 8  | 7  | 6  |
| Rain (mm)   | 10 | 10 | 20 | 40 | 60 | 40 | 10 | 30 | 80 | 5  | 5  | 1  |

### Berbera

|             | J  | F  | M  | A  | M  | J  | J  | A  | S  | O  | N  | D  |
|-------------|----|----|----|----|----|----|----|----|----|----|----|----|
| Av max (°C) | 28 | 28 | 32 | 30 | 36 | 42 | 42 | 41 | 40 | 33 | 31 | 29 |
| Av min (°C) | 20 | 22 | 23 | 25 | 28 | 30 | 31 | 30 | 29 | 25 | 22 | 20 |
| Rain (mm)   | 1  | 1  | 1  | 15 | 2  | 5  | 0  | 2  | 3  | 0  | 0  | 10 |

worthwhile archaeological sites, and one true gem in the form of the coast around the historic port of Zeila, not far from the Djibouti border. One alluring but very off-the-beaten-track possibility, if you are heading this way, would be to follow the rough tracks that run along the coast between Berbera and Zeila, a rough 4x4 expedition that takes at least two days and should ideally be done in convoy.

## TOUR OPERATORS

We are not aware of any international tour operators that currently run general-interest trips to Somaliland, but two highly regarded companies have run or intend to start running ornithological tours. These are **Birding Africa** (☏ +27 (0)21 531 9148/6405; e info@birdingafrica.com, birdingafricaoffice@gmail. com; www.birdingafrica.com) and **Birdquest UK** (☏ +44 1254 826317; e birders@ birdquest.co.uk; www.birdquest.co.uk). In addition, at least three reasonably reliable operations are based in Hargeisa, of which **Dalmar Tours** is a solid and relatively affordable option. **Nature Somaliland**, though a lot pricier, is the better bet for dedicated birders and other wildlife enthusiasts. See page 84 for further details.

# RED TAPE

All visitors to Somaliland require a valid passport, the expiry date of which should be at least six months after you intend to end your travels. A Somaliland visa (emphatically *not* the same thing as a Somali visa) must also be arranged in advance by all visitors. This is a requirement that is complicated by the fact Somaliland is not yet formally recognised as a country and thus lacks proper diplomatic representation any further afield than Addis Ababa, one of only two places where a visa can be collected outside the country, the other being the Somaliland Liaison Office in London (and do note that there is nowhere in Djibouti to get a Somaliland visa, nor can one be issued at the border). Another viable option for those flying to Hargeisa is to arrange a visa through the hotel where you will be staying.

## VISA PRIOR TO ARRIVAL

**Ethiopia** The most straightforward place to pick up a visa, especially for those travelling via Ethiopia, is the **Somaliland Embassy** in Addis Ababa. See *The Somaliland Embassy in Addis Ababa* on page 164 for full details.

**London** The **Somaliland Liaison Office** in London (*102 Cavel St, E1 2JA;* \ *020 7961 9098;* m *07960 287130;* e *slmission@hotmail.co.uk*) will usually issue a visa on the spot, although it is something of a one-man show, so it is best to call in advance to confirm when it will be open. It is theoretically possible for them to organise a visa remotely by posting or (safer) couriering them your passport, but we have had mixed reports about the efficiency of this, so do liaise with them first, and allow plenty of time for the passport to get there and back, and the visa to be processed.

**VISA ON ARRIVAL** Visas can be obtained on arrival only by prior arrangement with the immigration office in Hargeisa, and then only if you are landing at Hargeisa airport or coming overland from Djibouti with a recognised operator. The usual procedure is to email a scan of your passport to a contact in Hargeisa, ideally about two weeks prior to your arrival date, and then for two copies to be printed off and taken to the immigration office for processing. A visa will be issued on one of the printed scans, deposited at the airport and pasted into your actual passport after you land. It might be an idea to ask to have a copy of this visa emailed back to you so you can produce it on arrival. The Oriental Hotel/Dalmar Tours in Hargeisa has made arrangements of this sort in the past, as has the operator Nature Somaliland, and you could also try the Ambassador or Man-soor hotels.

**CUSTOMS AND IMMIGRATION** Provided you already have a visa, immigration is usually straightforward (but be warned that without a visa you will be refused entry). Up to 400 cigarettes, 40 cigars or 400g of tobacco can be brought into the country duty free, as can a reasonable amount of perfume for personal use. Alcoholic beverages of all kinds are illegal, and travellers caught importing any wine or spirits can at best expect it to be confiscated. We are not aware of any restriction on the import or export of currency.

# GETTING THERE AND AWAY

For many years, the easiest way to get to Somaliland from Europe, North America and almost anywhere else in the world was with Ethiopian Airlines, which has one of the most extensive international flight networks of any African carrier. Until

## VISAS FOR ETHIOPIA AND DJIBOUTI

A significant proportion of visitors to Somaliland travel overland from Ethiopia or Djibouti, so it is worth being aware of the visa requirements for both countries.

All visitors to Ethiopia require a visa, but citizens of the USA, Canada, Mexico, Brazil, New Zealand, Australia, South Africa, China, Japan, Korea, Israel, Russia, the UK and all other EU nations can buy a one-month single-entry visa upon arrival at Bole International Airport for around US$30. Other passport holders will need to arrange a visa in advance – if you live in a country where there is no Ethiopian embassy, and travel with Ethiopian Airways, you can apply for a visa through the airline office. If you plan to travel to Somaliland and then return to Ethiopia, you must either arrange a multiple-entry visa before you leave home (or through the immigration office on Churchill Avenue in Addis Ababa) or obtain a new single-entry visa at the Ethiopian Embassy in Hargeisa (see page 49).

If you are flying to Ethiopia, visas can be obtained upon arrival at Djibouti International Airport by any visitor with an EU, US, UK, Canadian or South African passport. A three-day transit visa, which costs US$30, is recommended if your main interest is Somaliland, but a three-month single-entry visa is also available for US$60. If you plan to return from Somaliland to Djibouti overland, there is nowhere to obtain a visa in Hargeisa, but a transit visa can be bought at the Looyada border post – except on Fridays, when the person in charge takes the day off and there is nobody available with the authority to issue a stamp. By contrast, if crossing between Ethiopia and Djibouti via the Ali Sabih border post, east of Dire Dawa, it is not normally possible to get a Djibouti visa on arrival, and you would need to sort this out in Addis Ababa.

2008, when these flights were suspended indefinitely in the wake of the embassy bombing, it also operated regular scheduled trips between Addis Ababa and Hargeisa. No major international airline has landed in Hargeisa since. Hopefully it is only a matter of time before Ethiopian Airlines resumes the Hargeisa flight and it is definitely worth checking this out before you look at any other options (either call the local representative, as listed on www.flyethiopian.com, or check the schedules on the same website).

In the meantime, the only viable option for flying into Somaliland is a handful of regional carriers of varying reliability that connect a limited selection of other cities in east Africa or Arabia to Hargeisa (HGA) and/or Berbera (BBO). The carriers in question are **African Express**, **Daallo Airlines**, **East African Safari Express**, **Jubba Airways** and **Punt Air**; collectively they connect Somaliland to three African cities, namely Addis Ababa (Ethiopia), Nairobi (Kenya) and Djibouti (Djibouti), as well as Dubai and Sharjah in the United Arab Emirates (for contact details see page 51).

It is also possible to fly into Addis Ababa, and then make your way to Somaliland overland, a popular option covered in greater detail in *Chapter 11*.

**VIA DJIBOUTI** Of the five regional gateways listed above, by far the closest to Somaliland is Djibouti, which lies about 30 minutes' drive away on the other side of the border from Zeila. Djibouti is connected directly to Paris by **Air France** (*www.airfrance.com*), and **Ethiopian Airlines** (*www.flyethiopian.com*) also flies there from Addis Ababa, which creates useful links to most major cities in Europe, North America, Asia and the rest of Africa. **Daallo Airlines** and **Jubba Airways** both fly from Djibouti to Hargeisa twice a week and tickets cost around US$120/235 one-way/return – significantly cheaper than flights from Nairobi or Dubai, although this will probably balance out against the higher cost of flights from Europe to Djibouti.

It is also possible to travel **overland** from Djibouti to Hargeisa in the 4x4s that serve as public transport between the two cities, possibly stopping *en route* at Zeila. However, this is a rough trip that might take anything from 14 hours in the dry season, to a couple of days after heavy rain. The departure point in Djibouti City is on Gammel Abdul Nasser Avenue, and it is conventional to book your seat in the morning and pay a deposit, then to return in the mid-afternoon for departure at around 16.00. When you get to Hargeisa, the driver should drop you at your hotel of choice for no extra charge. It's worth noting that the operator Nature Somaliland, which specialises in birding tours to Djibouti and/or Somaliland, frequently arranges for clients to fly into Djibouti and then travel overland to Hargeisa, as the road between the two cities offers the opportunity to see some key birds absent elsewhere in the country.

**VIA NAIROBI** Nairobi is served by an excellent global network of flights operated by the reputable national carrier **Kenya Airways** (*www.kenya-airways.com*) and numerous other well-known airlines. It is connected to Hargeisa by **East African Safari Express**, and to Berbera (with an optional free bus connection to Hargeisa) by **Africa Express** and **Jubba Airlines**. Flights are relatively expensive, however, at around US$220/440 one-way/return with East African Safari Express and Jubba Airlines, or US$350/450 one-way/return with Africa Express, although taxes usually push the return flight up to more than US$500.

**VIA DUBAI OR SHARJAH** Dubai International Airport is arguably even better connected than Nairobi, as it is the global hub of the national airline **Emirates** (*www.emirates.com*), which operates more than 2,000 flights per week to at least 100 destinations worldwide. Dubai is also connected to Hargeisa by **Daallo Airways**, and to Berbera (with an optional bus connection provided to Hargeisa) by **East African Safari Express** and **Jubba Airlines**. Flights are comparable in price with those from Nairobi – around US$500 return excluding taxes. Sharjah, by contrast, is relatively poorly connected in international terms, and the only airline connecting it to Somaliland is African Express, so it is probably not worth pursuing.

**VIA ADDIS ABABA** This option can probably be discounted by anybody hoping to jet directly into Somaliland, as the only carrier offering flights at the time of writing is Punt Air, a new company which has already acquired a reputation for unreliability. However, the paucity of international flights to Somaliland means a high proportion of visitors travel there **overland** from Addis Ababa, via Dire Dawa, Harar and/or Jijiga, which also has the additional advantage of allowing you to organise your visa in Addis Ababa. A compromise solution for those with limited time (or who don't fancy the long bus ride to eastern Ethiopia) is to catch an Ethiopian Airways flight from Addis Ababa to Jijiga, the closest town to the Somaliland border. See the chapter *Overland routes to Hargeisa from Addis Ababa* on page 156 for further details.

**AIRLINES SERVING SOMALILAND** Please note that the contacts below are booking details for head offices; the local contacts in Hargeisa are supplied on page 88. Bear in mind, too, that all flight departure times are prone to change, whether scheduled or unscheduled, and that none of these airlines can be regarded as punctual by, say, Swiss standards.

**African Express Airways** ☎+254 20 201 4746/239 0600; e afex@africanexpress.co.ke, afexnbo@gmail.com; www.africanexpress. co.ke. This Kenyan airline runs scheduled flights between Nairobi, Hargeisa, Berbera, Sharjah & Dubai. Flights from Nairobi to Berbera leave at 08.00 on Tue, Thu & Sun, taking about 4 hrs, while return flights leave Berbera at 11.00 on Mon, Wed & Fri, & take 5–6 hrs. The flight includes a free coach service from Berbera to Hargeisa.

**Daallo Airlines** ☎+971 4 299 4485/6; www. daallo.com. Based in Dubai, the official carrier for Somalia operates weekly flights to Hargeisa & Bosaso from Dubai & Djibouti. In theory, flights from Djibouti to Hargeisa operate on Mon & Thu, returning on Mon & Wed, while those from Hargeisa to Dubai are on Wed & Sun, returning Thu & Mon. Check departure times with the airline, which has a reputation for unreliability & for cancelling flights at the last minute if there are insufficient passengers.

**East African Safari Express** ☎+254 20 665 4321; e reservations@easa.co.ke; http:// eastafrican.easytravelpoint.com/ibe. Not to be confused with African Express, this airline runs what are probably the most reliable flights between Nairobi & Hargeisa, & it is the only carrier to fly there directly rather than landing in Berbera & bussing to Hargeisa. However, the plane stops briefly at Wajir, in northern Kenya,

for customs & security clearance, as direct flights from Somalia are not welcome at Nairobi. Flights in both directions currently operate on Tue & Sat only, leaving Nairobi at 08.00 & Hargeisa at 11.00, & taking around 3hrs one way. Online booking is planned for the near future but until that happens, the on-the-ball booking office in Nairobi (as listed above) is very helpful.

**Jubba Airways** ☎+971 4 222 6869; e jubba@ jubba-airways.com; www.jubba-airways.com. Generally regarded as more reliable than Daallo, & similar in price, this is probably the first choice for flights to & from Dubai & Djibouti. It operates twice-weekly connections to both, though do note that they actually land at Berbera, from where passengers are bussed to Hargeisa. Flights to & from Djibouti operate on Mon & Fri, leaving Djibouti at 08.30 & Hargeisa at 15.30. Jubba also offers flights to & from Nairobi, & is a little cheaper than the competition, but they take longer because the plane stops at a few places, including Mogadishu, *en route*, though you don't have to get out of the plane. It has a decent website, too, with full schedules posted & online booking facilities.

**Punt Air** ☎+251 1 620 921.This operates an affordable weekly return flight between Hargeisa & Addis Abba. Theoretically the flight is on Mon, but cancellations are frequent. You'd be better off using Ethiopian Airlines to get as far as Jijiga & travel overland from there.

## SAFETY

The first question to pass through the mind of many prospective visitors to Somaliland will be, 'Is it safe?'. To be honest, this question has no definitive answer. Officially, Somaliland is part of Somalia, undoubtedly one of the most lawless and dangerous countries in the world. As of May 2011, the US Department of State website (*www.travel.state.gov*) 'warns US citizens against all travel to Somalia, including the self-proclaimed "Independent Republic of Somaliland"', while the British Foreign Office travel advisory (*www.fco.gov.uk*) summarised the situation as follows, 'We advise against all travel to Somalia, including Somaliland. In the southern and central regions, there is ongoing serious violence, dangerous levels of criminal activity and general internal insecurity. We advise any British citizens in Somalia to leave'.

In practice, Somaliland functions as a completely separate country to Somalia or Puntland, and it is universally regarded to be far safer than either of these fractious neighbours. Within Somaliland itself, there have been instances of foreign aid workers being killed or kidnapped since independence in 1991, acts perpetrated by Al-Shabaab and other external groups hoping to destabilise their peaceful neighbour, but such incidents have been infrequent, and are evidently on the decrease. That said, Hargeisa and Bosaso were hit by six co-ordinated suicide bombings as recently as 2008, and the enduring instability of the entire Somali region precludes too many glib reassurances. Nevertheless, Somaliland is starting to attract a significant trickle of travellers from across the Ethiopian border, so far without incident, and the impression of every foreigner we met travelling or working in Somaliland is that visitors have little to worry about in terms of security, provided that they stick to regularly visited sites such as Hargeisa, Berbera and Las Geel, and ask local advice before heading further off the beaten track.

Also bearing on the issue of safety is the official requirement that all foreigners moving outside Hargeisa must be accompanied by an armed member of the Special Protection Unit (see box, *Travel with the SPU*, page 54). The official line seems to be that this is an ultra-conservative precaution against the devastating effect the killing of a foreigner would have on Somaliland's petition for international recognition. But it wouldn't be necessary, surely, unless there was a genuine risk associated with travel outside the capital? Perhaps, or is it simply misplaced paranoia? It has even been suggested that the SPU policy exists at the instigation of foreign UN and NGO workers with a vested interest in maintaining Somaliland's official high-risk status (it means that salaries are higher than in a more stable country). What can be said with confidence is that it is increasingly common for the Chief of Police in Hargeisa to issue a written waiver of SPU protection to backpackers upon request – an anomaly from which you can draw your own conclusions!

Whatever the actual risks associated with travel in Somaliland, the reality is that if you get into any sort of trouble there you'll be a lot more isolated than would normally be the case. There will be no embassy to help bail you out, since Ethiopia is the only country in the world with formal diplomatic representation in Hargeisa. Furthermore, most travel insurance policies explicitly exclude cover for countries subject to the FCO or US State Department travel warnings quoted above, in which case you will also be uninsured (for further advice, see the *Health* chapter, page 65).

Security issues aside, Somaliland is largely free of more conventional crime, such as pickpocketing, mugging and theft from hotel rooms. Indeed, we have heard of no such incident involving a traveller anywhere in Somaliland, and would regard the country to be as safe as anywhere we have visited in that respect. All the same, there is a significant disparity in wealth between most locals and visitors, so it might be viewed as tempting fate to wander along unlit streets alone at night, or to carry large sums of money or valuables publicly. And on the basis that it is preferable to err on the side of caution, below are a few tips that apply to travelling anywhere in Africa.

- Most casual thieves operate in busy markets and taxi parks. Keep a close watch on your possessions in such places, and avoid having valuables or large amounts of money loose in your daypack or pocket.
- Keep all your valuables and the bulk of your money in a hidden money belt. Never show this money belt in public. Keep any spare cash you might need elsewhere on your person.
- A buttoned-up pocket on the front of the shirt is one of the most secure places, as money cannot be snatched from it without the thief coming into view.
- Where the choice exists between carrying valuables on your person or leaving them in a locked room, we believe the latter is generally safer, assuming that the

A major ambiguity associated with travel in Somaliland is the erratically enforced requirement to travel everywhere outside Hargeisa accompanied by at least one member of the Special Protection Unit (SPU), an arm of the police force specially trained to protect foreigners. The exact rules regarding where and when SPU protection is required are almost impossible to pin down. The story seems to change from one day to the next (and one government department to another), so anything we state now may have changed by the time you get there.

As far as we can ascertain, the official requirement for all parts of the country east of Burao is that foreigners must travel privately in a convoy of at least two 4x4s, one for themselves and one containing at least two SPU guards. In practice, however, tourists are generally permitted to travel in one 4x4 with one SPU, although a second one may sometimes be required, depending on whether space is available. For travel west of Burao, one car (not necessarily 4x4) and one SPU is fine. It should be noted that many SPU guards will insist on taking the passenger seat – and if there is a second officer, a window seat in the back – which makes sense in terms of security, but does limit how much paying clients get to see through the window. On that basis, the argument for a second vehicle to carry the SPU is compelling, assuming you can afford it.

The rules surrounding travel on public transport are even more ambiguous. It seems to be universally agreed that no SPU protection is required on public transport between Hargeisa and the Ethiopian and Djiboutian borders, and it is equally clear at the time of writing that foreigners are forbidden outright from using public transport anywhere east of Burao, with or without SPU protection. Between Hargeisa, Berbera and Burao, it is permitted to use public transport, but only if you pay for SPU protection, otherwise you'll most likely

room is absolutely secure. However, some travellers' cheque companies will not refund cheques stolen from a room, or might reject the claim on a technicality, for instance if the door wasn't damaged during the robbery.
• Leave any jewellery of financial or sentimental value at home.

**BRIBERY AND BUREAUCRACY** Bribery is a fact of life for people doing business in many African countries, but it is seldom an issue for travellers and we neither heard nor experienced anything to suggest that visitors to Somaliland need be concerned about having to bribe their way out of a sticky situation.

However, the wheels of bureaucracy tend to turn rather slowly in Somaliland, and any serious dealings with officialdom are likely to be infused with the spirit of, 'why fill out in duplicate what can be filled out in triplicate?' This is especially true if you want to visit any attractions off the beaten track, which must normally be preceded by a visit to the nearest municipal office, police station, or both.

For travellers, most dealings with officials are at the ubiquitous roadblocks, which are normally straightforward and friendly encounters, provided you are accompanied by an SPU officer or have a waiver letter from the Chief of Police.

**LAND MINES** A grim legacy of the wars that gripped post-independence Somaliland between 1964 and 1991 is the large number of landmines – possibly be turned back at the first police roadblock (although people do sometimes get through without an SPU on board).

A further area of ambiguity relates to the rules for individual towns. The official ruling seems to be that you can walk or drive freely in Hargeisa without SPU protection at any time of day. In Berbera, it is permitted to walk or drive freely between 06.00 and 18.00, and while SPU protection is technically required after dark, this rule is often ignored. Elsewhere in the country, it is forbidden to walk or drive without SPU protection at any time, and you should not leave your hotel at all between 18.00 and sunrise.

SPU protection costs US$10–20 per guard per day, depending on who organises it and whether it's a day or overnight trip. In theory, travel expenses are covered by this fee but many SPU guards will expect the client to pay for their meals. In addition to being costly, some SPU officers are notoriously obstructive to any plan that interferes with their agenda (ie: chewing lots of *khat* and doing as little as possible), and you'll find that security risks are exaggerated or played down, and rules ignored, twisted, invented or heeded, on a somewhat self-serving basis. Unless you enjoy arguing with a man with a gun, this can become quite tiresome.

The good news for backpackers is that, over the months prior to publication of this guidebook, it became increasingly commonplace for the Chief of Police in Hargeisa to issue a written waiver on the spot to any traveller who asked. This allowed the bearer to travel freely to Berbera (and sometimes, upon request, to Burao) without SPU protection. We have not heard of anybody being permitted to travel in a private vehicle without SPU protection, but there is nothing stopping you from asking – and we'll post any developments based on reader feedback on our website: http://updates.bradtguides.com/somaliland.

as many as 100,000 in the vicinity of Hargeisa alone – that were laid and left unexploded when Somaliland declared itself independent. In the early 1990s, the US Department of State described the landmine situation in Somaliland as a 'very serious problem', and the International Red Cross ranked it third among the world's most severely mine-affected areas – with one amputee for every 652 persons, and an average of two mine victims per day being checked into Hargeisa Hospital. Since 1999, however, a number of international organisations, including the Halo Trust (*www.halotrust.org*), an NGO funded by the British and US governments among others, has been involved in a series of clearance operations that have rendered all but the most remote minefields benign. From a traveller's perspective, there is no significant chance of straying into a minefield provided you stick to the areas covered in this guidebook, but anybody thinking of heading out to more remote parts of the country should be alert to the possibility of unexploded ordnance and ask around in advance.

## WOMEN TRAVELLERS

Women travellers generally regard sub-equatorial Africa as one of the safest places to travel alone anywhere in the world, and Somaliland is probably no exception when it comes to gender-specific risks. That said, single women are advised to avoid hotels listed in the budget or shoestring category, in particular those with shared showers and toilets, which are highly unlikely to be frequented by local women. Likewise, it is unusual for local women to eat alone in restaurants, and female travellers who do so might become targets of unwanted curiosity or flirtation. Many female travellers to relatively conservative countries consider it to be a good idea to pretend you have a husband at home or in another town – and, ideally, a wedding ring as 'proof' of your status.

The biggest restriction on women travellers to Somaliland is the need to adhere to smothering local dress codes in all public places. For local women, the standard items of clothing are a loose-fitting, all-enveloping ankle-length dress called a *direh*, and a bonnet-like headscarf called a *hijab* that covers every last hair on their head. Some women also wear the more severe *abaya*, a long black or multi-coloured garment, reminiscent of a nun's habit, that leaves only the eyes, hands and feet exposed. Female travellers should dress similarly, at the very minimum wearing a loose ankle-length skirt, a top that is sufficiently baggy to mask the shape of their breasts, and a loose headscarf. Aside from being offensive to local sensibilities, any attire tighter or more revealing than this might, in a Somali context, create an unwanted impression of availability.

## GAY TRAVELLERS

Any act of male or female homosexuality is a criminal offence. Offenders risk imprisonment or, in extreme cases, capital punishment. That doesn't mean homosexuality doesn't exist (see *www.somaligaycommunity.org*), but out of necessity it is very clandestine. Setting aside the rights and wrongs of the matter, Somaliland clearly isn't a destination suited to single travellers in search of anything approximating a gay scene (or, for that matter, any other form of secular nightlife), and at risk of stating the blindingly obvious, gay couples who do visit the country should exercise maximum discretion.

## WHAT TO TAKE

**LUGGAGE** If you intend using public transport or doing much walking, it's best to carry your luggage on your back. There are three ways of doing this: with a purpose-made backpack, with a suitcase that converts to a rucksack, or with a large daypack. The choice between a convertible suitcase and a purpose-built backpack rests mainly on your style of travel. If you intend doing a lot of walking, you're definitely best off with a proper backpack. However, if you carry everything in a smaller 35 to 45-litre daypack, the advantages are manifold on public transport and in terms of overall mobility.

**CAMPING GEAR** Opportunities to camp in Somaliland are limited, and most people wouldn't want to bother with camping gear unless they plan on staying overnight in rural areas such as the Daallo Forest or Mount Wagar. If you are doing this with a local operator, best to get them to arrange any camping gear you require. Otherwise, the minimum requirements are a lightweight tent, a bedroll and a sheet sleeping bag.

**MONEY BELT** It is advisable to carry all your hard currency and credit cards, as well as your passport and other important documentation, in a money belt. The ideal money belt for Africa can be hidden beneath your clothing, as externally worn money belts are as good as telling thieves all your valuables are there for the taking.

Use a money belt made of cotton or another natural fibre, though bear in mind that such fabrics tend to soak up a lot of sweat and you will need to wrap plastic around everything inside.

**CLOTHING** If you're carrying your luggage on your back, restrict your clothes to the minimum, for example, two pairs of trousers for men or two long skirts for women, three loose-fitting shirts or T-shirts, at least one sweater (or similar) depending on when and where you are visiting, socks and underwear, one pair of solid shoes and one pair of flip-flops or sandals.

Ideally, bring light cotton or microfibre trousers. Jeans are great for durability, but they can be uncomfortable in hot weather and slow to dry after washing. Skirts, like trousers, are best made of a light fabric, and should reach the ankles. For men, any fast-drying, lightweight shirts are good, but ideally pack at least one with long sleeves for sun protection. Women should be conscious that any combination of shirt and bra (or no bra) that reveals an obvious bust shape, or even elbows, might offend local sensibilities. For general purposes, one warm sweater or fleece should be adequate.

Socks and underwear must be made from natural fabrics, and bear in mind that reusing them when sweaty will encourage fungal infections such as athlete's foot, as well as prickly heat in the groin. Socks and underpants are light and compact enough to make it worth bringing a week's supply. As for shoes, bulky hiking boots are probably over the top for most people, but a good pair of walking shoes, preferably with some ankle support, is recommended. It's also useful to carry sandals, flip-flops or other light shoes.

**OTHER USEFUL ITEMS** A mobile phone (unlocked – or get it unlocked in any city) will be useful. You can buy a local SIM card for next to nothing in Hargeisa, and credit is readily available and inexpensive. This also doubles as your alarm clock for any early starts.

Binoculars are essential for close up views of wildlife, especially birds. Compact binoculars are more backpack-friendly, but their restricted field of vision compared with that of traditional binoculars can make it difficult to pick up animals in thick bush. For most purposes, 7× magnification is fine, but birdwatchers might find a 10x magnification more useful. Be careful flashing your binoculars around any military installation, bridge, border post, roadblock, or other locality where it might be mistaken for a camera.

If you stay in local hotels, carry a padlock, as many places don't supply them. You should also carry a towel, soap, shampoo, toilet paper and any other toiletries you need, including tampons. A torch is essential as electricity is never guaranteed. Another perennial favourite is a Swiss Army knife or multi-purpose tool.

No English-language reading material is available in Somaliland, so if you tend to read a lot when you travel, bring a good supply of books or magazines. The same goes for any field guides or other background or interpretive literature you require. Novels can sometimes be exchanged with other travellers.

Medical kits and other health-related subjects are discussed in *Chapter 4, Health* on page 65, but do note that contact lens solutions may not be available, so bring enough to last the whole trip – and bring glasses in case the intense sun and dry climate irritates your eyes.

**ELECTRICAL** Electricity is 220V AC at 50Hz cycles and is available in most towns and cities across the country. British-style square three-pin plugs are in use. Hotels sometimes plug round-pin European plugs into the square holes, which works but is rather unsafe. It is a good idea to buy a suitable adaptor before you travel, although you should also be able to locate one in Hargeisa if need be. Stabilisers are required for sensitive devices, and adaptors for appliances using 110V. Batteries sold on the street are mostly of very poor quality, so bring any that you need with you.

**MAPS** The only commercially available map of Somaliland of which we are aware is ITMB's 1:1,170,000 Somalia & Djibouti. It is not as accurate as it might be, but is still worth carrying if you intend exploring off the beaten track. As far as we know, other than the ones included in this book which were prepared from scratch by the author, there are no town maps available for anywhere in Somaliland.

## $ MONEY AND BUDGETING

Day-to-day expenses in Somaliland are quite low if you stick to public transport. At the budget end of the price scale it is usually possible to find an adequate room for under US$10, and even the priciest hotels cost less than US$100. Food, drink and public transport are also quite cheap. However, if you plan to travel in a private 4x4, budget US$200 a day for a vehicle, driver and SPU protection. Note that all prices in this guide are likely to be subject to inflation over the life span of this edition. As a very rough estimate you might expect to pay 10–15% more than the price quoted for each passing calendar year.

The local currency is the Somaliland shilling, which is available in denominations of Ssh 500 and Ssh 100. It is trading at around Ssh 5,500 to the US dollar at the time of writing, which means that when you exchange a US$100 note into the local Somaliland currency, you'll receive 1,100 individual Ssh 500 banknotes (or, if you are really unlucky, 5,500 individual Ssh 100 notes!). As a result, the markets of Hargeisa are lined with foreign exchange stalls, piled high with bricks of local currency held together with elastic bands, where US dollars are traded freely with Somaliland shillings.

In practice, there is little need to change money in Somaliland, as US dollars and Somaliland shillings are used more or less interchangeably, and the path of least resistance is to pay for things in US dollars, accept change in either currency, but possibly to break US$10–20 into Ssh 500 notes on the day you arrive so you have some small change when it is required. For those who travel east of Burao, it is worth noting that the Somali shilling (the official currency of Somalia) is used more widely as you get further away from Hargeisa. At the time of writing the Somali shilling is about four times stronger than the Somaliland shilling.

Below are a few things you need to consider when preparing your finances for Somaliland.

- No credit cards or travellers' cheques are accepted anywhere in the country, so you need to bring funds for your trip in cash.
- While US dollars are universally recognised, other currencies – even euros and pounds sterling – are little known and are unlikely to be accepted outside Hargeisa, where the central branch of the Dahabshiil Bank represents your last opportunity to exchange them for US dollars or Somaliland shillings before heading out of the capital.
- US dollars issued before 2000 are simply not accepted as legal tender anywhere in the country, so avoid carrying them with you at all costs (and if possible, try to bring the newest notes you can locate, ideally issued within the past five years).

- Travellers with experience in Africa usually tend to carry high denomination US dollar bills (ie: US$50 and US$100), in the knowledge that they usually fetch a significantly better exchange rate than smaller ones. However, there is no such discrimination in Somaliland. Indeed, given that you will most likely make a lot of relatively small purchases in US dollars, and that change is often tricky to locate, it pays to carry a good stash of smaller denomination bills, such as US$1, US$5, US$10 and US$20.

For those who don't want to carry large amounts of cash around the country, or who will be spending a long time there, an ingenious and convenient alternative to credit cards (which are not accepted anywhere) is provided by **ZAAD** (*www. zaad.net*), a phone banking and payment service linked to the mobile provider Telesom. To register for this service, you must first buy a local Telesom SIM card, then visit any ZAAD office with a passport-size photograph to set up an account, deposit some money in it, and key in a four-digit activation key that allows you to set your own pin. Once active, you can pay most hotel, restaurant, filling station and other bills directly from your phone, and can then withdraw the balance from your account upon your departure from the country.

## GETTING AROUND

Although occasional flights do connect Hargeisa to other towns in Somaliland (check the Daallo and Jubba Air websites; see page 52 for details), the more normal mode of transport is by **road**. Conditions are variable. The main road from Borama via Hargeisa, Berbera, Sheikh, Burao and Oog (the Garoowe border post with Somalia) is surfaced and can easily be covered in any sedan car. All other roads, including the ones from Borama to Zeila, and Oog to Maydh via Erigavo, are unsurfaced and too rough to risk without a 4x4. There are no buses in Somaliland, but foreigners are usually permitted to use the inexpensive but jam-packed shared taxis that run along the stretch of road from Borama to Burao, via Hargeisa and Berbera, and also to travel in the 4x4s that connect Hargeisa and Burao to Zeila and the Djibouti border. Other parts of the country may only be visited in a 4x4 with a local driver, which can be rented through one of the agencies listed under Hargeisa (page 78). From what we know, self-drive car rental is not an option in Somaliland. It could be that overlanders with their own vehicle are permitted to drive themselves with SPU protection, but we have never heard from anybody who has done this.

## ⌂ ACCOMMODATION

Accommodation in Somaliland is generally far more varied and pleasant than one might reasonably expect, and by overall African standards it tends to be pretty good value, too. Detailed listings for specific towns are given in the regional part of the guide and graded into four categories: upmarket, moderate, budget and shoestring. The purpose of this categorisation is to break up long hotel listings that span a wide price range, and also to help readers isolate the range of hotels that will best suit their budget and taste. It is based as much on the feel of a hotel as its rates (which are quoted anyway) and placement may also be influenced by the standard of other accommodation in the same area.

**UPMARKET** This category includes the country's limited selection of Westernised hotels that might genuinely be considered as tourist class, although they would struggle to gain more than a two- to three-star ranking anywhere else in the world. Rates are typically around US$50–80 for an en-suite double room with television, Wi-Fi and air conditioning. This is the category to look at if you want the best room in town, irrespective of cost.

**MODERATE** Hotels in this category are a little too simple to be classified as upmarket but they are also a notch or two above the budget category in terms of price and/ or quality. In cities, expect unpretentious en-suite accommodation with hot water and possibly a television, a decent restaurant and English-speaking staff. Prices are generally in the US$25–40 range. This is the category to consider if you are travelling on a limited budget but still expect a reasonably high standard of accommodation.

**BUDGET** Accommodation in this category is aimed squarely at the local market and doesn't approach international standards, but is still reasonably clean and comfortable, often with a decent restaurant attached, and en-suite rooms with running cold or possibly hot water. Expect to pay around US$10–20, depending on the location, or less if you pitch a tent or stay in a dorm. If you are on a low budget but want to avoid total squalor, this is the category for you.

**SHOESTRING** This is the very bottom end of the market, and listings are usually small local guesthouses with simple rooms and shared showers and toilets. Running the gamut from pleasantly clean to decidedly squalid, these hotels typically charge less than US$10 for a room. It is the category for those basically looking to find the cheapest rooms in town.

# ✖ EATING AND DRINKING

**FOOD** Eating out in Somaliland tends to be an unceremonious activity, and the food is seldom anything to write home about. Local restaurants generally serve a limited selection of pre-cooked dishes, typically pasta and/or rice with vegetable or meat stew, with the most common meats being mutton, goat and camel. The choice is slightly greater at those moderate and upmarket hotels which have their own restaurant. In addition, Hargeisa and Berbera have a few adequate standalone restaurants catering to Western palates, with Berbera being a good place to break the regime of red meat with some fresh fish. Eating out in Somaliland may be problematic for vegetarians, since there is no guarantee that the vegetable sauce offered at most local restaurants will be strictly vegetarian (it often seems to contain small bits of meat, and even where it doesn't, it may well use some sort of meat stock). Outside of Hargeisa, strict vegetarians will most likely have to stick to bread, fresh market produce and whatever tinned items they can locate.

One distinctly Somali dish worth trying is *laxoox*, a filling pancake-like flatbread traditionally baked on a metallic circular stove called a *daawo*. It is usually eaten at breakfast with sweet Somali tea, or sometimes eggs, or sugar and lime, or even ghee. *Laxoox* is clearly a relation of Ethiopian *injera*, and has a similarly spongy texture, but it is made from wheat rather than tef, is less sour, and much smaller and floppier (you would normally eat three or four individual pancakes in one sitting). Fresh bread, known as *roodhi*, is also widely available in the mornings, either as a crusty roti-like flatbread *mofaa*, or more conventional rolls. Also popular are the greasy fried dough balls known as *khamiir*. There are also several Ethiopian restaurants in Somaliland, especially in Hargeisa, usually serving far spicier fare than is conventional for the Somali.

If you are shopping for a trip into remote areas, supermarkets in Hargeisa stock a fair range of imported goodies such as crisps, biscuits, chocolates and sweets. Elsewhere in the country, the selection is very limited. Fresh fruit and vegetables are widely available at markets.

**DRINKS** Now with its own bottling factory in Hargeisa, Coca-Cola is widely available in Somaliland, as are various other sweet carbonated drinks. You can buy packaged fruit juices in some supermarkets, but a more attractive (and very budget-friendly) option is the delicious freshly pureed or squeezed fruit juices made at stalls and restaurants in the larger towns. Another local favourite is Somali tea, which is often spiced and usually brewed with milk and a generous dose of sugar. If you prefer your tea free of milk and/or sugar, ask for Lipton. Bottled water is available, but make sure it's sealed. No alcoholic drinks are sold anywhere in Somaliland, although a few smarter restaurants and hotels stock alcohol-free beer.

## PUBLIC HOLIDAYS AND WEEKENDS

Somaliland follows the Islamic calendar and it is worth being aware that the weekend there – when government offices and financial institutions close – effectively falls over Thursday and Friday, but it's business as usual on Saturday and Sunday.

Public holidays fall into two categories: secular holidays celebrated on a specific date, and religious holidays where the date is based on the Islamic lunar calendar and changes every year. The following fall into the former category:

| | |
|---|---|
| 1 May | Labour Day |
| 18–19 May | Restoration of Somaliland Sovereignty |
| 26 June | Independence Day |

The following moveable Islamic holidays are recognised and will fall on the given dates over the life span of this edition:

| | 2012 | 2013 | 2014 |
|---|---|---|---|
| Maulid al-Nabi (Muhammad's birthday) | 4 February | 24 January | 13 January |
| Start of Ramadan | 20 July | 9 July | 28 June |
| Eid al-Fitri (end of Ramadan) | 19 August | 8 August | 28 July |
| Eid al-Adha | 26 October | 15 October | 4 October |
| Muslim New Year | 15 November | 4 November | 25 October |

## SHOPPING

**BARGAINING AND OVERCHARGING** The emphasis that some tourists place on bargaining can be a little over the top. Bargaining has its place, but the common assumption that everybody quotes inflated prices to tourists is nonsensical. Bartering is of little value at hotels, restaurants and supermarkets, but it may be necessary with taxis (shared or private) and markets, where some bargaining also goes on between locals. As ever, the better informed you are about prices at the start of the process, the more likely you are to be able to come to a mutually satisfying agreement, so it's worth asking at a few stalls to see what the norm is before starting the process. In addition you'll find that stallholders will be far more amenable if you are buying a range of produce rather than just one or two items. The key to bargaining is to be relaxed about it. Adopting an aggressive posture is only likely to irritate the other party and lower the likelihood of a successful conclusion to the whole business. And retain a sense of proportion: regardless of how poor you are in Western terms, you will mostly be a lot better off than the person you're dealing with.

## PHOTOGRAPHY

Photography is part and parcel of travelling, but it needs to be done with sensitivity. Taking wildlife photographs and scenic views is fine, but you do need to be a little more circumspect when photographing buildings and people. If you are caught taking photographs of military or government buildings, you may run into problems with the officials, and while it isn't illegal for non-Islamic visitors to photograph mosques and shrines, locals may object to it vociferously.

In towns, it is usually fine to snap general street scenes, but if it's clear that a significant number of people are disturbed by your camera, put it away. If people turn their face away from the camera or hide it behind their hand, point your lens in a different direction, as continuing to photograph will cause offence. It is also vital to always ask permission before photographing specific individuals – many people will be fine with it, but it is rude not to check first.

## MEDIA AND COMMUNICATIONS

**NEWSPAPERS** There are a few English-language newspapers printed in Somaliland; foreign papers are very difficult to locate.

**TELEVISION AND RADIO** There are a few local radio stations, but most broadcast mainly or exclusively in the Somali language, with the emphasis on religion and news programmes. Most hotels in the moderate and upmarket category offer a bouquet of Arabian satellite channels including Al Jazeera (*http://english.aljazeera.net*).

**TELEPHONE** The main service providers are Telesom (*www.telesom.net*) and Somtel, and a local SIM card for your mobile should cost US$5 and come with a full instruction sheet. A voucher for US$1 will most likely cover all the texting and phone requirements of those staying in the country for just a few days, but travellers heading across from Ethiopia may want to buy more credit to take advantage of the incredibly cheap international rates and call home. Our experience was that while it is no problem phoning outside Somaliland using a local SIM card, you cannot rely on text messages reaching the dialled number, even if a delivery notification is received.

**POST** There is no postal service to or from Somaliland.

**INTERNET** Online access is widely available and very cheap at internet cafés in Hargeisa, and there are also plenty of online facilities in Borama. Locals will often point out that the service is generally faster than in most parts of Ethiopia, which is true, albeit not setting the bar very high – it is pretty slow by any other standards. Several upmarket and moderate hotels offer a free Wi-Fi service to guests. Internet access is also available in Berbera, Burao and Erigavo but the number of cafés in these towns is limited, so don't rely on it too much.

## CULTURAL ETIQUETTE AND TRAVELLING POSITIVELY

**BEFORE YOU LEAVE** If you want to swot up beforehand on what it means to be a responsible tourist, a UK-based source of information is **Tourism Concern** (\ *020*

7753 3330; f 020 7753 3331; e info@tourismconcern.org.uk; www.tourismconcern. org.uk). It's also good to do some research about the country you're about to visit – not just its weather and its costs and hotels, but also what makes it tick: its history, culture, achievements, failures and so on. It can help to break the ice with local people if you know something (anything!) about their country and way of life.

**CARBON EMISSIONS** If you'd like to offset the carbon footprint of your flight, try www.carbonneutral.com, run by a UK organisation. The website has an easy-to-use emissions calculator and a range of offset programmes.

**IN SOMALILAND** Fancy terms such as 'cultural sensitivity' and 'low-impact tourism' often boil down to good old-fashioned respect and common sense. As a visitor, you should be willing to adapt to and respect local customs and traditions. For example, learn a bit of the local language, seek the permission of the community leader before roaming through villages, and ask before you take photographs. Be aware, too, that greeting procedures tend to be more formalised in Somaliland than in modern Western societies, and elderly people in particular should be treated with special respect. If you need to ask somebody directions, or anything else for that matter, it is considered very rude to blunder straight into interrogative mode without first exchanging greetings.

Somaliland is a strictly Islamic country and generally very conservative. It would be imprudent to get involved in religious discussions of any sort, and atheist or agnostic visitors will be better off saying they are Christian than declaring their lack of faith. Local clothing mores are conservative, for males and females, and should be followed closely by visitors. Be aware that Somalilanders, like most other Muslims, reserve the use of the left hand for ablutions, and the right hand for eating and other social activities. It is considered highly insulting to use one's left hand to pass or receive something, or to shake hands left handed. If you eat with your fingers, as is customary in Somaliland, use the right hand only, or you risk causing serious offence.

Also be careful to use energy resources such as water and electricity efficiently, not to wash in lakes or rivers (regardless of local practices, because of pollution) or get too close to the wildlife. Shop locally and use the services of local people whenever possible. Buy souvenirs from the craftspeople who made them rather than via middlemen who will siphon off profits, and patronise small street vendors rather than big supermarkets. Don't bargain unreasonably; the difference may be the cost of a drink to you but a whole family meal to the vendor. Use the services of a local guide, or a child who wants to help, and pay a fair rate.

Practical Information  CULTURAL ETIQUETTE AND TRAVELLING POSITIVELY

3

# 4

# Health
*with Dr Felicity Nicholson*

Like most of sub-Saharan Africa, Somaliland harbours an array of tropical diseases of varying degrees of severity and inconvenience. Although there's a fair possibility that you will become ill at some point on your trip, the cause is most likely to be either straightforward travellers' diarrhoea or a cold, and provided you receive the necessary immunisations before you travel, the only major cause for concern once you are in the country is malaria, which can be combated to a large extent by taking sensible precautions (see page 69).

## BEFORE YOU GO

**TRAVEL INSURANCE** Travel insurance should be one of your top priorities. This doesn't mean you should buy the dearest and most comprehensive policy you can find, but some degree of cover in case of accident or illness is essential. Most policies offer at least US$1 million in emergency medical expenses, and often a great deal more. They will also pay for you to be repatriated should the need arise. Whether or not you buy additional insurance – for baggage and personal belongings, for example – is up to you; weigh what you stand to lose against what you have to pay.

You can opt either for a tailor-made policy, priced according to your destination and the duration of your trip, or a multi-trip policy, which normally covers you for as many trips as you can squeeze into a year, provided that none exceeds a certain length. Most travel agents also sell travel insurance, although there is some concern over the cover provided by some of these and (as always) it pays to shop around. The internet has revolutionised insurance and there is a multitude of different companies out there which will be more than willing to sell you travel insurance. However, you will also need to check that the policy covers Somaliland, still officially part of war-torn Somalia, which won't be covered by any travel insurance policy that explicitly excludes countries subject to FCO or US State Department travel warnings (see *Chapter 3*, page 47). A recommended exception at the time of writing is World Nomads (*www.worldnomads.com*), whose policies cover you wherever you go, but do confirm this before paying.

**TRAVEL CLINICS AND HEALTH INFORMATION** A full list of current travel clinic websites worldwide is available on www.istm.org. For other journey preparation information, consult www.nathnac.org/ds/map_world.aspx. Information about various medications may be found on www.netdoctor.co.uk/travel.

## UK
**Berkeley Travel Clinic** 32 Berkeley St, London W1J 8EL (near Green Park tube station); ✆020 7629 6233; 🕐 10.00–18.00 Mon–Fri; 10.00–15.00 Sat

## LONG-HAUL FLIGHTS, CLOTS AND DVT

Any prolonged immobility including travel by land or air can result in deep vein thrombosis (DVT) with the risk of embolus to the lungs. Certain factors can increase the risk and these include: previous clot or close relative with a history; people over 40 (with an increased risk for those over 80 years); recent major operation or varicose vein surgery; cancer; stroke; heart disease; obesity; pregnancy; hormone therapy; heavy smokers; severe varicose veins; people who are very tall (over 6ft/1.8m) or short (under 5ft/1.5m).

A deep vein thrombosis (DVT) causes painful swelling and redness of the calf or sometimes the thigh. It is only dangerous if a clot travels to the lungs (pulmonary embolus). Symptoms of a pulmonary embolus (PE) include chest pain, shortness of breath, and sometimes coughing up small amounts of blood, and commonly symptoms start three to ten days after a long flight. Anyone who thinks that they might have a DVT needs to see a doctor immediately.

### Prevention of DVT
- Keep mobile before and during the flight; move around every couple of hours
- Drink plenty of fluids during the flight
- Avoid taking sleeping pills and drinking excessive tea, coffee and alcohol
- Consider wearing flight socks or support stockings (see www.legshealth.com)

If you think you are at increased risk of a clot, ask your doctor if it is safe to travel.

---

**Edinburgh Travel Health Clinic**
14 East Preston St, Newington, Edinburgh EH8 9QA; 0131 667 1030; www.edinburghtravelhealthclinic.co.uk; ⏱ 09.00–19.00 Mon–Wed, 09.00–18.00 Thu & Fri. Travel vaccinations & advice on all aspects of malaria prevention. All current UK prescribed anti-malaria tablets in stock.

**Fleet Street Travel Clinic** 29 Fleet St, London EC4Y 1AA; 020 7353 5678; e info@fleetstreetclinic.com; www.fleetstreetclinic.com; ⏱ 08.45–17.30 Mon–Fri. Injections, travel products & latest advice.

**Hospital for Tropical Diseases Travel Clinic** Mortimer Market Centre, Capper St (off Tottenham Court Rd), London WC1E 6JB; 020 7388 9600; www.thehtd.org; ⏱ 13.00–17.00 Wed, 09.00–13.00 Fri. Consultations are only for complex travellers or pre existing costumers. Travellers who have returned from the tropics & are unwell, with

fever or bloody diarrhoea, can attend the walk-in emergency clinic at the hospital without an appointment.

**InterHealth Travel Clinic** 111 Westminster Bridge Rd, London SE1 7HR, 020 7902 9000; e info@interhealth.org.uk; www.interhealth.org.uk; ⏱ 08.30–17.30 Mon–Fri. Competitively priced, one-stop travel health service by appointment only.

**MASTA** (Medical Advisory Service for Travellers Abroad) London School of Hygiene & Tropical Medicine, Keppel St, London WC1E 7HT; 0906 822 4100 (this is a premium number, charged at 60p per min); e enquiries@masta.org; www.masta-travel-health.com. For a fee, they will provide an individually tailored health brief, with up-to-date information on how to stay healthy, inoculations & what to take.

**MASTA pre-travel clinics** 01276 685040; www.masta-travel-health.com. Call or check the website for the nearest clinic; there are currently

50 in Britain. They also sell malaria prophylaxis, memory cards, treatment kits, bednets, net treatment kits, etc.

**NHS travel websites** www.fitfortravel.nhs.uk or www.fitfortravel.scot.nhs.uk . Provide country-by-country advice on immunisation & malaria prevention, plus details of recent developments, & a list of relevant health organisations.

**Nomad Travel Clinics** Flagship store: 3–4 Wellington Terrace, Turnpike Lane, London N8 0PX; ☎020 8889 7014; e turnpike@nomadtravel. co.uk; www.nomadtravel.co.uk; walk in or appointments ⊕ 09.15–17.00 every day with late night Thu. Also has clinics in west & central London, Bristol, Southampton & Manchester – see website for further information. As well as dispensing health advice, Nomad stocks mosquito nets & other anti-bug devices, & an excellent range of adventure travel gear. Runs a Travel Health Advice line on ☎0906 863 3414.

## Irish Republic

**Tropical Medical Bureau** 54 Grafton St, Dublin 2; ☎+353 1 271 5200; e graftonstreet@tmb. ie; www.tmb.ie; ⊕ until 20.00 Mon–Fri & Sat

## USA

**Centers for Disease Control** 1600 Clifton Rd, Atlanta, GA 30333; ☎(800) 232 4636 or (800) 232 6348; e cdcinfo@cdc.gov; www.cdc.gov/travel. The central source of travel information in the USA. Each summer they publish the invaluable *Health Information for International Travel*.

## Canada

**IAMAT** 10, 1287 St Clair Street West, Toronto, Ontario M6E 1B8; ☎416 652 0137; www.iamat.org

## Australia and New Zealand

**TMVC** (Travel Doctors Group) ☎1300 65 88 44; www.tmvc.com.au. 30 clinics in Australia & New Zealand, including: *Auckland* Canterbury Arcade, 174 Queen St, Auckland 1010, New Zealand; ☎(64) 9 373 3531; e auckland@traveldoctor. co.nz; *Brisbane* 75a Astor Terrace, Spring Hill, Brisbane, QLD 4000, Australia; ☎(07) 3815 6900; e brisbane@traveldoctor.com.au; *Melbourne* 393

**Trailfinders Immunisation Centre** 194 Kensington High St, London W8 7RG; ☎020 7938 3999; www.trailfinders.com/ travelessentials/travelclinic.htm; ⊕ 09.00– 17.00 Mon–Wed & Fri, 09.00–18.00 Thu, 10.00–17.15 Sat. No appointment necessary.

**The Travel Clinic Ltd, Cambridge** 41 Hills Rd, Cambridge CB2 1NT; ☎01223 367362; e enquiries@travelclinic.ltd.uk; www. travelcliniccambridge.co.uk; ⊕ 10.00–16.00 Mon, Tue & Sat, 12.00–19.00 Wed & Thu, 11.00–18.00 Fri

**The Travel Clinic Ltd, Ipswich** Gilmour Piper, 10 Fonnereau Rd, Ipswich IP1 3JP; ☎01223 367362; ⊕ 09.00–19.00 Wed, 09.00–13.00 Sat

**Travelpharm** www.travelpharm.com. The Travelpharm website offers up-to-date guidance on travel-related health & has a range of medications available through their online mini-pharmacy.

mornings. For other clinic locations, & useful information specific to tropical destinations, check their website.

**IAMAT** (**International Association for Medical Assistance to Travelers**) 1623 Military Rd, #279 Niagara Falls, NY 14304-1745; ☎716 754 4883; e info@iamat.org; www.iamat.org. A non-profit organisation with free membership that provides lists of English-speaking doctors abroad.

**TMVC** Suite 314, 1030 W Georgia St, Vancouver, BC V6E 2Y3; ☎(604) 681 5656; e vancouver@ tmvc.com; www.tmvc.com. One-stop medical clinic for all your international travel health & vaccination needs.

Little Bourke St, Melbourne, Vic 3000, Australia; ☎(03) 9935 8100; e melbourne@traveldoctor. com.au; *Sydney* 428 George St, Sydney, NSW 2000, Australia; ☎(2) 9221 7133; e sydney@ traveldoctor.com.au

**IAMAT** 206 Papanui Rd, Christchurch 5, New Zealand; www.iamat.org

## South Africa

**SAA-Netcare Travel Clinics** ✆ 011 802 0059; e travelinfo@netcare.co.za; www.travelclinic. co.za. 11 clinics throughout South Africa.

**TMVC** NHC Health Centre, Cnr Beyers Naude & Waugh Northcliff; ✆ 0861 300 911; e info@ traveldoctor.co.za; www.traveldoctor.co.za. Consult the website for clinic locations.

**MEDICAL KIT** Take a small medical kit with you. This should contain malaria tablets and a thermometer, soluble aspirin or paracetamol (good for gargling when you have a sore throat and for reducing fever and pains), plasters (band-aids), potassium permanganate crystals or another favoured antiseptic, iodine for sterilising water and cleaning wounds, sunblock, and condoms or femidoms. Depending on your travel plans, it is a good idea to carry a course of tablets as a cure for malaria; recommendations can change so seek specialist advice before travelling. As restaurant meals in Somaliland tend to be based around meat and carbohydrate, some people may like to carry vitamin pills.

**IMMUNISATIONS** Preparations to ensure a healthy trip to Somaliland require checks on your immunisation status: it is wise to be up to date on tetanus, polio and diphtheria (now given as an all-in-one vaccine, Revaxis, that lasts for ten years), and hepatitis A. Yellow fever is not considered a risk in Somaliland, and therefore vaccination would only be suggested if the traveller is entering Somaliland from another yellow fever country such as Ethiopia. Immunisation against **cholera** might also be advisable. Your GP or travel clinic should be able to advise you. The vaccine is a drink (Dukoral) that is recommended for adults and children aged six or above; it is taken as two doses at least one to six weeks apart and at least one week before entry. For children between two and six, three doses are needed, so it is best to plan your trip well in advance.

**Hepatitis A** vaccine (Havrix Monodose or Avaxim) comprises two injections given about a year apart. The course costs about £100, but may be available on the NHS; the vaccine protects for 25 years and can be administered even close to the time of departure. Hepatitis B vaccination should be considered for longer trips (two months or more) or for those working with children or in situations where contact with blood is likely. Three injections are needed for the best protection and can be given over a three-week period if time is short, for those aged 16 or over. Longer schedules give more sustained protection and are therefore preferred if time allows. Hepatitis A vaccine can also be given as a combination with hepatitis B as 'Twinrix', although two doses are needed at least seven days apart to be effective for the hepatitis A component, and three doses are needed for the hepatitis B. Again this schedule is only suitable for those aged 16 or over.

The newer injectable **typhoid** vaccines (eg: Typhim Vi) last for three years and are about 85% effective. Oral capsules (Vivotif) may also be available for those aged six and over. Three capsules over five days lasts for approximately three years but may be less effective than the injectable forms. They should be encouraged unless the traveller is leaving within a few days for a trip of a week or less, when the vaccine would not be effective in time.

**Meningitis** vaccine containing strains A, C, W and Y, is ideally recommended for all travellers, especially for trips of more than four weeks. The conjugated vaccine Menveo is preferable to the older polysaccharide vaccine as it offers superior cover.

Vaccinations for **rabies** are ideally advised for everyone, but are especially important for travellers visiting more remote areas, especially if you are more than

24 hours from medical help and definitely if you will be working with animals (see *Rabies*, page 72).

Experts differ over whether a BCG vaccination against **tuberculosis** (TB) is useful in adults: discuss this with your travel clinic.

In addition to the various vaccinations recommended above, it is important that travellers should be properly protected against malaria. For detailed advice, see below.

Ideally you should visit your own doctor or a specialist travel clinic (see page 65) to discuss your requirements, if possible at least eight weeks before you plan to travel.

## MEDICAL FACILITIES IN SOMALILAND

There are private clinics and/or hospitals in all the larger towns, but they tend to be under-equipped and overcrowded, the main exception being the private Edna Adan Maternity Hospital in Hargeisa (*www.ednahospital.org*). Pharmacies are also present in all the larger towns, and they are usually quite well stocked and staffed by an English-speaking pharmacist.

You should be able to buy such commonly required medicines as broad-spectrum antibiotics and Flagyl in any sizeable town. If you are wandering off the beaten track, it might be worth carrying the obvious with you. As for malaria tablets, whether for prophylaxis or treatment you would be wise to get them before you go as not all tablets are readily available.

If you are on any medication prior to departure, or you have specific needs relating to a known medical condition (for instance, if you are allergic to bee stings or are prone to asthma), then you are strongly advised to bring any related drugs and devices with you. Take the informational leaflets as well, just in case you're challenged.

## MALARIA

One of the main health risks to travellers is malaria, which is present throughout Somaliland all year round, although the risk of contraction is highest in the relatively wet summer months. This mosquito-borne disease is responsible for more than 350 million infections and one million deaths every year, of which around 85% will occur in sub-Saharan Africa. It is caused by protozoan parasites of the genus *Plasmodium*, and there are at least five strains known to be in Africa that infect humans – *P. falciparum*, *P. malariae*, *P. oval*. *P. knowlesei* and *P. vivax*. Of these five, *P. knowlesei*, *P. ovale* and *P. malariae* are comparatively rare, and an infection is most likely to be *P. falciparum* (which accounts for around 80% of the infections and 90% of the deaths) or *P. vivax* (which accounts for most of the rest). The *Anopheles* mosquito that transmits the parasite is very likely to be present anywhere in the country all year round, so it is important to protect yourself from the disease.

### AVOIDING MALARIA
**1) Avoid getting bitten** The simplest method of avoiding malaria is not to be bitten by an *Anopheles* mosquito. This is not an entirely practical objective, but there are ways of reducing the number of bites, and hence limiting your potential exposure to the parasite.

*Anopheles* is only active between dusk and dawn, and the female mosquitoes tend to hunt mostly just above ground level, so long trousers or skirts and thick socks (the mosquito is quite capable of biting through thin socks or tights) will help. Similarly, long sleeves will help limit the number of bites there, and shirts with collars may also help prevent bites to the neck.

Insect repellent should form a part of your armoury as well. Insect repellents containing **DEET** are an established method of protection. Different repellents contain different concentrations of DEET, but the recommended strength is 50–5% which is suitable for most adults and children. Impregnated armbands can be used around wrists and ankles to provide additional protection, both at night and during the day. There are now some effective natural repellents such as Incognito but you will need to reapply more regularly than with the DEET-based repellents. Whatever you choose, be aware that it is almost impossible to buy insect repellent in Somaliland so you'll have to bring it with you.

Like many insects, mosquitoes are drawn to direct light. In hotels, drawing curtains, closing doors and keeping the light off will help reduce the number of mosquitoes in your room at night. That said, some budget hotel rooms will host a serious accumulation of mosquitoes even before you check in. The best way to deal with this is to spray the room with a can of insect spray (easily bought locally) before you head out for dinner – and if the room is en suite, pay special attention to the bathroom. Mosquito coils can help reduce the number of bites you get, and are also available in the bigger towns.

Once in bed, your best source of protection is a treated mosquito net. Unfortunately, few hotels in Somaliland provide nets. If you bring your own net (and it's well worth having one in your rucksack), permethrin-treated nets are the best. Permethrin is a widely used broad-spectrum insecticide and you can buy permethrin liquid to treat your clothes – but be aware that after five or six washes it may no longer be effective. It's also worth packing a length of string for hanging the net.

## 2) Take malarial prophylactics
Limiting the risk of being bitten is all very well, but there is no way you will be able to avoid being bitten entirely, so it's essential that you take something to counter the malarial protozoa itself. Options include mefloquine (Lariam), malarone (proguanil and atovaquone) and the antibiotic doxycycline. All have their advantages and disadvantages, depending on how long you will be travelling for, and your susceptibility to certain side effects. (For instance, anyone who has been treated for depression or psychiatric problems, has diabetes controlled by oral therapy or who is epileptic (or who has suffered fits in the past) or has a close blood relative who is epileptic, should avoid mefloquine). The once popular combination of chloroquine and proguanil is no longer considered to be effective enough for most parts of Africa, but it may be considered as a last resort if nothing else is deemed suitable.

All tablets should be taken with or after the evening meal, washed down with plenty of fluid and, with the exception of Malarone (see page 70), continued for four weeks after leaving. It is important to be aware that no anti-malarial drug is 100% protective, although those on prophylactics who are unlucky enough to catch malaria are less likely to get rapidly into serious trouble.

There is the occasional traveller who opts to 'acquire resistance' to malaria rather than take preventive tablets, or who takes homeopathic prophylactics. Homeopathy theory dictates treating like with like so there is no place for prophylaxis or immunisation in a well person; bone fide homeopathists do not advocate it. Travellers to Africa cannot acquire any effective resistance to malaria, and those who don't make use of prophylactic drugs risk their life in a manner that is both foolish and unnecessary.

**3) Know the symptoms** As stated above, even if you are assiduous in avoiding bites and rigorous in taking your anti-malarials, there is still a risk of contracting a resistant strain of the parasite, so it's also worth knowing the likely symptoms. The most consistent of these is a fever of 38°C or more, and is usually accompanied by other symptoms such as a rash, diarrhoea, abdominal pain etc. Unfortunately, these symptoms are similar to those for many other diseases, so the ideal is to visit a local hospital and submit to a test, which usually takes no more than 15 minutes to produce a result. Where that is not possible, it is probably safest to assume you have malaria and act accordingly.

Malaria normally manifests itself between two and six weeks after the bite but in extreme cases the window might be anything from a week to a year. Bear this in mind after your return home – several of the British travellers who have died from malaria only developed the disease weeks or months after they returned to the UK and failed to recognise the symptoms as malaria. If you do think you may have malaria, seek medical attention at once, and specifically mention that you have recently visited a risk zone.

One very final thing: if you have the symptoms but the test is negative, this may be an indication of a typhoid infection and you should request a test for that. Also it is worth repeating the malaria test as sometimes they can give false negatives.

**4) Carry the curative regime** That way, if you test positive, or suspect you have malaria but can't get to a hospital to be tested, you can treat yourself without further ado.

Since the correct advice for treatment of malaria may well have changed since the time of writing, it is always best to seek current medical advice for the most up-to-date information.

Regardless of the curative regime you choose, you should make every effort to seek professional medical advice as soon as possible.

## OTHER DISEASES

**AIDS AND VENEREAL DISEASES** HIV and other venereal diseases are widespread in many parts of sub-Saharan Africa, with several countries having HIV-infection rates of higher than 10%. Somalia however, is something of an exception, with a rate of 0.2% (comparable with the UK or USA). Nevertheless, the risks involved in having unprotected casual sex barely need stating, and condoms and femidoms offer a high level of protection. Contrary to Western prejudices, health professionals in Africa are well aware of the dangers involved in using unsterilised needles. Supplies may not always be available, however, so if you need treatment in a really remote area, you might be glad to be carrying a few needles and hypodermic syringes.

**BILHARZIA OR SCHISTOSOMIASIS** *with thanks to Dr Vaughan Southgate of the Natural History Museum, London, & Dr Dick Stockley, The Surgery, Kampala*
Bilharzia or schistosomiasis is a disease that commonly afflicts the rural poor of the tropics. Two types exist in sub-Saharan Africa – *Schistosoma mansoni* and *Schistosoma haematobium*. It is an unpleasant problem that is worth avoiding, although it can be treated if you do get it. It is transmitted to humans by snails that live exclusively in freshwater, a commodity that is in relatively short supply in Somaliland, so you need be concerned only in the somewhat unlikely event that you wade or swim in a freshwater body other than a swimming pool. If that

happens, dry yourself off thoroughly with a towel, rubbing vigorously, and take a test six weeks after likely exposure, as symptoms are not always obvious.

**CHOLERA** Cholera is another disease that occurs in areas of poor sanitation where unprocessed sewage is released into waterways, which includes Somaliland. The main symptom is severe diarrhoea – sometimes accompanied by vomiting – which can cause dehydration and, in acute cases, death. An oral cholera vaccine (Dukoral) is now available from the UK (see page 68).

**HEPATITIS B** Hepatitis B is a serious viral disease that is present in the blood and body fluids of an infected individual. It attacks the liver (like hepatitis A) and can sometimes be fatal. Transmission is by unprotected sexual intercourse, unsterilised needles or through unscreened blood transfusions, which means that the measures recommended to combat HIV (see page 71) apply equally to minimise the risks of catching hepatitis B. The vaccine schedule has already been discussed above (see page 68).

**RABIES** Rabies can be carried by any mammal. The domestic dog is the species which most often passes it to humans, although it can be transmitted from any warm-blooded mammal. The most common route of infection is a bite from an infected animal, but a scratch or a lick over an open wound can also do it. Remember that the animal can look well so you have to assume that any mammal can have rabies.

The immunisation against rabies is highly effective, but once symptoms appear rabies is incurable, and the way that you die is so horrible that all doctors advise a post-exposure vaccine. Whether you have been immunised or not and there is any possibility that you have been exposed to a rabid animal, get to a doctor as soon as you can. The message, then, is to be immunised against rabies before a potential exposure (three doses ideally should be given over a minimum of 21 days) if you intend visiting remote places (ie: being away from medical help for more than 24 hours) or handling wild animals. Any wild animals that seem unusually tame should be assumed to be rabid: do not handle them.

All animal bites should be cleaned as protection against general infection. Scrub the wound with ordinary soap and bottled or boiled water for at least five minutes, then liberally apply povidone iodine or 40% (or higher) alcohol – even gin or whisky will do – or aqueous iodine. This can help to prevent the rabies virus from entering the body, and will guard against wound infection and the very real risk of catching tetanus.

The pre-exposure rabies vaccine course consists of three doses over a four-week period. Note that, even if you have been vaccinated against rabies, you will still require at two post-bite rabies injections. Unimmunised travellers will need a full course of injections plus the expensive rabies immunoglobulin (RIG), which will set you back around US$800–1,000. Unfortunately, RIG is seldom available in developing countries and so you would have to evacuate back to Europe – another good reason to take rabies vaccine before you go.

**TICKS AND TICKBITE FEVER** African ticks are not the rampant disease transmitters they are in the Americas, but they may spread tickbite fever and a few dangerous rarities. Tickbite fever is a flu-like illness that can easily be treated with doxycycline, but as there can be some serious complications it is important to visit a doctor.

Ticks should ideally be removed as soon as possible, as leaving them on the body increases the chance of infection. They should be removed with special tick tweezers

above     A man selling dates at the sprawling Hargeisa market (AVZ) page 87

right     Order a *bun* in Somaliland and you will be given a coffee. For bread, simply ask for *mofo* (AVZ) page 60

below     Chewing *khat*, a mildly narcotic leaf, is a national pastime in Somaliland (AVZ) page 88

above    Girls in traditional dress walk the streets of Burao, Somaliland's second largest city (AVZ) page 119

left    Money-sellers keeping the economy afloat in Burao: each block of 100 notes is worth under US$2 (AVZ) page 119

below    A colourful supermarket decorated by a local artist in Borama; art in Somaliland is used almost exclusively for commercial purposes (EL) page 30

*above*  Somalia claims to support the world's largest population of domestic camels, nicknamed by ancient Saharan traders as the 'Ship of the Desert' (EL) page 94

*right*  An elder from the town of Balligubadle, Galbeed province (EL)

*below left*  Henna is a popular form of body-decoration in Muslim parts of the East African coast, from Zanzibar to Berbera (AVZ)

*below right*  Somali woman with *qasil* on her face; a natural beauty product that also acts as a sun block (EL)

*above*    Usnea, or 'Old Man's Beard', hangs from the trees in the Daallo Escarpment (AVZ) page 132

*left*    The endangered dragon's blood tree, found in Daallo, manages to grow in the most unlikely crags (AVZ) page 133

*below*    The white-crowned starling (*Spreo albicapillus*) has been spotted alongside bustards and eagles in the plains surrounding Burao (AVZ) page 119

*above*    The only species of swine found in Somaliland, the desert warthog (*Phacochoerus aethiopicus*) is endemic to the Horn of Africa (AVZ) page 37

*right*    The endangered Speke's gazelle (*Gazella Spekei*) can be spotted in herds on the plains between Erigavo and Burao (AVZ) page 36

*bottom right*   Northern red-billed hornbill (*Tockus erythrorhynchus*); Somaliland is still relatively poorly known in ornithological terms, and new species are frequently recorded by visiting birders (EL) page 40

*left* **The unspoilt beach next to the Man-soor Hotel, just north of Berbera, is popular amongst locals** (EL) page 110

*below* **A herd of camels in the sparsely populated Sanaag region** (AVZ) page 125

*above*    Ga'an Libah, literally 'Lion's Paw', is a tall limestone ridge that rises to an elevation of 1,720m (AVZ) page 100

*below*    The ancient paintings at Las Geel are striking both for their vibrant colours and their rich complexity (AVZ) page 98

 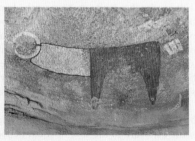

that can be bought in good travel shops. Failing that you can use your finger nails: grasp the tick as close to your body as possible and pull steadily and firmly away at right angles to your skin. The tick will then come away complete, as long as you do not jerk or twist. If possible douse the wound with alcohol (any spirit will do) or iodine. Irritants (eg: Olbas oil) or lit cigarettes are to be discouraged since they can cause the ticks to regurgitate and therefore increase the risk of disease. It is best to get a travelling companion to check you for ticks; if you are travelling with small children, remember to check their heads and particularly behind the ears.

Spreading redness around the bite and/or fever and/or aching joints after a tick bite implies you have an infection that requires antibiotic treatment, so seek advice.

## DIARRHOEA AND RELATED ILLNESSES

**Water sterilisation** You can fall ill from drinking contaminated water so try to drink from safe sources, such as bottled water, where available. If you are away from shops and your bottled water runs out, make tea, pour the remaining boiled water into a clean container and use it for drinking. Alternatively, water should be passed through a good bacteriological filter or purified with chlorine dioxide.

**Travellers' diarrhoea** Travelling in Somaliland carries a fairly high risk of getting a dose of travellers' diarrhoea, and the newer you are to tropical travel, the more likely you will be to suffer. By taking precautions against travellers' diarrhoea you will also avoid typhoid, paratyphoid, cholera, hepatitis, dysentery, worms, etc. Travellers' diarrhoea and the other faecal-oral diseases come from getting other peoples' faeces in your mouth. This most often happens from cooks not washing their hands after a trip to the toilet, but even if the restaurant chef does not understand basic hygiene you will be safe if your food has been properly cooked and arrives piping hot. The most important prevention strategy is to wash your hands before eating anything. You can pick up salmonella and shigella from toilet door handles and possibly bank notes. The maxim to remind you what you can safely eat is:

PEEL IT, BOIL IT, COOK IT OR FORGET IT.

This means that fruit you have washed and peeled yourself, and hot foods, should be safe, but raw foods, cold cooked foods, salads, fruit salads which have been prepared by others, ice cream and ice are all risky, and foods kept lukewarm in hotel buffets are often dangerous. That said, plenty of travellers and expatriates enjoy fruit and vegetables, so do keep a sense of perspective: food served in a fairly decent hotel in a large town or a place regularly frequented by expatriates is likely to be safe. If you are struck, see box (page 74) for treatment.

**SUN AND HEAT** The equatorial sun is vicious. Although it is impossible to avoid some exposure to the sun, it would be foolish to incur it needlessly. Tanning ages your skin and it can cause skin cancer. If you are coming to Somaliland from a less harsh climate, let your body get used to the sunlight gradually or you will end up with sunburn. Take things too far, and sunstroke – a potentially fatal condition – may be the result. Wear sunscreen and build up your exposure gradually, starting with no more than 20 minutes a day. Avoid exposing yourself for more than two hours in any day, and stay out of the sun between 12.00 and 15.00. Be particularly careful of sunburn when swimming or snorkelling. A shirt will protect your shoulders and a pair of shorts will protect the back of your thighs.

It is dehydration that makes you feel awful during a bout of diarrhoea and the most important part of treatment is drinking lots of clear fluids. Sachets of oral rehydration salts give the perfect biochemical mix to replace all that is pouring out of your bottom but other recipes taste nicer. Any dilute mixture of sugar and salt in water will do you good: try Coke or orange squash with a three-finger pinch of salt added to each glass (if you are salt-depleted you won't taste the salt). Otherwise, make a solution of a four-finger scoop of sugar with a three-finger pinch of salt in a 500ml glass. Or add eight level teaspoons of sugar (18g) and one level teaspoon of salt (3g) to one litre (five cups) of safe water. A squeeze of lemon or orange juice improves the taste and adds potassium, which is also lost in diarrhoea. Drink two large glasses after every bowel action, and more if you are thirsty. These solutions are still absorbed well if you are vomiting, but you will need to take sips at a time. If you are not eating you need to drink three litres a day plus whatever is pouring into the toilet. If you feel like eating, take a bland, high-carbohydrate diet. Heavy greasy foods will probably give you cramps.

If the diarrhoea is bad, or you are passing blood or slime, or you have a fever, you will almost certainly need antibiotics in addition to fluid replacement. A dose of norfloxacin or ciprofloxacin, repeated twice a day until better, may be appropriate (if you are planning to take an antibiotic with you, note that both norfloxacin and ciprofloxacin are available only on prescription in the UK). If the diarrhoea is greasy and bulky and is accompanied by sulphurous (eggy) burps, one likely cause is giardia. This is best treated with Tinidazole (four x 500mg in one dose, repeated seven days later if symptoms persist).

In hot parts of Somaliland, particularly along the coast, you may sweat more than you normally would. To counter the resultant loss of water and salt, you should drink more than normal and eat extra salt if you develop a taste for it (salt tablets are useless). Prickly heat, a rash caused by sweat trapped under the skin, is a harmless but highly uncomfortable and common problem when people used to temperate climates first enter the tropics. It will help if you wear 100% cotton clothing and splash yourself regularly with water, but avoid excessive use of soap.

Always wear clothes made from natural fabrics such as cotton. These help prevent fungal infections and other rashes. Athlete's foot is prevalent, so wear sandals in communal showers.

Small cuts are inclined to go septic in the tropics. Clean any lesion with a dilute solution of potassium permanganate two to three times daily. Antiseptic creams are not suitable for the tropics; wounds must be kept dry and covered.

## DANGEROUS ANIMALS

**INSECTS** Even if you are taking malaria tablets, you should take steps to avoid being bitten by insects, and by mosquitoes in particular. The most imperative reason for doing so is the increasing levels of resistance to preventative drugs. Whatever pills you take, there remains a significant risk of being infected by malaria in areas below 1,800m. Of much less concern, but still a risk, are several other mosquito-borne viral fevers that either are or else might be present in low and medium-altitude areas. **Dengue**, the only one of these diseases that is anything close to being common, is very nasty, with symptoms that include severe muscle cramps, high fever and a measles-like rash; fatalities are exceptional but medical help should be sought. The other diseases in this category are too rare to be a cause for serious concern. Nevertheless, they are difficult to treat, and some of them are potentially fatal.

To balance the warnings, it should be stressed that the overwhelming majority of insects don't bite people, and of those that do, the vast majority are entirely harmless. Mattresses quite often contain bedbugs and fleas, both of which are essentially harmless. For advice on avoiding insect bites, see the *Malaria* section on page 69.

**SNAKES** Although poisonous snakes are present in many parts of Somaliland, they pose little real threat to humans. The reason for this is that most snakes are very shy and secretive, and will move off at the slightest sign of humans.

The one place where you should be conscious of the possible presence of snakes is on rocky slopes and cliffs, particularly where you are scrambling up or down using your hands. This is because snakes respond to seismic vibrations – in most habitats they will sense your footsteps and slither away long before you get near them, but they may not on a rocky slope. You also have a greater danger of cornering a snake, or being unable to get away yourself, in a steep rocky habitat. Finally, rocky areas are the favoured dwelling place of Africa's most dangerous snake, the puff adder. Although this is not a particularly venomous species, it is capable of inflicting a fatal bite. The danger with puff adders is that they are unusually slothful, and the one species of venomous snake that doesn't generally move off in response to human foot treads.

As a general rule, you should wear trousers, socks and solid boots when you walk in the bush. Good boots will protect against the 50% of snakebites that occur below the ankle; trousers will help to deflect bites higher up on the leg. If you see a snake, wait to let it pass. If it rises to strike, the common advice is to stand dead still, as snakes strike in response to movement. This is far easier to say than to do and if you follow the instinctive reaction to retreat, this tactic usually works, too.

If the worst should happen, don't panic. Most snakes are non-venomous, and even with venomous snakes, the venom is only dispensed in about 50% of bites, and it is quite uncommon for a bite to contain enough venom to kill an adult. The chances are you will not come to any harm. Keep the victim still and calm; wash the wound with soap then wipe it gently with a clean cloth to remove any venom from the skin surface. Remove rings, bangles or watches in anticipation of swelling. If possible, splint the bitten limb, as movement quickens the rate of venom absorption, or if you have a crepe bandage apply this firmly from the end of the bitten extremity towards and over the site of the bite. Keep the bitten part below heart height. The victim should then be taken to a doctor or hospital, where they should be kept under observation. Antivenom will only be administered by a trained heath person if and when signs of envenomation occur. Having a positive identification of the snake will help effective treatment, but you should not attempt to catch it unless you are sure there is no risk of somebody else being bitten, bearing in mind that even a decapitated head can envenomate.

Finally, note that, after a snakebite, many 'traditional' first-aid measures will do more harm than good:

- DO NOT give alcohol or aspirin; paracetamol is safe
- DO NOT cut, incise or suck the wound; suction devices do not work
- DO NOT apply a tourniquet
- DO NOT apply potassium permanganate or ice

# Part Two

## THE GUIDE

# 5

# Hargeisa

Somaliland's largest town – one hesitates to use the word city – has a dusty low-rise feel more in line with a remote provincial administrative centre than a national capital. There's just one embassy in Hargeisa, no familiar airlines are represented, and other well-known international brands – be it McDonald's, Barclays or Hilton – are conspicuous by their collective absence. There are no trendy nightspots or sushi bars in Somaliland's capital, no neon lights or billboards, no overhead passes or traffic lights, no five-star hotels, no grandiose office blocks, no secular bookshops or flash tour operators, nor any cinemas, theatres or museums. Suffice to say that if cosmopolitan airs and transatlantic comforts feature highly on your list of travel priorities, humble little Hargeisa is bound to disappoint.

Therein lies much of Hargeisa's low-key charm. Rebuilt and resurrected from the ashes of recent war, this is a very pragmatic, take-me-as-I-am kind of city, one whose down-to-earth character and lack of architectural pomposity are epitomised by the use of a crashed MiG fighter jet as the centrepiece of its most important Civil War Memorial. Similarly, government offices in Hargeisa tend to be plainly decorated and informally signposted, and in most cases they effectively close shop at noon, after which the obligatory midday siesta morphs into an afternoon *khat*-chewing session. Indeed, the ubiquitous obsession with chewing this mildly narcotic leaf – every street corner seemingly has its own *khat* stall (see box, page 88) – gives Hargeisa a mild and rather likeable aura of decadence, one at odds with the stuffy images that many outsiders associate with Islamic Africa.

Overwhelmingly friendly and practically free of crime, Hargeisa in many respects feels more like an extension of the surrounding countryside than a proper urban conglomeration. Goats and sheep wander through the side roads, resting up wherever they find a sliver of shade, donkey carts jostle for road space with taxis and minibuses, and most people dress traditionally, in colourful flowing cloths. As is so often the case in small-town Africa, locals regularly stop you to ask your nationality and make small talk. Seldom, however, do such approaches appear to be motivated by anything other than plain curiosity – and, perhaps, the pleasurable implicit affirmation of nationhood associated with the presence of foreigners (who are often, and favourably, assumed to be journalists rather than tourists).

As national capitals go, Hargeisa is on the small side (it has an estimated population of 350,000) and is unusually manageable. Most activity takes place within a block or two of Independence Avenue, the strip of asphalt that snakes for several kilometres from the western outskirts of town to the east. The town centre, a tight grid of narrow roads studded with mosques and centred upon the venerable Oriental Hotel, is one vast sprawling market, with all the energy that implies. And while suburban Hargeisa is lacking in must-see attractions, it is always rewarding to explore the back roads on foot, drifting towards the fabulous camel market south of town, the green compound of the Man-soor Hotel in the northwest, or one of the city's many handsome mosques.

# HISTORY

Little is known about Hargeisa (literally 'the place where hide is sold') prior to the late 19th century. The town is built on the site of a venerable well, where desert nomads once congregated seasonally to water and feed their camels, and it was also entrenched as a watering stop along the ancient trade route from the Somali coast to the city of Harar. Lord Delamere, who later went on to be the most influential British settler in Kenya, undertook his first African hunting trip here in 1891, after which he returned annually to resume the hunt based out of a small bungalow he built at Hargeisa. The foundation of modern Hargeisa is generally credited to Sheikh Madar, a religious leader from Berbera who relocated to the interior in 1899, and reputedly lived in the bungalow built by Lord Delamere (which probably stood at what is now at the site of Sheikh Madar's Tomb).

By 1903, according to Major Swayne, who had passed through the area on several occasions since 1885, Sheikh Madar's settlement at Hargeisa was the largest in the interior of what is now Somaliland. Swayne described it as, 'a compact village of a few hundred *agal*, or permanent huts, surrounded by a high mat fence, and a square mile or two of sorghum cultivation belonging to different mullahs … built some five hundred yards from the right bank of the [Maroodi Jeex river] and at an elevation of thirty or forty feet above it.' Swayne also noted that it was:

> … situated on two important caravan routes [from Berbera], one from Ogaden and the other from Harar [and] supplies of rice, tobacco, and dates can sometimes be bought here in the trading season … There is abundance of good water in the bed of the river, and a masonry well has been built, and is kept in order by an Arab from Aden. The town is full of blind and lame people, who are under the protection of Sheikh Madar and his mullahs.

In 1941, Hargeisa replaced Berbera as capital of British Somaliland, a role it retained until independence in July 1960, when Mogadishu was chosen as the capital of the newly merged Somali Republic. Several impressive buildings were constructed during Hargeisa's tenure as colonial capital, among them the municipal building that still stands next to the Jama Mosque; and the State House, constructed on a vast estate to the southwest of the city centre in 1952 as a residence for Queen Elizabeth II on a planned visit to British Somaliland. This massive building later became the official residence of the British Governor and a guesthouse for visiting dignitaries prior to it being destroyed by fighting in 1988. After the war, State House Park was developed as an informal settlement for returned refugees and it now supports around 4,000 households.

Hargeisa was devastated by the Somali Civil War of the 1980s. An estimated 90% of the city was demolished in a series of bombings and other attacks by the Siad Barre regime in 1988. Tens of thousands of civilians were killed in the raids, and most of the survivors evacuated the city, either fleeing into the countryside, or across the border into Ethiopia or further afield. Hargeisa was liberated in 1991, after which the exiles started to return and rebuild the flattened city. In October 2008, the peaceful reconstruction process was briefly interrupted by a co-ordinated suicide bombing that targeted the Ethiopian Embassy, the presidential office and a UN compound, killing some 30 people and causing Ethiopian Airlines, the most important carrier to Hargeisa, to suspend all flights there on an indefinite basis. But this one tragic incident aside, the phoenix-like resurrection of Hargeisa from the ashes of war has been an African success story as remarkable as it is rare. As

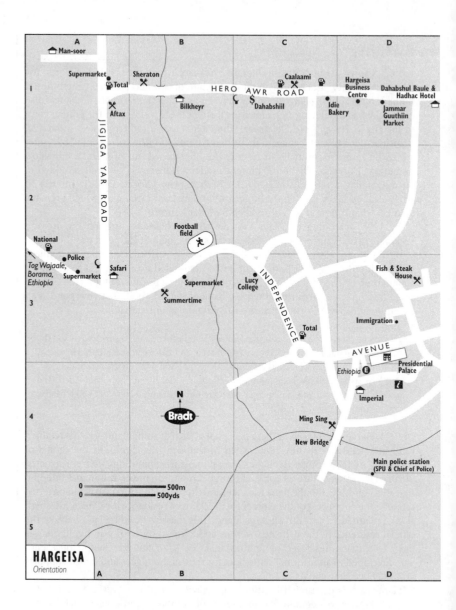

you walk the streets of Hargeisa today, it is humbling to recognise that almost every building you pass has been constructed from scratch or rebuilt from ruins since the early 1990s.

## GETTING THERE AND AWAY

What few international **flights** there are to Somaliland land at Hargeisa Egal International Airport, which lies immediately south of town, about 1km past the Ambassador Hotel. Most hotels listed in the upmarket or moderate categories can collect guests from the airport by prior arrangement and taxis are also available to

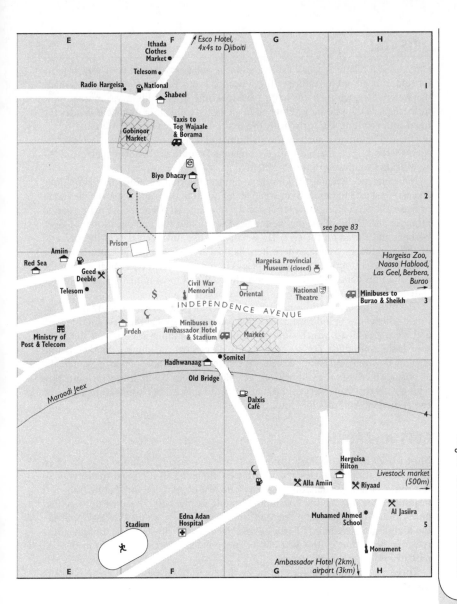

see page 83

Hargeisa Zoo,
Naaso Hablood,
Las Geel, Berbera,
Burao

INDEPENDENCE AVENUE

take you into town. Shared minibus taxis also run to the town from a bus station between the airport and the Ambassador Hotel.

Coming by **road**, a few 4x4s daily connect Djibouti and Zeila to Hargeisa via Borama. These leave from a taxi park about 1km north of Gobinoor Market and cost around US$38 for a cabin seat, US$28 to sit in the boot, and less for a perch on the roof. Regular shared taxis to or from Tog Wajaale (the main border with Ethiopia) and Borama leave from a park about 300m southeast of Gobinoor Market, and cost around US$5–6 per head. Shared taxis to Berbera cost US$5 and leave from a back road immediately north of the Jama Mosque, while those to Burao cost US$10 and depart from a park north of the police station and traffic circle about 200m further east.

# ORIENTATION

Hargeisa is a relatively small capital, and it is quite easy to find your way around. Its central geographic feature is the Maroodi Jeex ('Elephant Wadi'), a normally dry watercourse whose name harks back to a time when wildlife was more prolific in these parts than humans. Flowing in an easterly direction, the *wadi* divides the town into two uneven parts, with the main market area and centre lying to the north, and landmarks such as the stadium and airport to the south. Two bridges span Maroodi Jeex: the 'old bridge' immediately south of the town centre and the 'new bridge' southwest of the Presidential Palace.

Independence Avenue, the longest and most important thoroughfare, runs along an east–west axis for about 5km some 500m north of the *wadi*. Most vehicles enter or leave Hargeisa along Independence Avenue, since it becomes the main road to Ethiopia and Djibouti on the west side of town, and the main road to Las Geel, Berbera and Burao on the east. The small grid-like town centre is at the east end of Independence Avenue, where it is flanked by two important landmarks, the War Memorial (topped by a fighter plane) in the west and the Jama Mosque in the east. The Presidential Palace, Hargeisa Hospital and most ministries lie alongside Independence Avenue to the west of the town centre.

The most important thoroughfares north of Independence Avenue are Jigjiga Yar Road, which runs uphill for 1.5km to the Man-soor Hotel at the west end of town, and Hero Awr Road, which runs east from the Total filling station near the Man-soor Hotel (on Jigjiga Yar Road) to Radio Hargeisa and Gobinoor Market, before curving downhill and south to the town centre. South of Independence Avenue, the airport road crosses the 'old bridge' over Maroodi Jeex before hitting a T-junction with a road that runs west to the stadium and Edna Adan Hospital, or east to the camel market, Ambassador Hotel and airport.

# GETTING AROUND

Most places in central Hargeisa are within easy walking distance of each other. Alternatively, regular **buses** and **minibuses** run along all the main roads, with so few route variations that you are pretty safe just hopping on any public transport heading in the direction you want and hoping for the best. From the town centre, buses to Radio Hargeisa and the Man-soor Hotel leave from the taxi park opposite the Mandeeq Restaurant (a block behind the Oriental Hotel), while those heading towards the airport or the west end of Independence Avenue leave from the taxi park just north of the 'old bridge'.

There are several **taxi** ranks in the town centre, the most useful being opposite the Mandeeq Restaurant, next to Gobinoor Market, and on Independence Avenue perhaps 100m east of the Jama Mosque. Taxis can also usually be found parked outside the Ambassador and Man-soor hotels, or can be arranged through the reception desk of any hotel listed in the upmarket and moderate category. Fares are negotiable but shouldn't work out at more than US$5 for a one-way ride within the city limits.

# TOURIST INFORMATION

The tourist office, in the Ministry of Commerce, Industry & Tourism, lies in the dusty back streets behind the Presidential Palace [80 D3]. Headed up by Director of Tourism and Archaeology, Sada Mire, who contributed greatly to the research

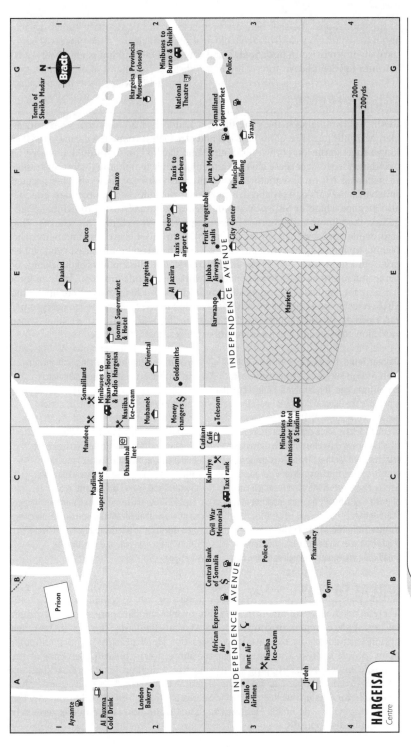

HARGEISA
Centre

Prison

Tomb of
Sheikh Madar

Hargeisa Provincial
Museum (closed)

Minibuses to
Burao & Sheikh

National
Theatre

Police

Somaliland
Supermarket

Siraay

Raaxo

Taxis to
Berbera

Jama Mosque

Municipal
Building

Duco

Daalad

Deero

Taxis to
airport

Fruit & vegetable
stalls

City Center

Somaliland

Minibuses to
Maan-Soor Hotel
& Radio Hargeisa

Joome Supermarket
& Hotel

Hargeisa

Al Jaziira

Jubba
Airways

Barwaaqo

INDEPENDENCE AVENUE

Mandeeq

Nasiiba
Ice-Cream

Mubanek

Oriental

Goldsmiths

Money
changers

Dhaambal
Inet

Madina
Supermarket

Cadtaani
Café

Telesom

Kalmiye

Taxi rank

Market

Minibuses to
Ambassador Hotel
& Stadium

Civil War
Memorial

Central Bank
of Somalia

Police

Pharmacy

African Express
Air

INDEPENDENCE AVENUE

Punt Air

Nasiiba
Ice-Cream

Gym

Daallo
Airlines

Jirdeh

Ayaante

Al Ruxma
Cold Drink

London
Bakery

0 ——— 200m
0 ——— 200yds

Bradt

N

83

of this guidebook, the staff here are very helpful and particularly knowledgeable about the country's wealth of archaeological sites, which are in the process of being formally inventoried in both Somali and English. Opening hours are 08.00–12.00 Saturday to Wednesday.

## TOUR OPERATORS

Recent years have seen the start up of a handful of low-key tour operators in Hargeisa, offering day trips to Las Geel and other sites around the capital, as well as longer tours to the likes of Berbera, Burao and Daallo Forest. It would, however, be misleading to think of these operators as comparable to upmarket safari companies elsewhere in Africa. Essentially they are all small one-man shows that use selected subcontracted cars or 4x4s and drivers, freelance guides where necessary, and will also arrange whatever SPU protection is required, usually using individual police guards they know and who have some experience travelling with tourists. That said, while working through an operator creates a lot more accountability than picking up an arbitrary car, driver and SPU off the street, in most cases you will be pretty much on your own once out of Hargeisa, and there is always the chance of being stuck with an SPU officer or driver with an attitude problem. The rate for a half-day tour to Las Geel is typically around US$80–120 for one person including SPU security and entrance fee, with an additional US$20 entrance fee charged per extra person, while 4x4 rental further afield usually works out at US$150–200 once you allow for fuel costs, driver's fee and expenses, and SPU protection.

**Dalmar Tours** [83 A3] ☏514999; m 412 9334 & 417 5535; e info@dalmartours.com; www. dalmartours.com. This reliable & flexible operator is based in the Oriental Hotel & is under the same hands-on management. They are very responsive to emails & have some experience arranging trips to Erigavo & Daallo. It's also a convenient starting point for those trying to team up with other travellers to save costs for a day trip to Las Geel or elsewhere, & the owner – when not out of town – can usually put together trips at very short notice.
**Nature Somaliland** m 413 8813; e info@naturesomaliland.com, abdi.jama@ ymail.com; www.naturesomaliland.com. Run

by a former National Geographic photographer, this small operator specialises in birding & wildlife tours personally guided by the super-knowledgeable owner-manager. It is a lot costlier than other operators, but also far more specialised, & should be the definite first choice for serious birders or wildlife lovers without budgetary restrictions. It is best to make arrangements as far in advance as possible.
**Somaliland Travel & Tourism** ☏524425; m 442 7766/440 6155; e info@somalilandtour. com; www.somalilandtour.com. This responsive new agency also offers day trips to Las Geel & tours further afield to the likes of Zeila & Erigavo.

 ## WHERE TO STAY

There is no shortage of hotels in Hargeisa, overall standards are surprisingly high and most places represent good value by African standards. The top-of-the-range option is undoubtedly the swanky Ambassador Hotel near the airport, although many people express a preference for the more down-to-earth Man-soor at the opposite end of town. Dropping slightly in price, a high proportion of backpackers crossing from Ethiopia end up at the Oriental Hotel, which is really good value, especially for single travellers, and also seems to be the best place to tune into the travel grapevine. The hotels Hadhwanaag and Amiin both stand out as genuinely pleasant budget options.

## UPMARKET

**⌂Ambassador Hotel** [81 H5] (45 rooms)
☎566666; e info@ambassadorhotelhargeisa.
com; www.ambassadorhotelhargeisa.com.
Situated about 5km south of the town centre &
1km from the airport, this is easily the smartest
hotel in Somaliland, set in large, secure &
reasonably attractive grounds below a hill.
Facilities include a fitness centre & tennis court,
an indoor swimming pool, a business centre,
fast free Wi-Fi, a free airport shuttle, & a well-
regarded restaurant with indoor & outdoor
seating. The non-smoking rooms all have a
comfortable queen-sized bed, writing table,
fridge, satellite TV, telephone & en-suite hot
shower. There are also comfortable villas aimed
at long-stay visitors. Despite being the priciest
hotel in the country, it is very reasonable by any
other standards, & good value. *US$53/79 B&B
sgl/dbl, or US$750 per month for a villa.*

**⌂Man-soor Hotel** [80 A1] (64 rooms)
☎527000/1/2; e mansoorhotel@hotmail.
com; www.man-soor.com. Set in a large green
compound on the northwest edge of town, this
is the only real rival to the Ambassador, & it has
a good range of facilities including a gym, a
business centre, a tennis court, online computers
for guest usage with Wi-Fi, a laundry service,
conference hall, & a decent airy restaurant that's
a popular rendezvous point for returned exiles &
expats. The comfortable tiled rooms are spacious
& all come with queen-sized bed, satellite TV &
telephone, while suites also have a proper sitting
area with sofas & armchairs. *US$45/80 dbl/suite.*

## MODERATE

**⌂Oriental Hotel** [83 D2] (30 rooms)
☎514999; m 412 9334 & 417 5535;
e orientalhotelhga@hotmail.com; www.
orientalhotelhargeisa.com. Founded in 1953 by
the father of the present owner-manager, this
is the oldest hotel in Hargeisa, with a couldn't-
be-more-central downtown location, & it has
been totally renovated since reopening after
the end of the civil war. The smart & reasonably
priced rooms are variable in size & quality, but all
come with en-suite hot showers, satellite TV &
telephone, & many also have a fridge, standing
fan & balcony. An attractive feature of the hotel
is its covered central courtyard restaurant,
which has satellite TV & free Wi-Fi, & tends to
be tolerably cool even on the hottest days. The
restaurant serves a varied selection of snacks
& meals in the US$3–4 range, as well as great
fruit juices, & is well entrenched as the main
travellers' congregation point in Somaliland. The
English-speaking staff are attentive & helpful, &
the hands-on owner, who also operates a tour
company & arranges car hire, is almost always
present & ready to answer your questions. The
only drawback is the sleep-shattering early
morning prayer call from the mosque on the
next block. *US$15/30 sgl/dbl, inc a good b/fast.*

**⌂Safari Hotel** [80 A3] (40 rooms)
☎570000; e info@safarihotelhargeisa.com,
safarihotelhargeisa@hotmail.com; www.
safarihotelhargeisa.com. Opened in 2010, this
modern multi-storey hotel on the corner of
Independence Av & the road uphill to the
Man-soor is one of the best options in town,
despite its non-central location. There is the
choice of sgl rooms (with three-quarter bed),
twins, dbls or suites (with king-sized bed), all
of which are reasonably spacious & come with
flat-screen satellite TV, telephone, en-suite
bathroom with hot water, & Wi-Fi. There is also a
good restaurant with indoor & outdoor seating.
*US$20/25/30/40 B&B sgl/twin/dbl/suite.*

**⌂Imperial Hotel** [80 D4] (21 rooms)
☎515000, 520524; e imperialhotel101@hotmail.
com. This pleasant & popular 2-storey is in a
quiet location a few paces from the Hargeisa
watercourse near the tourist office & main police
station, & about as far out of mosque earshot
as anywhere in town. The clean rooms come
with TV, roof fan & en-suite shower, & a decent
restaurant is attached. *US$20/25 sgl/dbl.*

**⌂City Center Hotel** [83 E3] (35 rooms)
☎510000; m 447 1733; e citycenterhotel@
hotmail.com. This central multi-storey hotel has
clean sgl & dbl rooms with 1 & 2 three-quarter
beds respectively, all en suite with hot water, as
well as TV, telephone & Wi-Fi. *US$15/25 B&B.*

## BUDGET

**⌂Barwaaqo Hotel** [83 E3] (40 rooms)
☏510077, 520000; e barwaaqohotel@hotmail.
com. This is an agreeable & central multi-storey
hotel, where the small but clean tiled rooms
come with dbl beds, TV & en-suite shower, but no
fan or AC. *US$12/20 sgl/dbl.*

**⌂Jirdeh Hotel** [83 A4] (20 rooms)
☏528792; m 411 1380. This good value hotel a
block south of Independence Av has large, cool,
tiled rooms, each with 2 sgl beds, TV & en-suite
hot shower. *US$10/15 sgl/dbl.*

## SHOESTRING

**⌂Amiin Hotel** [80 E3] (28 rooms)
☏520066; m 447 6476; e amiin1903@hotmail.
com. This multi-storey block, situated about
halfway between the town centre & the taxi park
for the Ethiopian border, has simple but clean
rooms with nets & in some cases balconies &/
or TV &/or en-suite shower. Dbls have a queen-
sized bed. The better rooms are very good value.
*US$7/10 sgl/dbl.*

**⌂Hadhac Hotel** [80 D1] (16 rooms)
☏518090; m 447 7478. This good value cheapie
is situated above the Dahabshiil Bank on the

**⌂Hotel Hadhwanaag** [81 F4]
(13 rooms) ☏521820. Situated in green
grounds on the north bank of the Hargeisa
watercourse, immediately south of the main
market area, this low-rise hotel has been warmly
praised for its helpful staff by several travellers.
The tiled rooms all come with TV, en-suite hot
shower, telephone & some cupboard space. And,
while they are undoubtedly a touch run down, it
would be ungenerous to complain at the price.
*US$8/12 sgl/dbl.*

main road connecting Radio Hargeisa to the
Man-soor Hotel. The rooms are basic but clean,
with a tiled floor & in some cases a balcony.
*US$4/6 sgl/twin using shared shower, US$10
en-suite dbl with hot shower.*

**⌂Shabeel Hotel** [81 F1] (8 rooms)
☏513311; m 406 8807. Situated on the traffic
circle close to the taxi parks for the Ethiopian
border & Djibouti, this basic place is worth
thinking about only if you are desperate to save
cash or you're catching a 4x4 to Djibouti early the
next morning. *US$4 dbl with en-suite cold shower.*

# ✘ WHERE TO EAT

Hargeisa, it can safely be said, isn't one of the world's great culinary cities. There are
very few restaurants, and most are identikit local places that serve up a small and
rather predictable selection of local staples, usually pasta and/or rice with a meat
stew. For greater variety, aside from the handful of places listed below, the best
options are generally the hotels listed in the upmarket and moderate categories,
all of which have their own restaurants (see *Where to stay*, page 84). Those at the
**Man-soor** and **Ambassador** are popular with expatriates, and neither is dauntingly
expensive, serving a varied range of beef, chicken, fish and vegetarian dishes for
around US$5. The **Oriental** is a reliable central option, and the substantial mains –
most of which cost US$4 – are supplemented with a starter of soup and fresh crusty
bread. The restaurant at the **Safari Hotel** is similarly priced and also comes highly
recommended. It is worth noting that nowhere in Hargeisa serves alcohol (if you
are desperate for the next best thing, the bars at the Man-soor and Ambassador
serve alcohol-free beer) but many places offer excellent freshly crushed fruit juice,
usually for less than US$1 per glass.

## MODERATE

**✘Fish & Steak House** [80 D3] ☏520440;
m 442 8773; ☉Sat–Thu. The main rival to Daus
as Hargeisa's top eatery is this longer serving &
somewhat pricier restaurant, which lies a few
hundred metres west of the town centre, & has

an abundance of outdoor seating, whether on
the covered balcony or in one of several huts
scattered around the pleasant little garden. It is
famed locally for its exceptional pizzas, which
cost around US$5–8 each, but should easily serve

2 people. Also on offer are fish, steak, chicken & burger dishes, fresh espresso coffee, & a selection of delicious desserts.

✘**Ming Sing Restaurant** [80 C4] ✆520501; m 402 2994. The only Chinese restaurant in Somaliland, this once popular place had been around for a while prior to closing in late 2010,

& the word locally is that it will eventually reopen following renovations. It is set in large grounds on the north bank of Maroodi Jeex, a few paces away from the Imperial Hotel (which also serves pretty good food if you pitch up & find it is still closed).

## BUDGET

✘**Aftax Restaurant** [80 A1] This simple restaurant opposite the Total garage near the Man-soor Hotel has been recommended as one of the best local eateries in town. Meals costs around US$2.

✘**Geed Deeble Restaurant** [81 E3] Another good local eatery, this has a central location more or less opposite the prison & it supplements the usual Somali dishes with adequate burgers, fruit juice & filter coffee.

✘**Mandeeq Restaurant** [83 D1] ✆521262; m 442 5567. It looks rather sleazy from the outside & the interior won't win over anybody who is phobic about flies, but this small eatery along the main road immediately north of the market area serves a decent plate of chicken, goat or fish for around US$3, & the juice is good too.

✘**Nasiiba Ice-Cream & Cafeteria** [83 D2] At least 2 branches of this café can be found in the town centre, as marked on the maps. Both serve a variety of snacks as well as burgers, ice cream cones, espresso coffee & imported fruit juices & alcohol-free beers. It might not stand out in another context, but there is nothing else like it in Hargeisa.

✘**Sheraton Restaurant** [80 B1] m 447 4722; e mesifinfree@yahoo.com. Named after the swankiest hotel in the Ethiopian capital Addis Ababa, this small & unassuming eatery near the Man-soor Hotel serves perhaps the best Ethiopian food in Somaliland. Dishes include *tibs* (fried meat) & *kai wat* (a red & very spicy stew) served with the Ethiopian staple *injera* (a large sour-tasting pancake). It also serves decent coffee. The owner speaks good English. Mains are in the US$1.50–2.50 range.

# SHOPPING

The whole of central Hargeisa functions as a gigantic, partially covered market but, unlike in most African capitals, there is little available in the way of handicrafts or other items of specific interest to travellers. The one arguable exception is the varied and generally quite inexpensive jewellery sold at the innumerable goldsmiths and silversmiths that line the roads immediately south of the Oriental Hotel. The main non-central market is Gobinoor near Radio Hargeisa.

For grocery shopping, there is no shortage of fresh produce available in the central market area, and numerous stalls also sell fresh bread and packaged items, such as mineral water, biscuits and tinned fruit, which might be worth stocking up on if you plan a trip to more remote parts of the country. There are also several supermarkets dotted around town. The ones in the national filling station near the Shabeel Hotel and the Total filling station near the Man-soor Hotel are particularly well stocked with luxury imported goodies, from crisps and fruit juices to chocolate bars and biscuits. Also good is the more central Madiina Supermarket.

**BOOKSHOPS** There are several stationery and religious bookshops dotted around town. The only place selling secular books is the **Red Sea Bookshop** on the ground floor of the Oriental Hotel [83 D2], and the English-language stock here is limited to a handful of titles about Somalia or Somaliland published by the Red Sea Press.

*Khat*, qat, chat, qaad, *Catha edulis*. The green, leafy stalks that lie somewhere on the continuum between vegetable and tree. Wrapped in bundles the size of a modest bouquet of flowers – for the boyfriend on a budget – these plastic-sheathed plants are perhaps Somaliland's most popular purchase. Brought into the country daily from the Ethiopian Highlands, the produce (ubiquitous and 100% legal in Somaliland) is rapidly unloaded from the arriving cargo planes/dump trucks/station wagons, and distributed to the thousands of little green street stalls that dot Hargeisa like the pox.

These resupply relays go on every single day with an efficiency that would make any paperboy blush. Chewed recreationally for its amphetamine effects, the *khat* is off the plane and in mouths all over Hargeisa in under an hour. This daily importation ritual is caused more by biological happenstance than anything else: the active ingredient starts to decline in potency from the moment it's harvested, so that within two days of being picked, a bundle of *khat* is no different from any other pile of leafy rubbish. Thus, it's imperative that the distributors get it to market as soon as possible and it's even been rumoured that one entrepreneur wants to start importing it via helicopter, reducing the delay between harvest and consumption to a couple of hours.

So with all this fuss, we must be talking about some pretty good stuff, right? Well, sort of. Chewing *khat* is an experience unto itself, and not necessarily because of its narcotic properties. Allow me to walk you through a typical afternoon session, step by step.

First, you head out to your local *khat* stall. With up to a dozen of these little green kiosks on any given block in Hargeisa, you've no shortage of options, and everybody has their favourite. But it's best to splash out and make a special trip downtown to Gafane 1 for some high-grade *Double Musbaar*. A *falad* is the standard portion, and it costs about Ssh35,000, or just under US$7. By contrast, for the same amount of cheapo 'bush weed' you'd pay just under US$2 and be rewarded with no feeling other than a sore jaw.

With a bundle of the quality stuff tucked under one arm, it's time to sort out the other accoutrements before we can begin. First on the docket is a trip to a corner shop, to pick up a Coca-Cola or two to counteract the *khat*'s bitterness, and three or four loose cigarettes if you're a smoker. Further down the street, you can grab a fresh thermos of sweet Somali tea, and you're sorted.

# OTHER PRACTICALITIES

**AIRLINES** The local offices for African Express, Daallo Airlines and Punt Air are clustered either side of Independence Avenue at the western end of the town centre. The office for Jubba is further east along Independence Avenue, next to the Barwaaqo Hotel. Full local contact details are included below.

**African Express Air** [83 A3] ✆583203; m 441 0248 or 442 2604; e gastravel@hotmail. com; www.africanexpress.co.ke
**Daallo Airlines** [83 A3] ✆523003, 573406; e hga@daallo.com, hga.reservations@gmail.

com; www.daallo.com
**Jubba Airways** [83 E3] ✆524022; e hargeisa@jubba-airways.com; www.jubba-airways.com

Having selected a spot to recline for a while, lay out your purchases in front of you. Unwrapping your bundle, you can begin right away, or if you're American-raised like myself, take your *khat* to the kitchen sink and give it a good rinse – after all, you never know what kind of chemicals it's been sprayed with. Then, pluck off a nice leaf or two and … chew.

The bitter taste is the first thing you'll notice. This puts a lot of people off, but you've got to work your way through it if you're going to have a proper chewing session. Personally, the first time I chewed, it didn't taste so great, but living in a country where *khat*-mastication is the closest thing to a national pastime, I was determined to persevere.

Working through a stalk every ten minutes or so, you quickly end up with a fat wad of green paste balled up in your cheek. And as saliva soaks into the cud-like ball, so the *khat* makes the epic journey into your bloodstream. Eventually, the moment of truth arrives – you've got a bunch of unhealthy snacks and a bitter-tasting gob of paste in your cheek, but what does this stuff actually *do*?

Truth be told, the first couple of times you chew, you may be at a loss to decipher the effects. Certainly, you feel more effects from a beer or two than after a whole bundle of *khat*. But the experience is also entirely different.

One of its principal effects is talkativeness. Once you're about halfway through your bundle, you'll find yourself in passionate discussions with your fellow chewers and intense, occasionally semi-manic conversations can go on for the rest of your session, and even after you've run out.

Otherwise, you may feel a little excitable, even somewhat wired, but at no point are you 'out of it' in the way associated with alcohol or other drugs. Somalis have a specific word for *khat*'s effects, always pronounced with a gleam in the speakers' eyes: *mirqaan* – a unique moment that encompasses every aspect of the experience, the excitement, the conversation, the piles of gross green guck, the lot.

*Mirqaan* is a very lucid experience, and because of that *khat* feels very mild when compared to any substance imbibed in the West. It's definitely a lot more work (and a lot less sexy) than pulling a corkscrew or cracking open a beer, but when you're in Somaliland, it's the only viable alternative to a social drink. So grab a friend, buy a bundle, and go *khat* each other up for the afternoon. And don't forget to cancel dinner – *khat* is an appetite suppressant, so you definitely won't be hungry.

**Punt Air** [83 A3] \518677; m 440 6864; e husenmf6@hotmail.com or alimtravel@gmail.com

**CAR RENTAL** No international car rental companies are represented in Hargeisa, and it is not generally possible to hire a car without a driver, partially for security reasons. Sedan cars and 4x4s with a driver can be rented through the tour operators listed on page 84. Alternatively, it is usually possible to charter a car and driver at any taxi park in Hargeisa, or elsewhere in the country; this will generally work out cheaper but you will need to negotiate and should clarify whether fuel and (for overnight excursions) driver expenses are covered in the agreed price. At the risk of stating the obvious, a private charter like this comes with far less accountability than a car rented through an operator.

**EMBASSIES** The only country with diplomatic representation in Hargeisa is Ethiopia, which maintains an embassy off Independence Avenue immediately west of the Presidential Palace. It is open 08.00–12.30 and 16.00–18.30 Monday to Thursday and Saturday, but you are strongly urged to visit in the morning if you need to arrange a visa for Ethiopia (see box, *Ethiopian visas*, page 91). Security at the Ethiopian Embassy is very tight, understandably so given that it was the target of a suicide bombing that claimed 20 lives in 2008, and you will be expected to leave all electronic devices, including mobile phones, outside.

**FOREIGN EXCHANGE** It is easiest to use US dollars for most purchases in Hargeisa and elsewhere in the country, and to accept change in local currency where necessary (see page 58). However, if you want to carry some Somaliland shillings to use as change, innumerable moneychangers can be found along the grid of roads around the Oriental Hotel, and they have a reputation for straight dealing. More complex financial requirements, such as international transfers, or changing euros or other non-US hard currencies into shillings or US dollars, are best dealt with at any of several branches of the Dahabshiil Bank.

**INTERNET AND EMAIL** Somalilanders are justifiably proud of the quality of internet service in Hargeisa, which is generally faster than in most parts of Ethiopia, although rather sluggish by other standards. Most of the better hotels offer free Wi-Fi to guests who have their own laptop (ask for an access code at reception), and some also have desktop computers permanently online for the use of guests free of charge. Alternatively, there must be a dozen internet cafés dotted around the town centre and rates for browsing are very cheap.

**MEDICAL FACILITIES** A prominent landmark in Hargeisa, situated south of Maroodi Jeex along the main road to the stadium, is the **Edna Adan Hospital** [81 F5] (✆ *525016;* m *441 6342;* e *ednahospital@yahoo.com; www.ednahospital.org).* This hospital was founded by the former Foreign Minister and prominent anti-FGM activist Edna Adan Ismail, who was awarded the French Legion of Honour in 2010 in recognition of her achievements, and is the director of the institution.

The hospital was established in 2002 to aid a country whose healthcare system had been destroyed by the civil war, leaving it with the world's highest rate of maternal and infant mortality. Today, it places strong emphasis on midwife training and it has the country's best maternity facilities, but it is also the medical facility favoured by UN staff and most other expats, and is the best place to head in an emergency. If you need a dentist, Dr Abdirahman, next to the Oriental Hotel, has been recommended.

**POLICE** The main police station [80 D4] has a somewhat remote location on the south bank of Maroodi Jeex and is best reached by following the road running south from Independence Avenue past the Imperial Hotel, crossing the 'new bridge' over the *wadi*, then taking the first left. It is here that SPU officers can be arranged for trips outside Hargeisa, and where you can try your luck obtaining a letter of waiver for SPU protection from the Chief of Police. For other police-related matters, such as reporting crimes, there is also a police station on the circle on Independence Avenue at the east end of the town centre.

**SAFETY** We heard nothing before, after or during our research trip to Somaliland to suggest that petty crime or mugging is a cause for worry. Indeed, from this point of view, Hargeisa must surely rank among the safest of African capitals. Nevertheless, it would be wise to exercise the same precautions one might in any city and avoid overt displays of wealth, such as wearing flashy jewellery or other expensive accessories, try not to carry significantly more money than you need for any given outing, and avoid walking around alone late at night, especially down quiet alleys.

Security, in particular terrorist activity, has to be regarded as a more serious concern than petty crime, especially given Somaliland's rather strained relationship with the rest of Somalia since secession in 1991. The only such incident in recent

## ETHIOPIAN VISAS

Unless they already have a valid multiple-entry visa, or an unused single-entry visa obtained elsewhere, all travellers who intend to cross from Somaliland into Ethiopia must get a visa in Hargeisa. This is not exactly a straightforward procedure, but can usually be completed in about two hours, provided all your paperwork is in order. Occasionally, however, the Ethiopian Embassy will only be prepared to issue a visa on the next working day after application, so it is advisable to allow for this in your planning.

It should also be noted that the Ethiopian Embassy is closed on Sunday, the Somaliland Immigration Office (which you need to visit to obtain a letter of request) is closed on Thursday and both are closed on Friday, so the full procedure can only be completed between Monday and Wednesday or on Saturday. The earlier you start the better, as both offices close for lunchtime siestas at 12.00 and there is no guarantee that the correct officials will return to their desks later in the day.

The first step, ideally completed an afternoon in advance, is to gather together all the bits and pieces required to complete the visa formalities: your passport, four identical passport photographs (these can be prepared in ten minutes at a photo studio along the road connecting the Oriental Hotel and Joome Supermarket), photocopies of the passport page with your photo and personal details as well as the page on which your Somaliland visa is stamped, the name and telephone number of your hotel in Hargeisa, as well as the visa fee of US$30 (other currencies may not be accepted).

Armed with this stash, you now need to head to the Somaliland Immigration Office to obtain the letter of request demanded by the Ethiopian Embassy. The Immigration Office is not easy to find, as it is tucked away and unsignposted, down a side road about 400m northeast of the Ethiopian Embassy. If in doubt, take a taxi. It is always open 08.00–12.00 Saturday to Wednesday, and may reopen in the afternoon, but don't count on it. The officials here will need two passport photos as well as the passport photocopies referred to above, and should be able to process the letter in 15–30 minutes.

The final stop is the Ethiopian Embassy (see page 90), hidden down an alley running south from Independence Avenue next to the Presidential Palace. Here you also need passport photos, your address in Hargeisa, and the US$30 fee, ideally in exact change. The visa is also usually issued on the spot, and you should be out again within 30 minutes, depending on how busy it is. If you are asked to come back the next day and you need a visa sooner, tell them it is urgent and the staff will almost certainly oblige the same day.

years occurred on 29 October 2008, when six co-ordinated suicide bombers attacked the Presidential Palace, the Ethiopian Embassy and the UNDP in Hargeisa, as well as the port of Bosaso in Puntland, killing at least 30 people. Whether travellers to Hargeisa are at any greater risk than in any other African city – or elsewhere in the world, for that matter – is impossible to say.

**TELEPHONE** A local SIM card for your mobile can be picked up at any branch of Telesom (*www.telesom.net*) or Somitel, as marked on the maps. If you don't have your own phone, the town centre is dotted with numerous kiosks and shops that offer inexpensive direct dialling overseas. Most hotels offer the same service but charges are higher.

## WHAT TO SEE

**TOWN CENTRE** Central Hargeisa is an agreeable and intriguing place to wander around, with a friendly easy-going atmosphere and no shortage of hustle and bustle around the market area. Architectural landmarks, however, are few and far between, so exploring the town centre is more a case of following your nose than sticking to a trail of prescribed sights. Nevertheless, a good starting point, standing prominently on the north side of Independence Avenue, is the **Hargeisa Civil War Memorial** [83 C3], which consists of a MiG fighter jet – which crashed close by during one of the regular aerial bombardments of the town – on a stand decorated with murals depicting the hardships of the civil war.

Immediately east of the war memorial is the main town centre and **central market** [83 E3], the latter a labyrinthine sprawl of covered and open stalls, laden with fresh fruit and vegetables, meat, packaged foods, local cloths and imported clothes, electronic goods, bricks of banknotes, and pretty much anything else you care to mention. The grid of roads north of Independence Avenue can come across like one large market, and are where you will find most of the town's famous goldsmiths, but the real market is actually south of the main road, and is most easily entered along the small road next to the City Center Hotel.

**Jama Mosque** [83 F3], the largest and most important of an estimated 350 scattered around town, stands prominently on the north side of Independence Avenue east of the market. It is unclear what war damage the mosque suffered, but it is in pristine shape today, with its whitewashed exterior, domed roof and tall twin balconied minarets. Next to it is the stone **Municipal Building** [83 F3], constructed in 1953 in anticipation of a planned visit to British Somaliland by Queen Elizabeth II (the visit was subsequently cancelled, but there's a plaque on the wall dedicated to her name).

At the traffic circle 100m or so past the mosque, a left turn leads you to two of the town's best-known landmarks, both on the left side of the road and semi-ruined after having been bombed in 1988. First up is the cavernous **National Theatre** [83 G2], a somewhat functional building that used to form the hub of the capital's cultural life, and will hopefully do so again once ongoing renovations are complete. Opposite this, the former **Hargeisa Provincial Museum** [83 G2], constructed with reinforced concrete in the form of four concentric circles in the 1970s, once housed an excellent ethnographic collection. The building itself is now partially rehabilitated and seems to serve as a clinic.

Another 200m uphill of this is an attractive whitewashed shrine and mosque centred on the **Tomb of Sheikh Madar** [83 F1], a celebrated religious leader who moved here from Berbera in 1899. In 1903, Swayne described Sheikh Madar as

Among the myriad moneychangers and innumerable bricks of Ssh500 notes that line the streets of Hargeisa, you'll pick out semi-discreet flashes of a glossier shade of green. Not money, but passports – brand new, completely blank, and with Somali Democratic Republic proudly emblazoned on the front cover. These are Somali (not Somaliland) passports, the issuance of which has semi-officially fallen into private hands since 1991.

In practice, this means almost anyone can wander downtown and get themselves a bona fide identity document, no questions asked. And it goes without saying that, living in a country with passports for sale on the streets, I couldn't pass up the opportunity to buy one.

Armed with some cash and a photo, I made my way downtown and started asking around for a '*baasaboor*'. As this is a true free-for-all private enterprise, prices vary wildly depending on who you ask. I soon settled on a US$60 model, in lovely institutional green. After I paid up, a stack of fresh blank passports was whisked out from a tattered black grocery bag, and I was handed my very own paint-by-numbers, do-it-yourself, fill-in-the-blanks passport.

'What about the stamps and signatures?', I queried. 'Ten dollar!', beamed Mr Moneychanger. Fair enough – it may be a disorganised free-for-all, but it still beats a trip to the DMV or post office.

After knocking US$2 off the stamp-and-signature fee, I was asked to fill in my personal details on a scrap piece of paper clearly torn out of a weekly planner several years out of date. Information in hand, my moneychanger-turned-citizenship officer disappeared around the corner, leaving myself and some bystanders in charge of his money piles.

In about as long as it takes to turn down a glass of tea, our faithful public servant was back with a stamped, signed and even laminated passport. Whoever he went to clearly ran a tight ship. With that, I bade farewell to Mr Moneychanger and various other congenial chatters, and headed off down the street, a Somali citizen in less than 30 minutes. I've had a tougher time getting a Chicago Public Library card – I wasn't even asked for any ID, the guy just filled in whatever information I gave him.

Of course, the issue of legitimate Somaliland (as opposed to Somalia) passports is more strictly regulated – much like getting a passport anywhere else. Ironically, however, this legitimate document is practically useless. Governments are unwilling to issue visas to citizens of a country whose existence they don't recognise, which means that a Somaliland passport is accepted nowhere in the world other than Ethiopia and Djibouti.

Perversely, a Somali passport that was printed who knows where, bought on the black market, and filled in by a moneychanger with a rubber stamp of mysterious origin, is a relatively legitimate document. Indeed, it is this very document that most Somalilanders wishing to travel abroad are forced to use. Not that I imagine getting a visa anywhere with a Somali passport is a walk in the park. Little wonder, really, that any Somalilander who can afford it will shell out for an Ethiopian passport instead.

'the chief of Hargeisa', adding that he was 'a pleasant-mannered man affecting Arab dress [who] reads and writes Arabic, and is a steady supporter of British interests'. He is regarded as the founder of modern Hargeisa by his many followers. Non-Muslims are usually permitted to peek through the compound entrance, but they may not cross the threshold, and photography may be forbidden.

## CAMELS

The ancient traders of the Sahara referred to the camel as the 'Ship of the Desert', while the Koran states that 'The Almighty in making animals created nothing preferable'. Others have been less kind and, 'a horse designed by a committee' is one famous putdown of the camel's faintly absurd, knock-kneed appearance. But it pays sufficient testament to the singularity of this desert-adapted beast, and its importance in Somali culture, that more than 40 different Somali words exist to describe various forms of camel, based on appearance, age, gender, use and various other subtleties.

The *Camelidae* evolved in North America about 45 million years ago, when forms as small as a rabbit and as tall as an elephant existed. Six more uniformly sized species are recognised today: four humpless South American varieties and two humped Old World ones. Of the latter, only the two-humped Bactrian camel persists in the wild, with fewer than 1,000 individuals left roaming the inhospitable Gobi Desert in Mongolia.

More numerous in a domestic state is the one-humped Arabian camel or dromedary (*Camelus dromedarius*), of which five Somali variants are recognised: Benadir, Dolbahanta, Guban, Mugugh and Ogaden. The Arabian camel might have been custom-made as a beast of burden suited to desert conditions, with its capacity to travel 100km daily bearing a load of up to 200kg. In ancient times, these camels were vital to overland trade in the arid Horn of Africa, and used to transport frankincense, spices and salt blocks from their inland source to the coastal ports.

Superficial desert adaptations include splayed feet for walking on sand, nostrils they can seal, and a double row of long eyelashes for protection in sandstorms. A camel can eat just about any vegetable matter, from grass and leaves to thorns and bark, and will also forage for carrion and bones. The hump stores fat, which can also be drawn upon for sustenance.

Most remarkable is the camel's capacity to survive for weeks without water. Sweat is minimal, the kidneys produce paste-like urine, and the faeces are so dry they can be used for fuel immediately. During long periods without drinking, a camel can lose up to one-third of its weight by recycling water stored in the body tissues; at the end of an enforced fast it can gulp down more than 100 litres of water in ten minutes, immediately absorbing it back into the dehydrated tissues.

Somalia – including Somaliland and Puntland – claims to support the world's largest population of domestic camels, estimated at around six million. Camels have long been a mainstay of the Somaliland economy (they are exported from Berbera to all over the Gulf of Arabia) and the country is the world's largest producer of camel milk. Camel milk is lower in fat than cow's milk, stays fresh for longer, and is rich in iron, potassium and several vitamins. The meat is also very healthy, being unusually low in cholesterol, and it is often served stewed or roasted in Somali restaurants.

**LIVESTOCK MARKET** [81 H5] Also known as the camel market, this bustling market, 30 minutes' walk south of the town centre, is well worth a visit, ideally between 08.00 and 11.00 when it is busiest. Multitudes of camels, goats and 'fat-tailed' sheep are all on sale here, and visitors are welcome to take photographs or to sit with the traders and sip a Somali tea in the shade. If you are thinking of buying, bargaining is definitely the order of the day, and word is that a camel might cost anything from US$1,000 for a strong fully grown stud to around US$300 for a punier three to four year old. By contrast, you can pick up a sheep or goat for a mere US$60–80.

To get here, follow the airport road south from the town centre, crossing the 'old bridge' over Maroodi Jeex, then continue for another 500m or so to a traffic circle and T-junction where you need to turn left. Continue along this road for another 1km, passing the Hargeisa Hilton on your left and the Al Jasiira Restaurant and junction for the airport on your right, until you reach the Dahabshiil Bank on your right and 50m further a small market on the left. Walk through the market for about 100m and the alley opens out into the large clearing where the livestock market is held. If in doubt ask for the *soukha geel* or *soukha seylada* (respectively 'camel market' and 'livestock market').

**HARGEISA ZOO** [81 H3] Tucked away down a residential side road about 500m east of the Jama Mosque, this private menagerie – signposted 'Beerta Xayawaanka' ('Animal Garden') in Somali – is a serious contender for the world's most unedifying zoo. The star attraction is a quartet of lions, brought to the zoo from Ethiopia by the government minister that owns it. They are now confined in tiny cages that stink of urine and rotting meat. The zoo's other inhabitants amount to a small flock of vultures and other raptors that get to clear up the meat scraps left by the lions, and that's about it. It is a truly depressing place, and impressions don't improve when you learn that one of the lions escaped and killed a local woman in 2008. The offending lion was subsequently shot by its owner, but visitors are still allowed to pet the giant paws of the survivors. If you really must visit, entrance costs less than US$1.

**NAASO HABLOOD** [81 H3] The pair of near-identical pyramidal hills known as Naaso Hablood (literally, 'Girl's Breasts') are a striking and aptly named Hargeisa landmark, rising to an altitude of 1,420m from a base of around 1,030m, some 5km northeast of the town centre. Local legend has it that the hills, with their step-like upper slopes, are manmade pyramids, the result of a cultural interchange with the ancient Egyptians when they visited the land of Punt 3,500 years ago. In fact, they are natural hills, made of granite and sand, though stone tools uncovered at a natural overhang on one of the peaks suggest it was settled by hunter-gatherers in prehistoric times.

To get here, follow the Berbera road out of town for precisely 2km past the Kaah fuel station (on the right side of the road), then turn left on to a rough dirt road which you need to follow for 3.5km to the base of the nearest hill (N 9°35.538, E 44°07.518). There's quite a bit of wildlife around, most visibly pairs of dik-dik, and the birdlife includes what appears to be a breeding colony of white-backed vultures in the gorge to the right of the track.

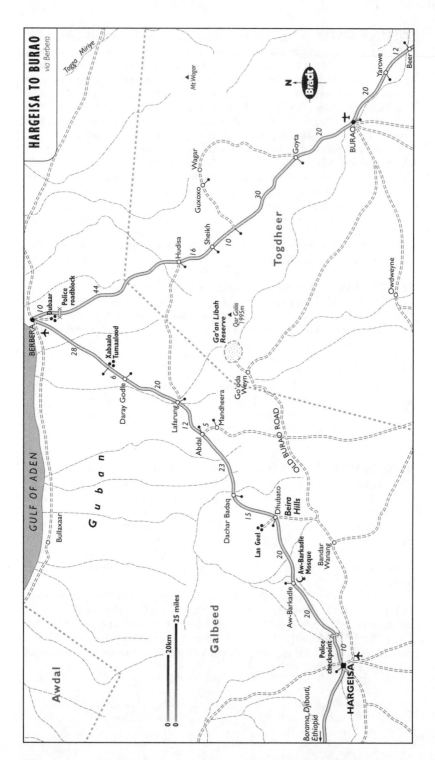

HARGEISA TO BURAO
*via Berbera*

GULF OF ADEN

Awdal

Galbeed

Togdheer

HARGEISA

BURAO

Beer

Yarowe

Goyta

Sheikh

Hudisa

Guxoxo

Wagar

Mt Wagar

Togga Miriye

Bullaxaar

Daray Godle

Xabaalo Tumaalood

Dubaar

Police roadblock

BERBERA

Lafarung

Abdal

Mandheera

Dachar Badaq

Las Geel

Aw-Barkadle Mosque

Aw-Barkadle

Bandar Wanang

Dhubato

Beira Hills

OLD BURAO ROAD

Go'oda Weyn

Ga'an Libah Reserve

Qar Golis 1995m

Owdweyne

Police checkpoint

Borama, Djibouti, Ethiopia

G u b a n

N

Bradt

10
12
20
20
30
16
10
44
28
6
20
12
5
23
15
20
20
10

0    20km
0    25 miles

# 6

# Las Geel and the Berbera Road

The 150km strip of asphalt running northeast from Hargeisa to Berbera is probably the best-maintained road in the country, and certainly the busiest. It passes through a characteristic Somali landscape of sandy, red dry plains covered in thirsty acacia scrub, criss-crossed by the occasional seasonal *wadi*, and set below a row of tall ridges and striking outcrops that look like the work of a giant child obsessed with creating piles of improbably balancing boulders. Surprisingly, perhaps, there is plenty of wildlife to be seen – baboon and dik-dik are virtually guaranteed, and you may also encounter desert warthog, gerenuk, gazelle, and colourful birds such as golden-breasted starling and bold yellow-breasted barbet.

In a private vehicle, the road to Berbera could be traversed in less than two hours, and it shouldn't take that much longer in a shared taxi, assuming that the numerous roadblocks don't detain you for too long. However, it also offers access to what is arguably the most compelling tourist attraction in Somaliland, the superb prehistoric rock art site at Las Geel, which lies a mere 55km north of Hargeisa along a 6km dirt track. Other sites of interest include the pre-Islamic stelae at Xabaalo Tumaalood, the historic Islamic shrine at Aw-Barkadle, and a set of hills whose slopes harbour the rare beira antelope. Further afield, Ga'an Libah is the most accessible wildlife-viewing site on the Golis Escarpment.

## AW-BARKADLE

Only 15 minutes' drive north of Hargeisa, close to the dry Dogor watercourse, lies the small village of Aw-Barkadle, which is named after Sharif Yusuf Barkadle, one of the most significant of the many Islamic saints that emigrated from Arabia to Somaliland in medieval times. Indeed, the shrine maintained at the burial site of Aw-Barkadle ('The Blessed Father') is among the most important and sacred Islamic sites in the Horn of Africa, to the extent that some Somalis regard three pilgrimages there to be equivalent to the Hajj to Mecca. Aw-Barkadle is often credited as the first saint who helped convert the Somali interior to Islam, partly though his invention of a vowel notation that allowed the Somalis to read Arabic texts. It is also said that he was responsible for introducing the variety of sheep most common in Somaliland today, a superficially goat-like breed distinguished by its short fat tail and black head.

Aw-Barkadle is strongly linked to the creation legend of the Yibbir, a small clan of nomadic mystics who customarily bless newborn Somali children and newlyweds. Local legend has it that when he first arrived in the village that now bears his name, Aw-Barkadle attempted to convert the incumbent Yibbir leader, a powerful pagan magician called Mohammed Hanif, to orthodox Islam. After his missionary approaches failed, Aw-Barkadle changed tack and challenged Hanif to a mutual test of their magical powers, a spiritual duel that resulted in him imprisoning his rival within a nearby hill, an act for which he compensated in keeping with Koranic law by paying the family *diyya* (blood money for killing a relative). This ancient legend clearly shows Islam prevailing over the older pagan ways of the Somali interior, but interestingly it is also cited as the rationale behind the extant custom of *samanyo*, which dictates that the parents of a newborn child or newlywed bride must pay a specified sum to the first Yibbir that approaches them to give his blessing.

That this legend has some basis in actual historical events is borne out by recent research undertaken by the Somali archaeologist Sada Mire, who writes:

> There are indications that Aw-Barkadle was also an important pre-Islamic site. It is surrounded by a number of burial mounds, dolmens, standing stones and stelae. Until relatively recently, fertility rituals were reportedly practised here: the participants washed themselves in a well, and then proceeded to a chalk pit where they daubed a white cross on their forehead, before entering a sacred enclosure and sitting on the fertility stone. This superimposition of revered landscapes has created one of the most archaeologically important sites in Somaliland, and is high on our list of potential World Heritage Sites.

**PRACTICALITIES** Aw-Barkadle village (N 9°41.460, E 44°18.549) straddles the Berbera road precisely 20km past the police roadblock on the northeast outskirts of Hargeisa. The medieval shrine to the eponymous saint, with its whitewashed walls, domed roof and green wooden doors, is situated about 1km southeast of the Berbera road, and is clearly visible from it. Nearby are the ruins of a mosque said to date from Aw-Barkadle's lifetime. Islamic pilgrims are welcomed, and if you fall into that category, the best time to visit is the first Thursday or Friday of the dark phase of the moon in the Islamic month of Jumada al-awwal – a feast day that attracts many thousands of pilgrims who hold a vigil at the tomb, accompanied by drumming and singing, on the Thursday night, and then the following morning climb the hill where Mohammed Hanif was reputedly imprisoned. Non-Islamic visitors are unlikely to be allowed within 500m of the tomb without written permission from the Department of Tourism & Archaeology in Hargeisa. Even then, it may be necessary to liaise with the Yibbir clan elders in order to obtain permission to visit.

# LAS GEEL

Estimated to be at least 5,000 years old, and quite possibly twice as ancient, the superb rock art at Las Geel ranks among the oldest and best preserved of its type anywhere in Africa. It comprises about a dozen individual painted shelters scattered on a granitic outcrop that rises from the confluence of two *wadis* (dry watercourses), a spot where the high water is reflected in the name Las Geel meaning 'Camel's Waterhole'. The paintings have been preserved *in situ* by their sheltered location and by the dry Somali climate, and they remain striking both for their vibrant colours and their rich complexity. Their presence also provides incontrovertible evidence that the pastoralist lifestyle was well established in the region thousands of years before it reached western Europe.

Easily visited as a day trip from Hargeisa or *en route* to Berbera, Las Geel is the most compelling tourist attraction in Somaliland, topping the Department of Tourism & Architecture's list of potential UNESCO World Heritage Sites. The site was also visited by the broadcaster Simon Reeve for the BBC programme *Places That Don't Exist*, broadcast in 2005. And yet, incredibly, the existence of this fantastic rock art remained unknown to the outside world until three years before that. Although locals had long held the site sacred, it was first documented in December 2002, when a team of French archaeologists under Professor Xavier Gutherz was led here by villagers from nearby Dhubato.

**GETTING THERE AND AWAY** Las Geel lies about 55km northeast of Hargeisa. To get here from the town centre, follow the main asphalt road to Berbera for about 50km, until you reach the village of Dhubato (N 9°44.370, E 44°27.925; exactly 40km past the main police roadblock outside Hargeisa). Here you need to turn left onto a rough unsignposted track that ideally requires a 4x4 but is just about manageable in a sedan car when dry. After 4.5km, the track reaches a police roadblock, from where it is another 1.5km drive to the site museum, which lies immediately below the main rock shelters, a walk of perhaps five minutes.

A popular half-day trip out of Hargeisa, Las Geel is sometimes visited in tandem with Naaso Hablood on the city outskirts. It can also be visited *en route* to Berbera (as mentioned above), assuming that you have **private transport**. Day **tours** can be organised through any hotel in Hargeisa, and tend to work out quite expensive for one or two people, but are better value for groups. The usual cost breakdown is around US$60–100 for the vehicle, another US$15–20 for the obligatory SPU guard, and another US$20 per person for entrance. Several travellers have reported getting a far better price by making arrangements directly with one of the **shared taxis** that cover the Hargeisa–Berbera route.

It is also technically possible to catch a shared taxi heading towards Berbera as far as Dhubato, then to walk the 6km to Las Geel and back, and hop on another shared taxi when you are done. We have not heard of anybody doing this, however, and the police roadblock at Dhubato might well react unfavourably to the idea. Be aware, too, that no drinking water is available at Las Geel or on the track from Dhubato, and it can get very hot in the midday sun, so aim for the earliest possible start. No accommodation exists in the vicinity of Las Geel.

**WHAT TO SEE** Most panels include a combination of monochromatic and polychromatic animal and human representations, with the most commonly used colours being red, black, white and yellow ochre. The most important shelter, on the southeast face of Las Geel, has an inclined ceiling where the almost 100m² surface is daubed with at least 350 individual paintings. Several other elaborately decorated shelters can be found on the same face of the outcrop, all within about ten minutes' walk of the car park, where there is a toilet, a small site museum, and little else in the way of facilities.

The most numerous figures at Las Geel, outnumbering humans, are humpless cattle, which – as is typical of rock art on the Horn of Africa – are always painted in profile, with only two legs visible, a pronounced udder, a plastron or other decorations around the neck, and lyre-shaped horns shown as if seen from above. Larger bovine figures tend to be more colourful and elaborately decorated, but some panels also include smaller monochrome cows, usually in black or red. Also very common are human or other anthropomorphic figures, which more often tend to be monochrome, and are sometimes shown carrying weapons and accompanied by hunting dogs. The anthropomorphic figures tend to be rather stylised, with a small round head sometimes adorned by a crown or headdress, a wide thorax draped in a loose vertically-striped robe and spindly lower limbs (rather like stick-men, as drawn by children). Aside from dogs and cows, other animals represented include antelope, goats and giraffes.

6

There is something rather eerie about emerging from a nondescript tract of dry Somali scrub to be confronted by a panel of paintings, executed by an unknown artist or artists, possibly thousands of years before the time of Muhammad, Christ, Moses or Abraham. True, these ancient panels may lack the linear perspective to which our eyes are accustomed, but still one can hardly fail to be impressed by the fine detail of the portraits, or to wonder at their occasional forays into apparent surrealism. Almost invariably, first exposure to these charismatic works of ancient art prompts three questions: how old are they, who were the artists and what was their intent?

When, who and why? The simple answers are that nobody really knows. The broadest time frame, induced from the earliest time that domestic cattle could have been introduced to the region, and the clear differentiation of this art from any Sabaean or Axumite tradition, is that they are at least 3,000 years old, although most archaeologists favour a significantly earlier date, somewhere in the ballpark of 5,000 to 10,000 years ago. The artists were clearly pastoralists, predominantly herding cattle (although some paintings also depict sheep and goats), but the presence of hunting tools and dogs in many panels indicates their lifestyle still included an element of hunter-gathering.

The most intriguing of the questions surrounding Africa's ancient rock art is the intent of its creators. One obstacle to determining this is that nobody knows how representative the surviving legacy might be. Most extant rock art is located in overhangs, simply because a painting on any more exposed site would have been wiped clean by the elements long ago. We also have no record of whether the artists dabbled on canvases less durable than rock, but unless one assumes that posterity was a conscious goal, it seems more than likely they did. In which case, the few precious galleries that survive might represent a mere fraction of a percentage of the art executed at the time.

# GA'AN LIBAH RESERVE

A southwesterly extension of the Golis Range – the long escarpment that also includes Mount Wagar and the Daallo Forest – Ga'an Libah (sometimes transcribed as Gacan Libaax) is a tall limestone ridge that rises to an elevation of 1,720m within the triangle formed by the surfaced roads connecting Berbera to Hargeisa and Burao. The British colonial administration set aside the area as a 130km² forest reserve in 1952, and so it remained until civil war broke out in 1988. In the 1990s, the reserve suffered badly from overgrazing, erosion and charcoal-burning, but it has since been revived under the auspices of the Candlelight organisation, which started a community-based Integrated Environmental Management Project here in 2001.

The slopes of Ga'an Libah (literally 'Lion's Paw') support stands of thick woodland and relict forest patches, thanks to the combination of a relatively high summer rainfall (around 400mm per annum) supplemented by airborne winter moisture in the form of mists created by rising maritime air. The dominant tree, known locally as *dayib*, is the coniferous *Juniperus procera*, but there are also areas of evergreen woodland containing various *Ficus* species alongside wild olives (*Olea africana*) and *Euphorbia abyssinica*, a spectacular spike-leaved succulent that grows up to

Two broad schools of thought surround the interpretation of Africa's ancient rock art. The first has it that the paintings were essentially recreational, documentary or expressive in intent – art for art's sake if you like – while the second regards them to be mystical or proto-religious works of ritual significance. The only instance where we are in some position to let the artists interpret for themselves is in the uKhahlamba-Drakensberg region of South Africa, where almost 50,000 individual images make up the largest repository of rock art anywhere on the continent. Uniquely in Africa, while some panels in the uKhahlamba-Drakensberg are thousands of years old, others are so recent that they depict ox-wagons, uniformed soldiers and other figures associated with European settlement, indicating that the hunter-gatherer artists were still actively painting right up until their extermination by settlers in the late 19th century.

Formerly viewed as a simple visual account of day-to-day hunter-gatherer life, the rock art of southern Africa is now understood to be altogether less prosaic in intent, thanks largely to the research of David Lewis-Williams, which is based partially on the 19th-century ethnographic notes made by sympathetic settlers, and partially on encounters with surviving hunter-gatherer people on the Kalahari. Lewis-Williams has concluded that rock art of the uKhahlamba-Drakensberg depicts ritual trances experienced by shamanic spiritual leaders (whose state of altered consciousness has been compared to a hallucinogenic drug experience), as well as reflecting their complex relationship with the eland antelope, the animal they most revered. Viewed in this light, and in the absence of any evidence to the contrary, it is tempting to think that the rock art at Las Geel might be similar in intent, representing some sort of religious link between the pastoralist artists and the cows they so clearly idolised. It's a theory, anyway – but then an integral part of the rock art's charisma is that while we can speculate to our heart's content, we will never know the whole truth.

5m tall. The upper slopes of Ga'an Libah also form an important watershed to the surrounding plains, and it is the main source of the seasonal Togdheer River, which runs past Burao and provides winter sustenance to the arid Nogal Valley.

The reserve could feasibly be visited as a day trip from either Berbera or Hargeisa, but that makes for a long slog, and would force you to do any hiking in the midday heat, so an overnight trip is recommended.

**GETTING THERE AND AWAY** There are two main routes to Ga'an Libah, and the drive takes around five hours from either Hargeisa or Berbera. No public transport goes to the reserve, and a **4x4** is strongly recommended, especially after rain, as the road is rough in parts. Both routes branch east from the main road between Hargeisa and Berbera, and they converge at the village of Go'oda Weyn (also known as Go Weyn; N 9°47.257, E 44°54.489), where you need to check in at the police station before proceeding. From Go'oda Weyn, it is a 15km ascent to the Ga'an Libah entrance gate, and just past that is the old forestry camp that now serves as the reserve headquarters.

Coming from Hargeisa, you need to follow the surfaced Berbera road as far as Dhubato (also the junction village for Las Geel), then turn right onto a rather rough dirt track that connects with the old Hargeisa–Burao road after about 20km at the small village of Gadhka-Warsame-Haad. The track beyond Gadhka-Warsame-Haad heads through open plains, with Ga'an Libah looming on the distant eastern horizon, then there's a lightly wooded stretch. Just after crossing a large *wadi* (the one that drains Ga'an Libah Mountain itself), you go up a windy track that eventually passes through Go'oda Weyn.

Coming from Berbera, you are better turning left off the Hargeisa road at the signposted junction for Mandhera at Abdal (N 9°57.038, E 44°41.497), 62km southwest of the police roadblock outside Berbera. From here, it is 5km to Mandhera (N 9°54.899, E 44°42.767), the site of a police training academy and large jail, then another 45km to Go'oda Weyn.

**WHERE TO STAY AND EAT** There is no formal accommodation for tourists, but you can stay overnight in a basic unequipped **hut** at the reserve headquarters, where **camping** is also permitted, assuming you have suitable equipment. There is no charge in either case, but you will be expected to offer a 'service fee' – in essence a tip – to the staff there. There are reputedly plans to build a proper guesthouse for tourists, but our impression is that this is unlikely to come to anything in the near future. No food is available in the reserve, so you will need to be self-sufficient. Before heading this way, you might want to check the current situation with the Candlelight office in Hargeisa (\ 523146; m 442 6069; e *candasli@yahoo.com or aiawaleh@hotmail.com; www.candlelightsomal.org*).

**WHAT TO SEE** A century ago, Ga'an Libah supported large herds of elephant as well as a significant population of the lions for which it is named. There's nothing quite as exciting there today, but it still protects relatively dense populations of greater and lesser kudu, Speke's gazelle, dik-dik, gerenuk, beira, klipspringer and desert warthog. The cliffs are home to baboon, and confirmed predators include leopard, caracal, spotted hyena, black-backed jackal and bat-eared fox.

Easily explored on foot along a network of informal trails, Ga'an Libah is a popular site with birdwatchers, as it's the closest patch of forest to Hargeisa. Birdlife includes the endemic Somali thrush and Archer's buzzard, as well as the near-endemic Somali starling, and several other woodland birds with a limited distribution in Somaliland, for instance African scops owl, Alpine swift, Nyanza swift, Hemprich's hornbill, white-bellied go-away bird, greater honeyguide, white-rumped babbler, brown-rumped seedeater, Ethiopian boubou and various bee-eaters, barbets, woodpeckers and warblers.

Even if you are not interested in wildlife, the clifftop viewpoint about 1km from the headquarters is spectacular, offering sweeping views across the arid plains below. Other attractions of these limestone hills include a network of caves, some of which are reputedly decorated with prehistoric rock art, and a number of other archaeological sites, including pre-Islamic stelae and other grave markers.

## BEIRA HILLS

The rocky hills of the Somali interior are home to the beira, a small and little-known antelope that is near-endemic to Somaliland (see box page 103). In most parts of its range is it very secretive and difficult to find, but it is usually located with relative ease in the so-called 'Beira Hills' that lie to the southeast of the Berbera road, about an hour's drive from Hargeisa. You'll probably need to make contact with the local scout, who monitors the site in association with Nature Somaliland (see page 84), to stand a real chance of finding the antelope quickly.

**GETTING THERE AND AWAY** Callan Cohen and Mike Mills provided the following directions. From Dhubato (the junction village for Las Geel), continue driving towards Berbera for about 1.5 km and then turn south onto a dirt road (N 9°44.676, E 44.°28.657). After about 2km you pass between two low hills. Park in the *wadi* (N 9°44.382, E 44°44.382) and scan the sparsely wooded slopes all around. Hopefully, you will soon be met by the local scout who will lead you to the best areas should you need to walk into the hills.

## XABAALO TUMAALOOD

Straddling the Hargeisa–Berbera road, about 6km past the small village of Daray Godle and 28km before the junction with the road for Burao, Xabaalo Tumaalood (N 10°12.626, E 44°52.923) is the most accessible of numerous pre-Islamic burial sites that scatter the Somali countryside. It lies about 500m south of a small roadside mosque that often supports a temporary nomad settlement when the grass is high.

The undecorated stelae that mark the graves stand up to 2m tall, and many are enclosed in circular clearings demarcated by a ring of stones. The age of this unexcavated site is undetermined, but since it pre-dates the introduction of Islam to the interior, it must be at least 700 years old.

---

### BEIRA ANTELOPE

Placed in a monospecific genus, the beira *Dorcatragus megalotis* is a handsome long-legged antelope, intermediate in size between the dik-diks and klipspringer, and distantly related to both. It has a grizzled grey back and flanks, separated from the tan legs and belly by a black side stripe, and a red face with bold white circles around the eyes, as well as a bushy white tail. The horns, present in the male only, are straight and short, but it has unusually large ears, which gives it exceptional hearing. It can obtain all the water it requires from its diet of leaves and grass.

Listed as 'Vulnerable' by the IUCN, the beira is near-endemic to Somaliland, where the estimated population of a few thousand individuals probably represents more than 95% of the global total. Its core range is focused on the mountains of the escarpment, but it does occur on isolated rocky hills elsewhere in the country. Outside Somaliland, it is present in small numbers on the other side of the unofficial borders with Puntland and Somalia, and its historical range also extends into Djibouti and the far east of Ethiopia, where its current status is uncertain. Unlike most other small antelope, it lives in small herds, typically comprising one or two males and up to five females, although groups of more than a dozen have been recorded.

A resident of rocky slopes, where it tends to be highly territorial, the beira is a wary creature, ever ready to flee, using its rather goat-like hoofs to manoeuvre across scree and larger rocks. Its existence was first made known to Western science by Captain Swayne, a dedicated hunter who heard word of a 'small, red antelope [with the] habits of a klipspringer' from Somali hunters, who knew it as a behra, in the early 1880s. Despite his prowess with the gun, Swayne was never able to bag a specimen himself, and eventually he paid some local hunters for the two type specimens he sent to the Zoological Society of London in 1894.

# 7

# Berbera and Surrounds

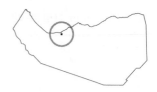

The historic town of Berbera has been a centre of maritime trade since ancient times, and it lies on the Gulf of Aden opposite Yemen. This was a strategic location for the trade route between the Red Sea and India, and more recently during the Cold War. Indeed, in the 1970s it was an important base for the USSR, which built the 4km runway (one of the longest anywhere in Africa) that somewhat redundantly graces the international airport a few kilometres south of town. Today, Berbera is the main commercial seaport in Somaliland, serving not only the capital Hargeisa, about 150km to the south, but also bordering parts of eastern Ethiopia.

Boasting an idyllic swimming beach and access to innumerable well-preserved coral reefs, Berbera has enormous potential for tourist development, although this remains largely unrealised at the time of writing, with just one operational resort hotel and dive centre in place. Also of great interest is the old quarter of town, where the wealth of crumbling pre-20th century architectural gems – most in urgent need of restoration work – would make it a shoo-in candidate as a UNESCO World Heritage Site were Somaliland ever to gain UN recognition. Even in its present semi-ruinous state, Berbera is an absorbing place, and it doesn't seem wildly fanciful to see a rehabilitated incarnation of the old town one day forming a Somali counterpart to such iconic cultural tourist hubs as Ilha do Moçambique, Gorée Island or Lamu.

As things stand, Berbera tends to make a less-than-favourable first impression, particularly when you arrive in the harsh light of early afternoon via an extensive and unsightly litter belt of scrubby thorn trees, draped with thin plastic bags. It doesn't help that the town's only proper tourist facility, the out-of-town Mansoor Hotel, has the stark and unfinished appearance of a beachfront construction site. Or that the town can be intolerably hot in the summer (May to September), when daytime temperatures routinely nudge above 45°C, with typical nocturnal minimums of 30–35°C, all but necessitating a room with air conditioning.

Once settled in, however, Berbera is thoroughly appealing, at least it is during the relatively cool winter months, when average temperatures, although not exactly arctic, are almost 10°C lower. The compact old town, its alleys lined with attractive mosques and other relics of the Ottoman occupation, is great fun to explore, and the sandy out-of-town beach is genuinely refreshing. Further afield, the surrounding reefs offer superb diving and snorkelling, while the ancient waterworks at the Dubaar Springs – overlooked by old Ottoman fortification – make for a worthwhile day out. Berbera could also be used as a base for exploring the likes of Mount Wagar and Ga'an Libah.

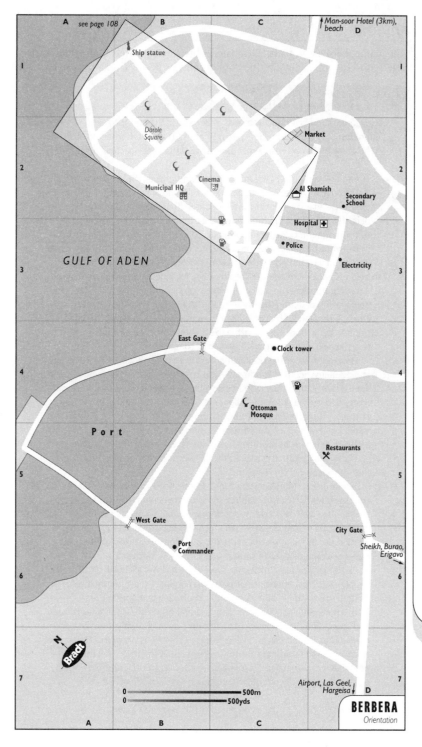

Man-soor Hotel (3km), beach

Ship statue

Dorole Square

Market

Municipal HQ

Cinema

Al Shamish

Secondary School

Hospital

Police

Electricity

GULF OF ADEN

East Gate

Clock tower

Ottoman Mosque

Port

Restaurants

West Gate

City Gate

Sheikh, Burao, Erigavo

Port Commander

N

Bradt

0          500m
0          500yds

Airport, Las Geel, Hargeisa

**BERBERA**
*Orientation*

Berbera and Surrounds

7

# HISTORY

The name Berbera is truly antiquated. The ancient Greeks and Phoenicians referred to the inhabitants of the Somali coast as Berbers, a name referenced in

## BERBERA IN THE MID 19TH CENTURY

Two illuminating first-hand accounts of Berbera in the mid 19th century survive. The oldest was written by Lieutenant Charles Cruttenden, who visited Berbera in the early 1840s and who wrote extensively about the seasonal trade fair:

The annual fair is one of the most interesting sights on the coast, if only from the fact of many different and distant tribes being drawn together for a short time, to be again scattered in all directions ... The place from April to the early part of October was utterly deserted, not even a fisherman being found there; but no sooner did the season change, than the inland tribes commenced moving down towards the coast, and preparing their huts for their expected visitors. Small craft from Yemen, anxious to have an opportunity of purchasing before vessels from the Gulf could arrive, hastened across, followed about a fortnight to three weeks later by their larger brethren from Muscat, Soor, Bahrain, Bussorah, and Graen. Lastly, the fat and wealthy Banian traders, from Porebunder, Mandalay, and Bombay ... elbowed themselves into a permanent position in the front tier of craft in the harbour, and by their superior capital, cunning, and influence soon distanced all competitors.

During the height of the fair, Berbera is a perfect Babel, in confusion as in languages: no chief is acknowledged, and the customs of bygone days are the laws of the place. Disputes between the inland tribes daily arise, and are settled by the spear and dagger, the combatants retiring to the beach at a short distance from the town, in order that they may not disturb the trade. Long strings of camels are arriving and departing day and night, escorted generally by women alone, until at a distance from the town; and an occasional group of dusky and travel-worn children marks the arrival of the slave caravan from Harar and Efat.

At Berbera, the Gurague and Harar slave merchant meets his correspondent from [Arabia] ... and the [tribesman], his head tastefully ornamented with a scarlet sheepskin in lieu of a wig, is seen peacefully bartering his ostrich feathers and gums with the smooth-spoken Banian ... who prudently living on board his ark ... exhibits but a small portion of his wares at a time, under a miserable mat spread on the beach.

By the end of March the fair is nearly at a close, and craft of all kinds, deeply laden, commence their homeward journey ... By the first week in April, Berbera is again deserted, nothing being left to mark the site of a town lately containing 20,000 inhabitants, beyond bones of slaughtered camels and sheep, and the framework of a few huts ... carefully piled on the beach in readiness for the ensuing year. Beasts of prey now take the opportunity to approach the sea: lions are commonly seen at the town well during the hot weather; and in April last year, but a week after the fair had ended, I observed three ostriches quietly walking on the beach.

The other, more acerbic, account from this period was written by Richard the medieval Arabic name for the Horn of Africa, Bilad al Barbar (literally, 'Land of Berbers'). Back then, however, the name Berbera was applied to the entire southern coast of the Gulf of Aden, and it is unclear when it became associated with one specific port.

Burton, who visited Berbera on his return from Harar in 1855, and was impressed more by its potential than the actuality at the time:

> The 'Mother of the Poor', as the Arabs call [Berbera], in position resembles Zayla. The town – if such name can be given to what is now a wretched clump of dirty mat-huts – is situated on the northern edge of alluvial ground, sloping almost imperceptibly from the base of the southern hills … [It has] contracted its dimensions to about one sixth of its former extent: for nearly a mile around, the now desert land is strewed with bits of glass and broken pottery. Their ignorance has chosen the worst position: 'Mos Majorum' is the Somali code, where father built there the son builds, and there shall the grandson build.
>
> To the south and east lies a saline sand-flat, partially overflowed by high tides: here are the wells of bitter water, and the filth and garbage make the spot truly offensive. Northwards the sea strand has become a huge cemetery, crowded with graves whose dimensions explain the Somali legend that once there were giants in the land … Westward, close up to the town, runs the creek which forms the wealth of Berbera. A long strip of sand and limestone – the general formation of the coast – defends its length from the northern gales, the breadth is about three quarters of a mile, and the depth varies from six to fifteen fathoms near the Ras or Spit at which ships anchor before putting out to sea …
>
> The present decadence of Berbera is caused by petty internal feuds. [Two] powerful tribes assert a claim to the customs and profits of the port on the grounds that they jointly conquered it from the Galla … a blood feud rages, and the commerce of the place suffers from the dissensions of the owners … Moreover the [dominant] tribe is not without internal feuds. Two kindred septs … established themselves originally at Berbera. The more numerous [sept] admitted the [other] for some years to a participation of profits, but when Aden, occupied by the British, rendered the trade valuable, they drove out the weaker sept, and declared themselves sole 'Abbans' to strangers during the fair. A war ensued …
>
> The Emporium of Eastern Africa has a salubrious climate, abundance of sweet water … a mild monsoon, a fine open country, an excellent harbour, and a soil highly productive. It is the meeting-place of commerce, has few rivals, and with half the sums lavished in Arabia upon engineer follies of stone and lime, the environs might at this time have been covered with houses, gardens, and trees … Occupation [by Britain] has been advised for many reasons … Berbera is the true key of the Red Sea, the centre of East African traffic, and the only safe place for shipping upon the western Erythraean shore, from Suez to Ras Guardafui. Backed by lands capable of cultivation, and by hills covered with pine and other valuable trees … this harbour has been coveted by many a foreign conqueror. Circumstances have thrown it as it were into our arms, and, if we refuse the chance, another and a rival nation will not be so blind.

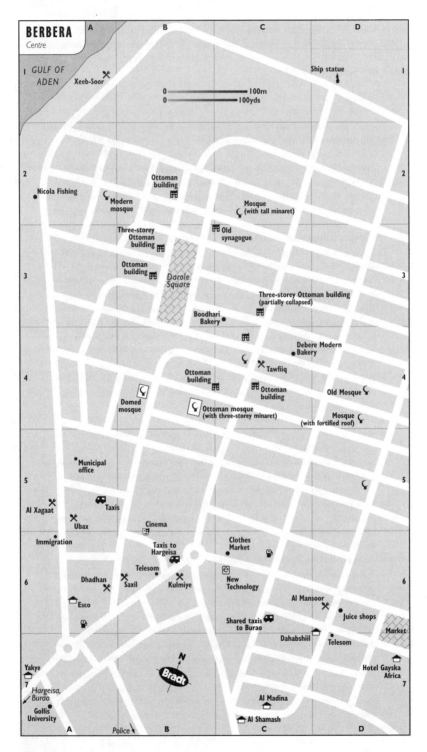

# BERBERA
## Centre

**GULF OF ADEN**

Xeeb-Soor

Ship statue

0 ———— 100m
0 ———— 100yds

Nicola Fishing

Modern mosque

Ottoman building

Mosque (with tall minaret)

Three-storey Ottoman building

Old synagogue

Ottoman building

Darole Square

Three-storey Ottoman building (partially collapsed)

Boodhari Bakery

Debere Modern Bakery

Tawfiiq

Ottoman building

Ottoman building

Old Mosque

Domed mosque

Ottoman mosque (with three-storey minaret)

Mosque (with fortified roof)

Municipal office

Taxis

Al Xagaat

Ubax

Cinema

Immigration

Taxis to Hargeisa

Clothes Market

Dhadhan

Saxil

Telesom

Kulmiye

New Technology

Al Mansoor

Esco

Shared taxis to Burao

Juice shops

Market

Dahabshiil

Telesom

Yakye

N

*Bradt*

Hotel Gayska Africa

Hargeisa, Burao

Gollis University

Police

Al Madina

Al Shamash

The age of present-day Berbera is difficult to determine. It might well have been one of the ports involved in the ancient trade between the east coast of Africa and Egypt (see *Somaliland and the Land of Punt*, page 4) and it is almost certainly synonymous with the port of Malao, described in the 1st century AD *Periplus of the Erythraean Sea* as, 'After Avalites there is another market town, better than this, called Malao, distant a sail of about 800 stadia. The anchorage is an open roadstead, sheltered by a spit running out from the east. Here the natives are more peaceable.'

Berbera is also a prime candidate for the port described in 9th and 12th-century Chinese documents as Boboli, which traded in ivory, incense and female slaves (for further details, see *Medieval Somaliland*, page 7). Surprisingly, perhaps, there are no overt references to Berbera in Arabic literature of this period. It is first mentioned by name in the writings of the early 13th-century geographer Ibn Said, and again by the legendary globetrotter Ibn Battuta, who visited the region in 1331 and noted that the sultan of the 'exceedingly large city' of Mogadishu originated from Berbera.

In the late medieval period, Berbera was certainly an important trade port, although largely subservient to Zeila, as it was situated at the eastern boundary of the Adal Sultanate. The most detailed surviving description of Berbera from this time, penned by Bartema, who mistook it for an island, states that 'it is not great but fruitful and well peopled: it hath abundance of flesh. The inhabitants are of colour inclining to black. All their riches is in herds of cattle ... the prince [thereof] is a Mohammedan'.

In 1518, Berbera was sacked by a Portuguese expedition led by Antonio de Saldanha. It swiftly recovered from this blow, however, to become part of the Ottoman Empire in 1546, and by the end of the 16th century it had replaced Zeila as the main centre of trade and Islamic culture along the Somali coast. For the next three centuries, Berbera's (mostly good) fortunes rested on a legendary annual trade fair, held during the relatively cool winter months of November to March (see box, *Berbera in the mid 19th century*, page 106). The port mushroomed during the fair, when it supported a temporary population of up to 20,000, as caravans incorporating several thousand camels arrived from Harar to trade with merchant boats from Arabia and Asia. The key export during this period was livestock, in particular the surrounding region's famously tasty sheep, but British traders who visited Berbera in 1840 noted items such as coffee, gum, myrrh, ivory and ostrich feathers on sale.

Britain took control of Berbera in 1884, following the withdrawal of the Ottoman Egyptian garrison to fight the Mahdist Rebellion in Sudan. Berbera was made the capital of British Somaliland in 1888, a role it retained until 1941, when the administration relocated to Hargeisa. Post-independence, a modernised deep-sea harbour was completed in Berbera in 1962, assisted by a US$55 million loan with generous repayment terms from the USSR, which also established a naval base at the port and built the airport outside town.

In 1980, Somalia switched its Cold War allegiance from the USSR to the USA, which took over the naval base and allocated the airport as an emergency landing strip for its space shuttle programme. Since the closure of the border between Eritrea, and the Ethiopian War of the late 1990s, Berbera's port has emerged as a major export terminus for Ethiopia, and the leading source of foreign revenue for Somaliland. Today, it supports a population of at least 30,000 people, probably more like 70,000, depending on which source you choose to believe.

## GETTING THERE AND AWAY

Berbera International Airport [81 H5], a few kilometres out of town along the Hargeisa road, doesn't receive the sort of traffic that justifies a runway length of 4km, but a few international **flights** land there weekly, offering connections to Dubai, Nairobi and Djibouti. See *Getting There and Away* in *Chapter 3* (page 49) for details.

The 150km road from Berbera to Hargeisa is surfaced in its entirety. Allowing for police roadblocks, but not for other stops, the direct drive should take less than two hours in a **private car**. It might take a bit longer in a **shared taxi**, which costs US$5 per person. The taxis leave Hargeisa from a back road behind the Jama Mosque, and Berbera from the main road connecting the two traffic circles at the southern end of town. It is usually possible to negotiate a private hire with one of these taxis for around US$30–50, depending on whether you incorporate a stop at Las Geel. Technically, an SPU officer must accompany all foreigners travelling between Hargeisa and Berbera, but it's increasingly common for the Chief of Police in Hargeisa to issue a letter of waiver upon request.

Rough tracks run along the coast west and east of Berbera connecting it to Zeila and Maydh. There is no public transport in either direction, but except after heavy rain it is usually possible to drive to Zeila in a private 4x4 over two days, ideally in convoy. The best place to hire a **4x4** for this trip is Hargeisa, but you could also ask for advice at the dive centre at the Man-soor Hotel (see below). We have also heard of travellers heading to Zeila by camel, a trip that would take a couple of weeks. We have no information about the coastal road towards Maydh.

Details of onward travel to Burao and Sheikh are covered in *Chapter 8*.

## GETTING AROUND

The town centre is very compact and it is easy to **walk** everywhere. The Man-soor Hotel and associated swimming beach [105 D1] is quite a way from the town centre; if you don't fancy walking there, you can pick up a **taxi** at the rank for Berbera or Burao [108 C6].

## TOURIST INFORMATION

There is no tourist office as such, but anybody wanting to visit the port or Dubaar waterworks will first need to visit the municipal office [108 A5] to obtain permission from the mayor. This can be quite a tedious process, and an early start is advised, as like most government offices it is only reliably open from 08.00–12.00 Saturday to Wednesday, and you are unlikely to locate the mayor outside these hours.

##  WHERE TO STAY

There are fewer hotels than might be expected in Berbera, and only one – the out-of-town and relatively upmarket Man-soor – caters primarily to tourists. The other hotels can be found at the southern end of the town centre, and while none truly stands out, the Esco and Yakye are both perfectly acceptable.

### UPMARKET

**Man-soor Hotel** [105 D1] (24 rooms) m 441 9423; e mansoorhotel@hotmail.com; www.man-soor.com. Affiliated to its namesake in Hargeisa, this is the closest thing in Somaliland to a resort hotel, boasting a semi-beachfront location in the heart of the litter belt, some 3.5km northeast of central Berbera. It is also the site of the country's only dive centre. Unfortunately, however, it makes few concessions to aesthetics, consisting as it does of a large rectangular compound dominated by grass & concrete & 2 blandly institutional-looking rows of square semi-detached bungalows. In contrast to the utilitarian exterior, the rooms are very pleasant & come with dbl beds, mosquito netting, dining table, AC, & satellite TV. There is also a good restaurant serving a varied selection of seafood & meat dishes in the US$3.50–6 range, as well as a few vegetarian options. It is

set just too far back from the beach to offer much of a sea view, but still it couldn't be more convenient in terms of beach access. *US$50/60 B&B sgl/dbl.*

## MODERATE

🏠**Dahabshiil Hotel**  [108 D6] (6 rooms) m 444 6917; e guure917@hotmail.com. Placed in this category based on price rather than quality, this small 1st-floor hotel has clean but

gloomy twin rooms with fan, AC, fridge, satellite TV & free Wi-Fi. Toilets & showers are shared. Rather poor value. *US$25 twin.*

## BUDGET

🏠**Yakye Hotel**  [108 A7] (30 rooms) m 441 0098. The pick of Berbera's cheapies, this clean modern hotel lies at the southern end of the town centre along the main road, just around the corner from the taxi park for Hargeisa. There is the choice of an en-suite room with 1 three-quarter bed, or a twin with shared shower. All

rooms have a fan, net & optional AC. *US$10 for a sgl or dbl, US$20 if switch on the AC.*

🏠**Esco Hotel**  [108 A6] (14 rooms) m 442 6554. Around the corner from the Yakye & of a similar standard, this has clean en-suite rooms with cold water only. *US$9 dbl.*

## SHOESTRING

🏠**Al Madina Hotel**  [108 C7] (30 rooms) ☎740254; m 444 8291. This basic but quite pleasant single-storey hotel has a design & feel reminiscent of many guesthouses in East Africa. Rooms range from unadorned sgls to en-suite dbls with AC, & all rooms seem to have nets. *US$5/8 sgl/dbl using shared showers, US$10/30 en-suite dbl with fan/AC.*

🏠**Al Shamash Hotel**  [108 C7] (12 rooms) This unsignposted 2-storey building is your best bet if the Al Madina, around the corner, is full. *Basic rooms with shared showers cost US$5.*

🏠**Hotel Gayska Afrika**  [108 D7] m 441 6532. About the most rudimentary lodge in town, this place can be found in the market area & has simple twin rooms with shared showers. *US$5.*

# ✕ WHERE TO EAT

Many visitors stay at the Man-soor Hotel [105 D1], and most eat there, too, if only because it is some distance out of town. The food at the hotel is pretty good, but there are also plenty of decent eateries in town, of which the two below are outstanding.

✕**Al Xagaat Restaurant**  [108 A5] Situated on the seafront near the southern end of the town centre, this is the top restaurant in Berbera. It serves excellent whole or filleted fish, as well as decent steaks, with pasta or chips, for around US$4 per plate. The whole fish is sensational, easily the best meal we had anywhere in Somaliland, & the fruit juice is also superb.

✕**Xeeb-Soor Restaurant**  [108 A1] ☎740 055; m 444 6418. This seafront restaurant at the northern end of town is a lively & likeable spot at sunset, when it offers attractive views of the port. There is outdoor seating right on the waterfront, & the menu consists of generous portions of fish or pasta that cost around US$4. There's good fruit juice, too.

# OTHER PRACTICALITIES

**FOREIGN EXCHANGE** There don't seem to be any bespoke foreign exchange facilities in Berbera but, as with most other towns in the country, US dollars and Somaliland shillings are used more or less interchangeably.

**INTERNET AND EMAIL** Internet facilities are less prevalent than in most other large towns in Somaliland. The **Man-soor** [105 D1] and **Dahabshiil** [108 D6] hotels both have free Wi-Fi for guests, but if you are staying elsewhere or don't carry a laptop, your best bet is the **New Technology Internet Café** [108 C6] near the main circle at the southern end of town.

**SAFETY** Berbera comes across as a very safe city and we have heard nothing to suggest visitors are at any appreciable risk of being robbed or otherwise attacked. Nevertheless, while foreigners are permitted to walk around town freely by day, it is technically forbidden to leave your hotel without SPU protection between 18.00 and 06.00. However, a permit from the Chief of Police allowing you to travel to Berbera without SPU protection would presumably nullify this ruling, and many travellers simply choose to ignore it anyway. Should the local police spot you walking around without SPU protection after dark, they might well stop you, but the worst that is likely to happen is that you'll be told off or escorted back to your hotel.

## WHAT TO SEE

The oldest quarter of Berbera, known locally as **Darole**, is also the most northerly part of town, hemmed in by the old port to the west, a series of tidal flats to the north, and several recently resettled suburbs to the south and east. Darole itself can be divided into two distinct districts, with a rough boundary being the road that runs eastwards from the municipal building. The more northerly of these two districts, essentially the former residential quarter, is centred on old Darole Square and is studded with venerable mosques and other architecturally noteworthy buildings. By contrast, the southern district, stretching west from the main market, is less architecturally distinguished and more commercially oriented, making it closer in feel to other modern Somali towns such as Burao or Hargeisa.

Strong on character but remarkably run down and poorly documented, the narrow roads and alleys that run through the older part of Darole are lined with handsome pastel-coloured buildings dating back to the Ottoman era. Among the most striking of these, as marked on the map on page 108, are the **Ottoman Mosque** [108 B4] (with three-storey minaret), the row of single-story **homesteads** opposite it, the buildings that enclose **Darole Square** [108 B3], and several other dispersed two and three-storey **mansions** in varying states of repair and disrepair. Architectural oddities include the buildings marked '**domed mosque**' and '**old synagogue**' (the latter reputedly boarded up by departing Jews during World War I), and several **flat-roofed mosques**, vaguely reminiscent of certain west African Islamic architectural styles, in the backstreets to the east of the main road.

We've been unable to determine the age of any of Darole's buildings, or for that matter any other pertinent historical details about them. It seems logical to assume, however, that most of these buildings post-date Burton's description of Berbera as a 'wretched clump of dirty mat-huts' (see box, *Berbera in the mid 19th century*, page 106) and also that they pre-date the withdrawal of Ottoman Egypt. This would suggest that they are predominantly from the period 1860–80, but this hasn't been confirmed. It is also unclear to what extent the current semi-ruinous state of many of these buildings is attributable to bombing and other military activity associated with the civil war c1989–91, or simply the result of decades of neglect. Whatever the case, the architecturally fascinating northern quarter of Darole rewards casual exploration, revealing new sights at every turn, and one can't help but be conscious of its immense potential for rehabilitation and restoration.

Possibly the most famous of 20th-century Somali love poets, Elmi Boodhari was born in 1907 into a family of Berbera bakers whose shop stood just half a block from Darole Square. As a young man, sometime during the early 1930s, Elmi fell hopelessly in love with a beautiful woman called Hodan Cabdulle, who walked into the shop late one afternoon to buy bread. Unfortunately for Elmi, the object of his love displayed no interest in him; worse still, she came from a family that was both wealthier than his, and of higher social status.

Initially the baker's son was unfazed, and he tried to woo Hodan with effusive poetry, but when this failed, his family became concerned at his state of mind and reminded him of his social standing, and they tried to convince him to look for a more suitable partner. Eventually the family invited a dozen eligible and beautiful girls to persuade him to forget Hodan and settle for one of them instead. Elmi responded by writing what is widely agreed to be his most beautiful poem, the opening line translates roughly as, 'If beauty could do something, or make a heart calm ...'

Heartbroken and bedridden, Elmi Boodhari died in 1941, after Hodan married somebody else. However, his memory lives on as one of the most beloved and influential Somali poets of all time, and the family bakery, only a few paces east of Darole Square, still bears the Boodhari name, churns our fresh bread daily, and welcomes interested visitors.

Central Berbera is also bursting with human interest. Most people still dress in the traditional style and they are exceptionally friendly, particularly the giggling gangs of camera-loving children that will sooner or later attach themselves to any stray traveller. The market area [108 D6], although more subdued than you might expect, is well worth a look, and plenty of small local eateries and juice stalls offer shade and refreshment when you are ready to escape the afternoon heat. The arid location of this isolated old port town is underscored by the camel herds that mill around the alleys, holding up the traffic as they feed from a low branch or thoughtfully contemplate a change of direction. We were told by locals that the males occasionally become a little aggressive and frisky when approached the wrong way – probably not a huge concern, but still reason enough to give them a few metres berth.

Outside the old town, the most interesting part of Berbera is the district of **Sha'ab**, running out towards the new port. The **Ottoman Mosque** [105 C4] here has a balconied minaret similar to the one in the town centre, and it is said locally to be one of the oldest buildings in Berbera, although its age cannot be confirmed. The **new port** [105 B4] – like Malao some 2,000 years ago, 'sheltered by a spit running out from the east' – is worth a look, but you'll need to obtain permission from the Municipal Headquarters first, and possibly the harbourmaster, too.

## AROUND BERBERA

**DUBAR WATERWORKS** The main source of freshwater for Berbera since time immemorial has been the palm-lined **Dubar Springs** (N 10°20.467, E 45°08.081), which lie about 12km out of town at the base of the eponymous mountains, and are fed by their drainage. Prior to the Ottoman occupation, the people of Berbera would have had to fetch drinking water from the springs on camelback, to supplement the meagre supply of sour brackish water in wells closer to town. That all changed, however, when the Ottoman rulers built a rock and limestone-plaster aqueduct that connected the springs to the town, using the slight downward gradient created by a 180m drop in altitude to transport the water.

It is unclear when exactly the aqueduct to Dubar was built, but it had evidently fallen into disuse when Cruttenden visited the area in the 1840s, and was so far gone when Burton visited in 1855 that he was unable to trace it to more than 10m of its head. During the colonial era the aqueduct was rehabilitated and maintained by the British, who also built the stone collective chambers that still surround several wells there. The aqueduct filled with rubble during the civil war, and fell into disuse thereafter, but it was restored to working order in 2009 with the assistance of UNICEF and various other donors.

Burton explored Dubar extensively, and noted that there were two main springs in the area. The larger of these, Dubar Wena ('Great Dubar') was a 'dry bed of a watercourse overgrown with bright green rushes ... about half a mile long', its surface 'white with impure nitre' but with 'tolerably sweet' water in 'numerous pits' that 'abundantly supplied the flocks and herds'. At Dubar Yirr ('Little Dubar') by contrast, 'a spring of warm and bitter water flowed from the hill over the surface to a distance of 400 or 500 yards, where it was absorbed by the soil' and formed a 'rushy swamp'. According to Burton, 'the rocks behind these springs were covered with ruins of mosques and houses', but no such structures survive today.

Visible from miles around are the imposing ruins of an old **stone fort**, whose outer walls stand 2–3m tall and enclose an area of around 400m². The fort stands sentinel on a steep, rocky hill overlooking the springs and reputedly dates to the Ottoman era, but the smaller house-like structure in its centre was clearly built or renovated during the British colonial era. As is so often the case with archaeological sites in Somaliland, the fort is unexcavated and the limited information available regarding its history is somewhat contradictory. It is said locally to date to the 19th century, but Cruttenden described it as a ruin of 'considerable antiquity ... different [in style] to any houses now found on the Somali coast' in the 1840s, suggesting a much older construction date. Either way, it is an interesting ruin to explore, offering a superb vantage point over the palm-studded springs and surrounding plains.

In order to visit Dubar you first need permission from the Mayor of Berbera, which can be obtained by visiting the municipal office in town before midday, and you may also need to get the thumbs-up from the Department of Water. Once these permits are in place, follow the Burao road out of town for 2km past the junction with the Hargeisa road, then turn right onto an unsignposted but conspicuous dirt track and follow this for another 10km, forking to the left at the only real junction. You can park right next to the waterworks, and the climb up a loose rocky slope to the hilltop fort shouldn't take longer than ten minutes in either direction.

**BERBERA MARINE PARK** The Somaliland coast can justifiably lay claim to being one of the world's best-kept marine secrets, lined as it is with a series of reefs whose potential as a diving and snorkelling destination is on a par with the better-publicised and more developed Red Sea and East African coastline that flank it. Despite some recent habitat deterioration and loss of marine resources due to unregulated overfishing, especially in the vicinity of Zeila, these reefs remain in excellent condition and support a wide range of underwater wildlife, ranging from a dazzling variety of brightly coloured and bizarrely shaped small reef-dwellers to such marine giants as the whale shark and manta ray, alongside several species of dolphin and sea turtle (see *Marine Wildlife*, page 44).

Offered no formal protection until recent years, the Somaliland coast is now the site of two official marine parks, designated by the Ministries of Fisheries and Tourism, and run by an IUCN-affiliated organisation called Somaliland Marine Parks, in collaboration with the government of Somaliland. The most accessible of these is the 30km² **Berbera Marine Park**, which safeguards a 10km coral reef running west from the port of Berbera, an area known for its kaleidoscopic wealth of reef fish and dense dolphin population. The other more remote protected area is the 50km² **Sa'ad ad-Din Marine Park**, which protects the eponymous archipelago offshore from Zeila, close to the border with Djibouti.

Tourist development is a major stated aim of Somaliland Marine Parks, as it is believed to be an important way of creating sustainable economic benefits for local communities living in the vicinity of protected areas. At present, the only place running commercial dives is the **Mansoor Dive School (m** *413 8607 (Somaliland) or +44 (0)7830 161880/(0)7794 462684 (UK);* **e** *info@somalilandmarineparks.org; www. somalilandmarineparks.org)*, which is under the same management as Somaliland Marine Parks, and based out of the Man-soor Hotel in Berbera (see *Where to stay*, page 110). It offers single dives for US$30 per person, and a variety of packages including six dives over three days for US$135, ten dives over five days for US$200, and weekend breaks, inclusive of four dives, accommodation and meals at the Man-soor Hotel, for US$160 per person. Snorkelling gear can also be rented for US$10 a day. At the moment all dives are focused in and around Berbera, but there are plans to develop Sa'ad ad-Din Marine Park properly and run trips there using a tented camp near Zeila.

It is strongly advised to make advance contact with the dive school, especially if you will be there during the week, as most of its custom currently consists of weekend breaks from Hargeisa, and the rest of the week is usually set aside for research and conservation work.

**DHAMBALIN ROCK ART SITE** This remarkable rock art site, situated about 100km east of Berbera, was unknown to the outside world until October 2007, when the archaeologist Sada Mire was persuaded to visit it by two residents of the nearby village of Beenyo. It is the only such site in Somaliland where sheep are depicted, alongside wild animals including giraffe, lion, baboon, and even a marine turtle. There are also many human figures, clearly wearing headgear, holding a bow and arrow, and accompanied by dogs, in what appear to be hunting scenes. A pair of pre-Islamic burial sites faces the paintings, and while they are too modern to be associated with the artists, who lived 3,000–5,000 years ago, their presence might suggest that the paintings were held sacred by subsequent inhabitants of the area. The site is unlikely to open to tourists until a landmine field *en route* has been properly cleared.

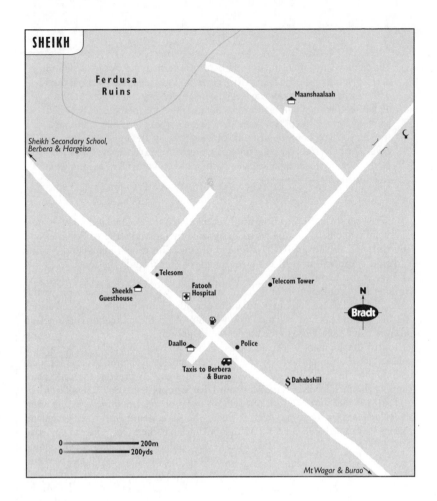

# 8

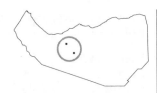

# Sheikh and Burao

These two inherently humdrum towns, in the central region of Togdheer, are of interest to travellers for three possible reasons. For those dependent on public transport, Burao has the 'because it's there' allure of being the farthest-flung Somali town that can be reached with ease from Hargeisa, and it is increasingly common for backpackers to be allowed to visit without SPU protection, provided they obtain a letter of permission from the Chief of Police in Hargeisa. For those with private transport, Burao is the most commonly recommended overnight stop before embarking on the long and dusty trip to Erigavo in Sanaag.

The smaller town of Sheikh, between Berbera and Burao, is the one place where a surfaced trunk road breaches the spectacular Golis Escarpment, as well as being the springboard for trips to remote forested Mount Wagar, one of the highest points along this escarpment.

## SHEIKH

The small town of Sheikh lies at a relatively lofty altitude of 1,470m in the Golis Range, a mountainous escarpment that separates the coastal plain from the main Somali Plateau. Also sometimes spelled Sheekh or Shiikh, the town straddles the 120km surfaced road that runs southeast from Berbera to Burao, and lies exactly halfway between these two larger towns. The ascent here from Berbera along the Sheikh Pass follows one of the most dramatic roads in Somaliland, starting from the village of Hudisa at the base of the Golis Range, then climbing some 700m over a 10km series of switchbacks that offer fantastic views of the plains below.

Sheikh is relatively well watered and the surrounding hillsides are often thrillingly green after the rains, although they tend to look somewhat bare and arid in the dry season. The town itself boasts little in the way of sightseeing, the main exception being the Ferdusa Ruins on its northern outskirts, although even these are less than compelling. An alluring excursion from Sheikh, particularly for birdwatchers, is a day trip to Mount Wagar, the highest point in the Golis Range. This is only really practical, however, in a private 4x4 (see below).

**GETTING THERE AND AWAY** Sheikh is 60km from Berbera and the same distance from Burao, along a good surfaced road. In a **private vehicle**, the drive in either direction should take comfortably less than one hour, but a little longer in a **shared taxi**, allowing for roadblocks. Transport for Sheikh leaves Hargeisa from the taxi park near the police station at the eastern end of the town centre, while taxis from Berbera leave from the southern end of the town centre (two blocks west of the market); and those from Burao from the main circle. All transport in and out of Sheikh stops on the main road in front of the police station to drop and collect passengers.

## ⌂ WHERE TO STAY
### Moderate
⌂**Sheekh Guesthouse** (6 rooms) ☎730077. This clean, pleasant & newly furnished guesthouse on the main road comprises 2 cottages, each with one en-suite dbl & 2 en-suite twins. The cottages sleep up to 6 people & have a dining area & a sitting room with TV. It is excellent value for small groups, but is a little costly for solo travellers as the bedrooms are not let out individually. *US$50 per cottage.*

### Budget
⌂**Maanshaalaah Hotel** (60 rooms) ☎730164. This unexpectedly large hotel is set around a leafy courtyard on the edge of town about 500m north of the main road. There is the choice of reasonably clean but small & austere sgls, some with a balcony &/or a fan, & a few larger dbls with net, fan, TV & balcony. There is no restaurant, all rooms use the shared showers, & it feels somewhat rundown, but still it's not bad value for the price. *US$5/10 sgl/dbl.*

✖ **WHERE TO EAT** Neither of the hotels listed above has a restaurant but there are a few options dotted along the main road, none of which is likely to offer anything more inspiring than standard pasta or rice with sauce and a lump of meat.

**OTHER PRACTICALITIES** There is a branch of **Dahabshiil Bank** if you need to change money, and also a **filling station** on the main road. It is advisable to check in with the police before heading out to Mount Wagar.

### WHAT TO SEE
**Around town** The main point of interest in Sheikh is the extensive **Ferdusa Ruins**, which lie on the northern outskirts of town, not even five minutes' walk from the Maanshaalaah Hotel. As accessible as the unexcavated site is, however, not a great deal is known about it, other than it represents the remains of a stone city that flourished about 400 years ago. It is also unlikely that the surviving jumble of stone mounds – each one presumably a house that has crumbled to ground level – will convey much to anybody but a trained archaeologist.

Major Swayne, who travelled through the area in the 1880s, stated that Sheikh 'takes its name from the tomb of a sheikh built in the form of a sugarloaf plastered with a white substance, which forms a conspicuous landmark at the top of the pass'. We strongly suspect that this is the same prominent white hilltop shrine that can be seen clearly from the site of the ruins, but were unable to confirm this.

A short distance out of town, **Sheikh Secondary School** was established as a boarding school in the colonial era and was often referred to as the Eton of Somaliland – having educated several students who would become prominent post-independence political figures in Somalia and elsewhere in the Horn – prior to its enforced closure in 1989 after several buildings were destroyed by fighting. The school has flourished since it reopened in 2003 under the auspices of the non-profit international children's charity SOS, despite the brutal murder of supervisors Richard and Enid Eyington in October of that same year (a gang of eight Islamic extremists was tried and found guilty of their murder two years later).

Another educational institution of note is the small EU-funded **Sheikh Technical Veterinary School (STVS)**, which opened in 2000 and made local headlines when its first two female students graduated in 2010.

**Mount Wagar** *with Abdi Jama of Nature Somaliland (www.naturesomaliland. com)* One of the highest points on the Golis Range, the 2,004m Mount Wagar (also known as Buuraha Wagar), supports an extensive cover of Afromontane forest, dominated by the coniferous *Juniperus procera* and evergreen *Buxus hildebrantii*, while the lower slopes support patches of the prehistoric-looking succulent *Euphorbia candelabra*. Although the forest cover on Wagar remains significant, recent reports suggest it is gradually shrinking as a result of charcoal burning. Furthermore, the undergrowth and lower vegetation have been hammered in places by grazing cattle and goats, which come up from the lower plains especially in the dry season.

At one time Mount Wagar was home to a profusion of large mammals, including elephant and lion, and while these are long gone, local farmers claim that leopards still prowl the forests, alongside the likes of Hamadryas baboon, greater kudu, lesser kudu and various small antelope. Listed as part of the same Important Bird Area as Ga'an Libah, Wagar also supports a varied selection of forest and other montane birds. The localised chestnut-naped francolin, Gambaga flycatcher and brown-tailed rock chat are near-definite ticks, and the latter is worth careful scrutiny as Wagar is the only site outside Ethiopia where the similar sombre rock chat has been recorded. Other endemics present in the area include Somali wheatear, Somali thrush and Somali starling. A mysterious 'montane form' of scops owl collected here (and also reported based on a recent visual record at Daallo) represents probably the only African populations of the Arabian scops owl.

Wagar has been little visited in recent years, and there are no facilities whatsoever for tourists. Realistically, the long sustained walk to the top necessitates at least one night's stay on the mountain, which means that you need to bring camping gear. Alternatively, it can be visited with the earliest possible start from Sheikh (the closest place with proper accommodation) but you will need to stick to the footslopes to do the round trip in one day. The hiking is very pleasant, although arguably no match to Daallo or Ga'an Libah, and if you make it up the strenuous series of ridges that lead to the final shoulder over the escarpment, the 360° view from there is stupendous.

Mount Wagar lies 25km east of Sheikh as the crow flies, but the shortest feasible road route is about twice that distance, and the drive takes around one hour, depending on road conditions. It is advisable to check in at the police station in Sheikh before heading this way. The unsignposted junction (N 9°51.965, E 45°15.566) to Wagar lies exactly 10km from Sheikh on the left side of the surfaced road towards Burao (about 1km past the Durbur Bridge). From here, you need to follow a rougher track to the village of Gugoxo at the base of the mountain, where you may be able to arrange a local guide.

# BURAO

The second-largest city in Somaliland and capital of Togdheer Province, Burao – transliterated as 'Burco' in Somali – lies 100km east of Hargeisa as the crow flies, but more than twice that distance along the only surfaced road, through Berbera and Sheikh. The population, estimated at between 300,000 and 400,000, comprises the Habar Yoonis and Habar Jeclo subclans of the Isaq clan, whose propensity for outbursts of inter-subclan violence has often flared up in the post-independence era. The town straddles the seasonal Togdheer (literally 'Long River'), a watercourse that is dry for most of the year, and is spanned by Burao Bridge in the north and Deero Bridge in the east.

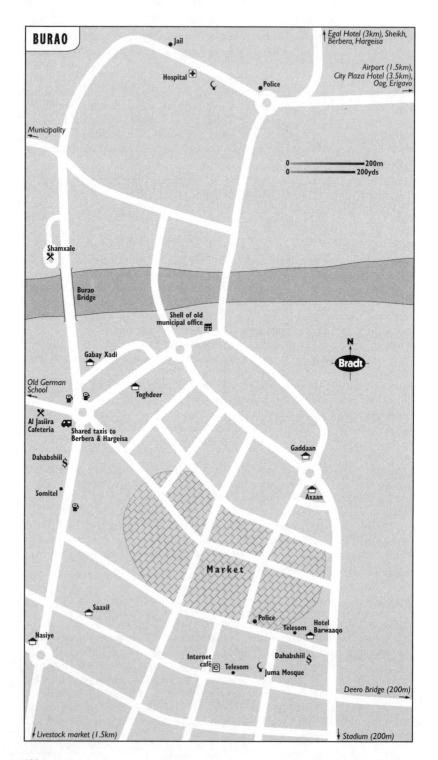

BURAO

Jail

Hospital

Police

Egal Hotel (3km), Sheikh,
Berbera, Hargeisa

Airport (1.5km),
City Plaza Hotel (3.5km),
Oog, Erigavo

Municipality

0            200m
0            200yds

Shamxale

Burao
Bridge

Shell of old
municipal office

N

Bradt

Gabay Xadi

Old German
School

Toghdeer

Al Jasiira
Cafeteria

Shared taxis to
Berbera & Hargeisa

Gaddaan

Dahabshiil

Axaan

Somitel

Market

Saaxil

Police

Telesom

Hotel
Barwaaqo

Nasiye

Internet
café

Telesom

Dahabshiil

Juma Mosque

Deero Bridge (200m)

Livestock market (1.5km)

Stadium (200m)

Today Burao, like most other towns in Somaliland, offers little in the way of prescribed sightseeing, the one exception being its famous livestock market. That said, it is a pleasant enough spot, with a decent selection of hotels and other amenities, and for many visitors it might be worth visiting simply because it is the furthest east you can easily travel in Somaliland without public transport. Burao is also the starting point for 4x4 trips further afield to Erigavo and Daallo Forest, a drive that's sufficiently long and daunting to make an overnight stop here as good as obligatory.

**HISTORY** Little is known about the early history of Burao but it has clearly long been the site of an important well (see box, *Burao in 1885*, page 123), and it was an administrative centre and the location for several anti-colonial riots during the British era. In 1988, the town was more or less abandoned as a result of the civil war, when most residents fled across the border to a refugee camp in Ethiopia. Burao's main claim to fame in modern Somali history is as the site of the Grand Conference of the Northern Peoples that led to Somaliland's unilateral secession from the rest of Somalia in May 1991.

Shortly after the 1991 conference, the refugees flooded back to Burao but, after three years of bombardment and abandonment, most of the buildings they had left behind were ruined or roofless, and the streets were overgrown with invasive vegetation. Reconstruction started almost immediately and, despite conflict-related disruptions in 1992 and 1994–95 (the latter nearly derailing Somaliland's emerging democracy), the town has experienced a dramatic economic recovery over the past two decades. Public services are also largely rehabilitated: Burao now has a reliable electricity and groundwater supply, and its youth are serviced by a remarkable tally of more than 30 primary schools, seven secondary schools and a university.

**GETTING THERE AND AWAY** Burao lies 260km from Hargeisa along the surfaced road that runs via Berbera and Sheikh, respectively 120km and 60km away. Depending on roadblocks, expect the drive from Hargeisa to take around four hours in a **private vehicle** and about half that time again in a **shared taxi**. Shared taxis for Burao leave Hargeisa from the station on the east side of the town centre, close to a police station, and they cost US$10. Those from Berbera leave from the southern end of the town centre. All inbound and outbound taxis to or from Burao congregate on the main circle in front of the Al Jarisa Café. This is also where **4x4s** leave for Erigavo every other day (usually in the early morning), a trip that costs US$50 per person.

Foreign visitors to Burao are technically required to travel with at least one SPU guard, whether in a private vehicle or on public transport – a ruling that is almost certain to be enforced at roadblocks unless you have a waiver letter from the Chief of Police in Hargeisa (see page 90). We have yet to hear of anybody being granted such a letter to travel beyond Burao to Erigavo, nor of any traveller who has used public transport along this route.

**GETTING AROUND** Burao is a small town and it's easy to get around **on foot**, but you may want to hire a **tuctuc** to visit the livestock market, 15 minutes south of the town centre, or to get to the out-of-town City Plaza or Egal Hotel. Fares shouldn't be more than US$3. Shared **minibus taxis** also run along a couple of the main roads and cost next to nothing

## WHERE TO STAY
### Moderate

**City Plaza Hotel** (10 rooms) ☎710658; m 435 1539; e cityplaza03@hotmail.com; www.buraocityplaza.com (website under construction at the time of writing). One of the nicest hotels in the country, the City Plaza lies in small but green grounds alive with birdsong some 3.5km east of the town centre along the main road to Erigavo. The smart twin rooms have comfortable beds, AC & a piping hot en-suite shower, while suites are larger & come with satellite TV. It's also far enough from the nearest mosque that you can contemplate a proper lie-in. There is a very pleasant outdoor seating area with satellite TV, as well as an indoor restaurant, & there's free Wi-Fi throughout. The varied menu caters to Western palates; most main dishes are in the US$3–5 range (including soup) & the fruit juices are excellent. The only real downer for those using public transport is the distance from town, but tuctucs are available to take you out there cheaply. After a few days in the wilds around Erigavo, this place seems truly luxurious & superb value. *US$20 twin, US$35 dbl suite, b/fast costs an additional US$4 pp.*

**Egal Hotel** (27 rooms) ☎715624; m 431 1169. Situated 3km out of town along the Hargeisa road, this doesn't come close to matching the standard of the City Plaza but it is probably a notch or two above any of the more central places. The rooms are clean, large & adequately furnished, & they all come with TV, standing fan, mosquito net & en-suite hot shower. The restaurant has a good reputation & you can eat indoors or in the dusty gardens. *US$10 sgl (with a three-quarter bed), US$15 dbl, US$20 twin.*

### Budget

**Nasiye Hotel** (20 rooms) ☎715963; m 443 1187. Probably the best bet in the town centre, situated on the main road towards the livestock market, 5mins south of the taxi park. This 3-storey hotel has spacious, clean rooms with TV, standing fan & en-suite cold (but usually sun-heated) shower. It also has one of the best restaurants in town, which may be a factor if the 18.00 curfew for foreigners is enforced. *US$10/14/15 sgl/twin/dbl.*

**Hotel Barwaaqo** (56 rooms) ☎715700; e barwaaqocentralhotel@hotmail.com. There's nothing wrong with this new multi-storey hotel, set in the market area about 5mins' walk southeast of the main circle & taxi park. Clean, tiled single rooms come with a three-quarter bed, TV, telephone & en-suite cold shower, while the spacious doubles have 1 three-quarter bed & 2 sgl beds. There is a 1st-floor restaurant but it doesn't look very appealing. Decent value. *US$10/15 sgl/dbl.*

### Shoestring

**Gabay Xadi Hotel** (33 rooms) ☎710527; m 431 5886; e kh.mly@hotmail.com. This is the option closest to the taxi park, rather reminiscent in design to the ubiquitous 'guesthouses' in Tanzania & Kenya. Although it seems a bit run down & scruffy compared with the other places listed, it is still quite pleasant & very affordable, with the bonus of a manager who speaks very good English. The choice is between a cell-like sgl using shared showers, or a larger room with a dbl bed, standing fan & en-suite cold shower. *US$5/10 sgl/dbl.*

**Togdheer Hotel** (15 rooms) One of a few rock-bottom cheapies scattered around the town centre, this is very close to the taxi park. *US$3 for a basic sgl.*

## WHERE TO EAT
The **City Plaza Hotel** has the best restaurant in town, certainly if you are looking for a break from the usual Somali fare, but it is only convenient for those who are staying there or who have their own transport. The **Egal Hotel** has also been recommended but is similarly isolated. The best bet in the town centre is the ground floor restaurant at the **Nasiye Hotel**, which supplements the usual Somali dishes with a selection of steak and chicken options, as well as good fruit juice and espresso coffee. Of the more emphatically local eateries, the **Shamxale Restaurant** has indoor and outdoor seating, a great setting in the riparian greenery

along the north side of the Togdheer watercourse, and a selection of pasta and rice dishes with roast goat an occasional speciality. The busy **Al Jasiira Cafeteria** behind the taxi park is popular for fruit juices and snacks.

## OTHER PRACTICALITIES

**Foreign exchange**  Several banks and private moneychangers are dotted around the town centre.

**Internet and email**  There are fewer internet cafés than might be expected, but the one next to the Juma Mosque is pretty reliable.

**Safety**  Foreigners travelling to Burao require SPU protection, whether they use private or public transport, and they are almost certain to be turned back at one of the roadblocks *en route* without it. However, we have heard several recent reports of travellers being granted a waiver from the Chief of Police in Hargeisa to visit Burao on public transport without an SPU officer, in which case you should get through without a problem. Once in Burao, the rule seems to be that you can only walk around in daylight in the company of an SPU officer, and travellers must stay in their hotel from 18.00 until sunrise. The police waiver referred to above would clearly allow you to walk around without an SPU guard by day, but you may well be grounded at night, in which case it makes sense to stay in a hotel with its own restaurant.

### BURAO IN 1885

One of the first Westerners to visit Burao was F L James, whose report of an exploratory expedition from Berbera to the Wabe Shebelle River (in southern Somalia), quoted below, was originally published in the Proceedings of the Royal Geographic Society in 1885.

The first day's journey after we reached the top of the mountains took us well away from the hills, and we entered the level stoneless plain, which stretches without interruption for 200 miles south. At first our route lay along the course of the Tug Dayr (Togdheer) till we reached a well called Burao ... [where we] procured extra camels to carry water, as we were told we had a waterless stretch, variously estimated at from seven to nine days to cross, at the end of which time we might find a little water by digging, but if not, three days farther would bring us to a well.

On our arrival at Burao, Sultan Aoud collected his people in our honour, and they went through some well-executed evolutions on horseback before our zariba; charging in a body – there were about 200 of them – and with wild shouts flinging their spears into the air, and then all reining up their horses on their haunches close to our enclosure, shouted *Mort, mort* ('Welcome, welcome'), to which we replied *Kul leban* ('Thanks').

Another day the Midgans, a low-caste tribe who carry bows and poisoned arrows, came with numbers of tame ostriches, whose feathers they pluck and send to Berbera. Their bows were decorated with white ostrich feathers, and they went through a curious dance. These Midgans are found living among all the Somali tribes, and are very much looked down upon. There are two other low castes: the Tomals, workers in iron, and the Ebir, workers in leather charms.

**WHAT TO SEE** If you arrive in Burao expecting superlatives, you've come to the wrong place. In most respects, this pleasant town comes across as a scaled down and even dustier version of the capital, centred upon a bustling central market area where town dwellers and rural visitors get on with the day-to-day business of Somali life. The most important landmark in the town centre is the **Juma Mosque**, a large but unadorned modern building of limited architectural interest.

It pays great testament to subsequent reconstruction efforts that so few reminders of the civil war remain, but a bombed-out old municipal office still stands a short distance east of the main circle, while the impressive **ruins** of what must once have been a very large German school lie about 500m to the west. This school opened in 1969 and flourished for 20 years before the civil war forced its closure in 1989; several roofless double-storey classrooms and an old church are still standing.

Burao's **livestock market**, situated about 1.5km south of the town centre, is claimed to be the largest in the country, attracting nomadic traders from as far afield as northern Kenya, Djibouti and Somalia. It is well worth a look, especially between 09.00 and 11.00, when trade activity peaks. If our visit is representative, however, the market isn't nearly as busy as its Hargeisa counterpart, and it specialises in goats and sheep rather than camels.

For those interested in birdwatching, Callan Cohen and Mike Mills found that the area around Burao offers some good birding. The mixture of acacia scrub and plains around town supports species such as little brown bustard, magpie starling, white-crowned starling, tawny eagle, northern carmine bee-eater and Somali long-billed crombec. Lying almost exactly 20km due southwest of town, the Arorih plains are an excellent place to find the endemic Somali lark, and the secretary-bird may also be found here.

# 9

# Sanaag

The largest, most sparsely populated and least developed of Somaliland's five administrative regions, Sanaag extends over approximately 54,000km² and supports a population estimated at around 200,000, most of whom are nomadic pastoralists. There are few towns of any substance here – the regional capital Erigavo would be little more than an overgrown village in any other context – and much of the terrain is as bereft of topographic interest as it is standing water. Thanks to its location on the disputed border with Puntland, Sanaag is also the least stable region of Somaliland, with all areas east of the road (or, more accurately, dirt track) between Oog and Erigavo being more or less off limits to travel.

For all that, Sanaag is arguably the most alluring region of Somaliland for visitors. The long sandy track to Erigavo passes through an archetypal Somali landscape of boundless badlands, inhabited by lonesome camel-herders, occasional herds of gazelle, baboon troops and several rare desert birds. North of Erigavo, the Daallo Forest, set on a spectacular stretch of escarpment rising to 2,416m above the coastal plain below, is a prime contender as Somaliland's first national park, thanks to its wealth of endemic flora, abundant birdlife and rich (albeit unrealised) potential for hiking and rambling. Below the escarpment stands the tiny but historic port of Maydh, a major exporter of frankincense for millennia, and the site of several important early Islamic and pre-Islamic tombs.

It should be stressed that this part of Somaliland remains potentially volatile, and that independent travel is forbidden at the time of writing. However, the area can easily be explored in a vehicle rented from Hargeisa – though you will need SPU protection – and the existence of limited public transport between Burao, Erigavo and Maydh may open it up to budget exploration in the future.

## BURAO TO ERIGAVO

Few visitors to Somaliland make it further east than Burao, but for those who do, the most enticing sights are the scenic Daallo Forest and the coast around Maydh, both of which are accessed from the small and remote highland town of Erigavo, the unlikely capital of the periodically unstable province of Sanaag. The journey from Burao to Erigavo is best approached as an adventure in its own right, taking as it does the best part of a day in a 4x4, following some of the roughest and dustiest roads you'll encounter anywhere in Africa.

Comfortable it isn't, but the trip to Erigavo – whichever route you follow – passes through some of Africa's most hauntingly empty landscapes. These include the Saraar Plains and Nogal Valley, vast arid expanses of stone and sand studded with giant termite hills, hemmed in by jagged rocky mountains, populated mainly by nomadic camel-herders, and punctuated by a few scattered oases and associated one-road settlements. The most important individual points of interest *en route* are

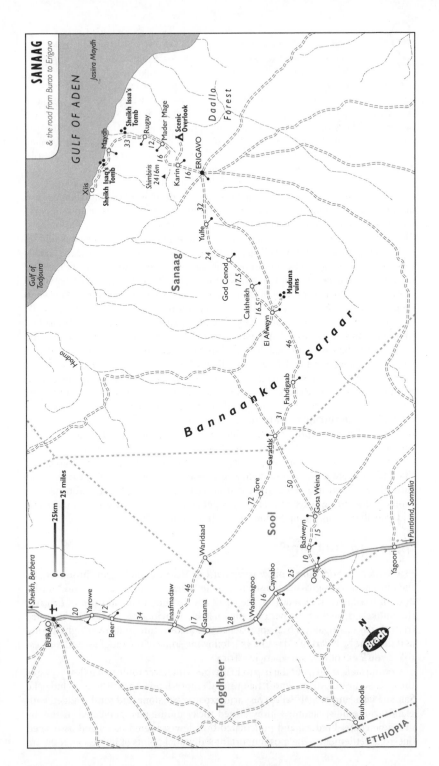

SANAAG
& the road from Burao to Erigavo

GULF OF ADEN

Jasira Maydh

Gulf of
Tadjoura

Hadma

Sheikh, Berbera

25km

25 miles

Xiis

Maydh

Sheikh Isaq's
Tomb

Sheikh Issa's
Tomb

33

Rugay

12

Mader Mage

16

Scenic
Overlook

Daallo
Forest

Shimbiris
2416m

Karin

16

ERIGAVO

Yulfe

32

24

God Cenod

17.5

Calsheikh

16.5

Maduna
ruins

El Afweyn

46

Sanaag

Fahdigaab

31

Garadak

Bannaanka
Saraar

Tore

72

50

Waridaad

Sool

Gosa Weina

Badweyn

15

Caynabo

25

Oog

10

BURAO

20

Yarowe

12

Beer

34

Inaafmadaw

46

17

Gataama

28

Wadamagoo

16

Wadamagoo

Yagoori

Puntland, Somalia

Togdheer

N

Bradt

Buuhoodle

ETHIOPIA

126

Gosa Weina Oasis, on the track connecting Oog to Garadak, and the well-preserved ruins of Maduna, a few kilometres outside El Afweyn.

Unexpectedly, perhaps, both main routes to Erigavo can provide some worthwhile wildlife viewing. The near-endemic Speke's gazelle is quite common, particularly on the amazingly barren stretch of the Nogal Valley between Waridaad and Tore. Other mammals likely to be seen include desert warthog (especially between God Cenod and Yulfe), unstriped ground squirrel, common jackal and, to a lesser extent, black-backed jackal, bat-eared fox, spotted hyena, Salt's dik-dik and gerenuk. The main attraction for birders is the presence of three localised bustards (Hueglin's, buff-crested and little brown), along with various sandgrouse and larks. The main road between Burao and Oog also skirts the so-called red-sand plains, home to the little-known dibatag antelope and collared lark, but both species are more likely to be seen east of Oog.

**PRACTICALITIES** The trip from Burao to Erigavo usually takes between eight and ten hours, depending on how fast you drive and which of the two main routes you use. A **4x4** with decent clearance is almost mandatory, and some areas may be impassable after rain. Some people recommend travelling in a convoy of two 4x4s, partly for security reasons (the SPU escort will usually travel separately in the front vehicle) and partly because the area is so remote that there is little hope of quick assistance in the event of a breakdown. Especially if you travel in one vehicle, it's advisable to leave as early in the day as possible, as any unexpected delays might leave you on the road after dark – a situation best avoided.

The two main routes to Erigavo both branch north from the main surfaced road that runs east from Burao towards the Somalia border post at Garoowe (and eventually on to Mogadishu). The two routes connect at Garadak.

## The two main routes to Gardak
**Burao to Garadak via Oog** The longer but probably faster of the two routes, covering a total of 395km, entails following the Mogadishu road out of Burao, through the roadside villages of Yarowe, Beer, Inaafmadaw, Gataama, Wadaamagoo (notable for the giant fig tree in the middle of the main road) and Caynabo, until after 152km you reach the small town of Oog (N 8°56.066, E 46°37.190). Here, you need to turn left onto a wide, flat, sandy track that runs north through Badweyn (N 8°59.789, E 46°39.368) after 10km and passes Gosa Weina (N 9°05.299, E 46°46.350) after another 15km, before arriving at the junction village of Garadak (N 9°29.181, E 46°52.018) after another 50km.

**Burao to Garadak via Inaafmadaw** This more direct route cuts about 65km off the option outlined above, but entails an extra 45km on dirt. It also follows the Mogadishu road east out of Burao, but turns left after 66km at Inaafmadaw (N 9°08.679, E 45°57.149). This journey follows a criss-crossing and occasionally confusing network of unsignposted tracks that pass through Waridaad (46km past Inaafmadaw; N 9°17.025, E 46°15.183) and then tiny Tore with its disproportionately large mosque (50km further; N 9°22.094, E 46°42.727) before connecting with the track from Oog at Garadak after another 22km.

**Garadak to Erigavo** The 166km road north of Garadak is less distinct, but there are a few small settlements along the way to help you stay orientated. These are Fahdigaab (31km past Garadak; N 9°39.855, E 47°01.314), the relatively substantial town of El Afweyn (45km further; N 9°55.629, E 47°12.898), and then Calsheikh

Published in the 1894 Journal of the Royal Geographic Society, Lieutenant E J E Swayne's *Expedition to the Nogal Valley*, an account of a 1891 trip undertaken with his brother Major H G C Swayne, describes something of the Somali customs associated with the usage of wells such as Gosa Weina in the days before motorised pumps:

> The sub-tribes each have their own separate pastures and watering-places, and will not drink at each other's wells unless on terms of intimate friendship. With such thousands of camels, goats, sheep, and ponies, the watering has to be done very methodically, different hours for this being allotted to different families. The men descend into the wells, say, 20 feet down, and water is passed up from man to man in skin buckets, and poured into skins arranged in the form of basins with sticks, and propped up by stones. The herds are then driven up to drink, and driven off again to give place to others. All the time the men engaged in the wells are singing songs, and others sing and whistle encouragement to the camels. The white gypsum rock in the vicinity of the wells is ground into dust by the continual passage of beasts, and is glaring, and very trying to the eyes. At sunset all the beasts are driven off, and collected by families inside thick thorn fences; fires are lighted, sheep killed, and songs and dances kept up until a late hour. The position of each sub-tribe is marked by 30 or 40 brown zerebas, inside which camel-mats, rigged up on sticks, afford shelter to the women and children.

(16.5km further; N 10°04.067, E 47°12.342), God Cenod (17.5km further; N 10°11.596, E 47°11.748) and Yulfe (24km further; N 10°22.429, E 47°11.766). From Yulfe it is only 32km to Erigavo.

## WHAT TO SEE

**Oog and surrounds** Situated in the periodically unsettled province of Sool, the endearingly named town of Oog is of little interest to travellers except as the main junction for the more popular of the two routes to Erigavo (see above). The presence of two adequate hotels also makes it a potential overnight alternative to Burao prior to undertaking the long drive north, allowing you more time to stop along the way. The better of the two lodgings is the **Hotel Sool** (*12 rooms;* \ *721022;* m *414 3334*), which charges US$4 for a single or US$6 a double, and has a reasonable local restaurant where the outdoor seating attracts a fair selection of dry-country birds.

Only 10km along the Erigavo road north of Oog, **Badweyn** is a small town most obviously notable for its substantial mosque and the isolated multiple-trunked tree that stands alongside the main track. Given the rather generic name – Badweyn literally means 'Big well' – it is unclear whether this is the same place described in Lieutenant Swayne's *Expedition to the Nogal Valley* (see box on page 128), as the 'tank at Badwein … an oblong hole quarried out of gypsum rock, about 120 yards long and 80 yards wide, with perpendicular rocky sides'.

Another 15km along this road, it is well worth stopping at the tiny oasis of **Gosa Weina** ('Well of Clans'), a site that was definitely visited by Swayne. Gosa Weina is centred upon the largest and most reliable freshwater source for many miles around, a deep well whose water used to be brought to the surface in buckets, but is now pumped into a trough that attracts nomadic camel herders from all over the region.

In periods of drought, hundreds of camels might aggregate at this oasis at any one time, and it is fascinating to watch them march to the watering trough and back.

### Birdwatching around Oog  *Callan Cohen & Mike Mills*

South of Oog, the rough roads that run southwards from the main surfaced road to the Ethiopian border pass through the northern reaches of the Haud, a vast desert that stretches deep into the Ogaden region of Ethiopia. The endemic dibatag antelope was once common here, but we couldn't locate it on a 2010 visit and know of no other recent records. Also found on the red sands here is the rare collared lark, a very shy bird that occurs between patches of spiny acacia scrub. A good area to look for this bird is along the road to Qorigulud, which branches southwards from the asphalt between Kiridh and Oog.

## Maduna and El Afweyn  The enigmatic abandoned Islamic city of **Maduna** (N 9°50.121, E 47°15.578), near El Afweyn, is the most substantial and impressive accessible ruin of its type in Somaliland. Its most important feature is a large rectangular **mosque**, the 3m-high walls of which are still intact and contain a mihrab along with perhaps a dozen smaller arched niches. This central building is surrounded by several dozen old houses, most of which still have partially intact walls, and the baobab on the slope immediately below is sufficiently large to suggest it was planted when the city was still inhabited.

An aura of mystery overhangs Maduna – unsurprisingly, perhaps, when so little is known about its history. The dry-stone architectural style suggests that the ruined city was a contemporary of Amoud and Abasa (see page 148), so presumably it once formed part of the Adal Sultanate. As far as we know, however, the site has never been excavated and no historical records pertaining to it survive. Also perplexing, according to archaeologist Sada Mire's article in *World Archaeology*, are several 'dome-shaped structures without doors or windows' whose 'only entrance was via a small opening at the top'. Mire suggests these rooms may have been prison cells of some type, but we can only speculate.

The closest town to Maduna is **El Afweyn**, perched at an altitude of 1,050m some 90km south of Erigavo. A sandy but driveable 8km track runs eastwards from the town to Maduna, although the lack of obvious landmarks along the way means the ruins may be difficult to locate without GPS or a local guide. There is no caretaker

---

### TALEH

This town of around 40,000 inhabitants, situated some 50km north of the main road between Oog and Garoowe, is too close to the Puntland border to be safe to visit at the time of writing. Taleh (also transcribed as Taleex), is, however, of great historic interest as the former headquarters of the early 20th century anti-colonial movement led by the 'Mad Mullah' Mohammed Abdullah Hassan, who built an immense stone fort there that was partially destroyed by a British aerial bombardment in 1920. We have no recent reports as to the state of the ruined fort, but photographs taken in the 1980s, immediately before the civil war, suggest it was still in impressive shape then, with most of the 2m wall, along with at least one domed roof and several tall arched doorways, still intact. More recent feedback from any adventurers who head to this little-visited area would be appreciated.

at the site, nor any entrance fee charged, but local sensitivities mean it is advisable to go to the municipal office in El Afweyn for written permission before you visit. The ruins are supposed to house a large number of poisonous snakes, so it probably pays to put on solid footwear before you start clambering about.

El Afweyn, sometimes transliterated as Ceel Afweyn, has a relatively cool climate thanks to the lower-lying plains further south, and it is reputedly the third-largest town in Sanaag Province, although it feels a lot smaller that the population estimate of 60,000 would suggest. There is no formal accommodation but the **NGO Guesthouse** on the Erigavo side of town will put travellers up in its very basic rooms for a 'donation' (expect to be asked for US$10 per person, which feels very exorbitant for what you get), and there are plenty of local eateries serving pasta, bread and other simple dishes. The **Afweyn** (well) for which the town is named, set on its eastern outskirts, feeds a small dam that forms a congregation point for Egyptian vultures (small numbers of which are common around towns and cliffs in this region) and other raptors.

# ERIGAVO

The administrative capital of Sanaag, Erigavo (also spelled Ceerigaabo) is an unassuming highland town of around 200,000 people. It has a somewhat isolated and parochial feel, a kind of African Siberia surrounded by sand rather than snow, thanks partly to the almost total lack of public transport heading to or from the direction of the capital. The town also has perhaps the most agreeable climate in Somaliland, set at a lofty altitude of 1,770m close to Mount Shimbiris, the country's tallest peak, and receiving sufficient rainfall to support a surrounding belt of low-scale seasonal agriculture.

**GETTING THERE AND AWAY** The fascinating but gruelling 4x4 drive from Burao to Erigavo is covered in the previous section. In a private vehicle, the **drive** from Burao takes at least eight hours and an early start is highly recommended. Allow two days to get to Erigavo from Berbera or Hargeisa. **Public transport** is limited to a few 4x4s that leave from Burao every other day, usually at around 05.00, and charge US$50 per person. We have yet to hear of a traveller being permitted to use this service, but it can't hurt to ask for permission from the Chief of Police in Hargeisa (see page 90).

**GETTING AROUND** Everything of importance is within a few hundred metres of the main square so it is easy enough to get around **on foot** – assuming that you are allowed to (see *Safety* on page 52).

## WHERE TO STAY
### Budget

**Daallo Hotel** (6 rooms) m 420 0965. The newest & ostensibly the smartest option in town, this unsignposted 3-storey hotel overlooking the main square leaves much to be desired. The rooms are dirty, poorly maintained & madly overpriced, the staff are unhelpful when they can be located, & the lack of a restaurant means you need to eat dinner before the 18.00 curfew is (enthusiastically) enforced, & to postpone breakfast until your SPU decides he is ready to collect you from behind the locked door. *US$20 for a twin using the shared cold shower, US$30 for an en-suite dbl.*

**Sanaag Hotel** This basic hotel near the police station is no better than the Daallo, but if you are going to be locked in overnight, the green compound does give it a slight edge. *US$10/20 sgl/dbl with shared shower.*

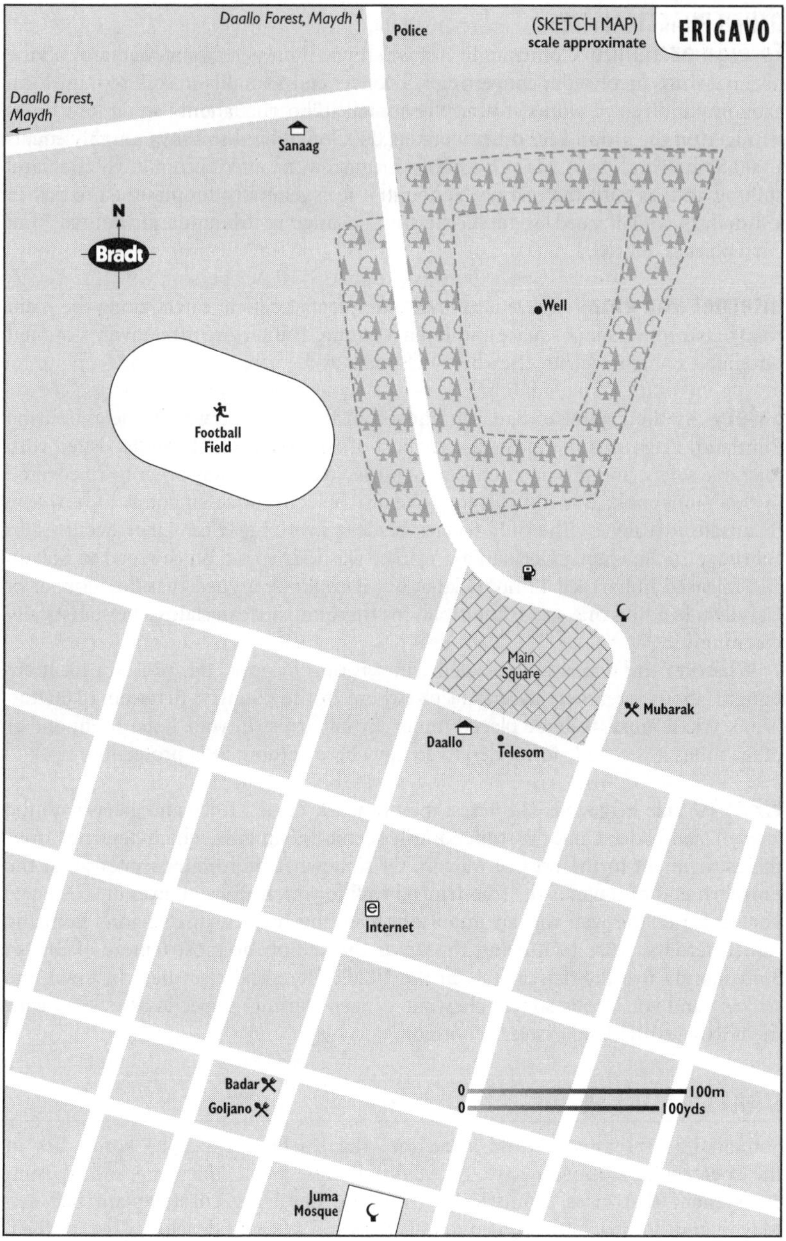

ERIGAVO
(SKETCH MAP)
scale approximate
Daallo Forest, Maydh
Daallo Forest, Maydh
Police
Sanaag
N
Bradt
Well
Football Field
Main Square
Mubarak
Daallo
Telesom
Internet
Badar
Goljano
0
100m
0
100yds
Juma Mosque

**WHERE TO EAT** The only place where our SPU allowed us to eat was the **Mubarak Restaurant** on the main circle, which serves typically unexciting Somali fare of pasta or rice, with vegetable slop or roast camel or goat meat. The **Badar** and **Goljano** restaurants near the Juma Mosque are reputedly better, although neither looks very inspiring from the outside. Excellent fresh bread is widely available.

## OTHER PRACTICALITIES

**Foreign exchange** Confusingly, just when you'll have got your head around the decimal shifts involved in converting US dollars and Somaliland shillings, the local economy in Erigavo works around the Somali shilling, currently about four times stronger on the ground (in other words, 4,000 Somaliland shillings roughly equals 1,000 Somali shillings). Many people in Erigavo won't even accept the Somaliland shilling and, as with the rest of the country, it is generally simplest just to pay in US dollars, and if need be to accept small change in whatever of the two local currencies is offered.

**Internet and email** There is at least one internet café in town, along the main road between the main square and Juma Mosque. The service is relatively slow and unreliable compared with elsewhere in Somaliland.

**Safety** As the capital of Sanaag, whose borders are disputed by neighbouring Puntland, Erigavo is the most easterly part of Somaliland that can be visited with tolerable safety, and it is potentially a lot more volatile than any other town covered in this guidebook. It is difficult to make any objective assessment as to how safe or unsafe it really is. The only recent incident involving a foreigner occurred in February 2008, when a German aid worker was kidnapped on the road to Maydh and released unharmed 12 hours later, but it could be argued that the number of travellers heading this way is too small for this almost clean slate to be statistically meaningful.

Whatever the real risk associated with visiting Erigavo, the SPU is a lot more uptight about foreigners here than elsewhere in the country. Between 18.00 and 07.00, you'll most likely be placed under virtual arrest in your hotel room and at other times it is strictly forbidden to go anywhere without SPU protection.

**WHAT TO SEE** Erigavo is of interest mainly as the closest town and gateway to the lovely Daallo Forest and the stupendously scenic Tabah Pass, which descends from the escarpment to the port of Maydh. Of somewhat more minor interest, at the northern end of town, is the tree-fringed well to which Erigavo owes its existence. For centuries the well was an important watering hole for the region's nomadic camel-herders, prior to it being chosen as the site of the most remote of British Somaliland's five district capitals in the 1920s. Here and elsewhere in town, the striking and vociferous Somali chestnut-winged starling, a species associated with the northern highlands, is very common.

## DAALLO FOREST

Somaliland's foremost natural attraction, the Daallo (or Daloh) Forest lies in the spectacular Calmadow (or Al Mado) Range, a tall limestone and gypsum escarpment that rises dramatically from the low-lying coastal plain between Maydh and Bosaso. Little known to outsiders and as yet undeveloped for tourism, Daallo is less than an hour's drive north of Erigavo, close to the base of Mount Shimbiris, the highest point anywhere in Somalia. The main attractions of Daallo are the stupendous clifftop views from the top of the escarpment to the distant Gulf of Aden more than 2,000m below, and a rich biodiversity that includes at least 200 endemic plant species, along with many woodland birds and other animals whose range is confined to the Somali region.

Biologically, Daallo represents the most accessible and largest semi-pristine relict of Somali Montane Xeric Woodland, an eco-region confined to the 300km-long escarpment running inland from the northern Somali coast. Isolated from other similar habitats by the vast swathes of desert that cover the Somali interior and the far east of Ethiopia, this important centre of endemism supports a unique combination of plant species, with links to the Afromontane, Mediterranean and Micronesian regions, and much of it remains unexplored in scientific terms. Plans to set aside the forest as a national park have been in the pipeline for years but, as things stand, it is not accorded any formal protection and large stands of woodland have been chopped down in recent years by charcoal burners.

Daallo is the wettest part of Somaliland, receiving a mean annual rainfall of around 750mm, most of which falls between April and October, when the well-watered lower slopes form the country's main centre of agriculture. During the drier winter months, sea fogs and mist are an important supplementary source of water for common high-altitude trees such as *Juniperus procera*, *Buxus hildebrantii*, *Olea chrysophylla* and *Sideroxylon buxifolium*. A striking plant associated with Daallo is the endangered Gabel Elba dragon's blood tree (*Dracaena ombet*), a thick-stemmed, spike-leaved succulent that manages to grow in the most unlikely crags and is known locally as *mooli*. The lower slopes of the escarpment also support large stands of *Boswellia frereana*, whose resin is used to make frankincense (see box, page 135).

Daallo supports the densest and perhaps the richest fauna of the Somali region. It is of particular interest to birdwatchers as the best place to see a host of endemics and other localised specials, including Archer's buzzard, Archer's francolin, Somali thrush, Warsangli linnet and Somali golden-winged grosbeak, as well as more typical African highland and forest species, ranging from the busy Abyssinian white-eye to the stunning Narina trogon. Mammals are more elusive but include Hamadryas baboon, two species of hyrax and the endearing Speke's pectinator. The endemic beira antelope was once resident in the region, but we know of no recent sightings. The forest also supports a varied selection of secretive predators – locals claim that leopard and spotted hyena are quite common – and we had a magnificent view of a striped hyena lying in the middle of the road shortly after dusk.

**GETTING THERE AND AWAY** The gateway village to Daallo Forest is tiny **Karin**, which consists of a few dozen dwellings and a handsome mosque, set scenically at an altitude of 2,070m on the edge of the Daallo Escarpment below Mount Shimbiris. Karin lies 16km north of Erigavo, along a dirt road best driven in a **high clearance vehicle**, and the drive takes 40 minutes without stops. Immediately before the police checkpoint at Karin, a right turn leads through the most accessible block of escarpment forest for 6km, before emerging at the Scenic Overlook Campsite (N 10°46.217, E 47°17.973). The short stretch of road between Karin and the campsite is worth taking slowly and it could be rewarding to explore on foot. Alternatively, Karin also marks the start of the 30km Tabah Pass, a spectacular dirt road that descends to the escarpment base at Rugay, and then continues along the coastal plain to Maydh.

We've not heard of anybody trying to get to Daallo without a **private vehicle**, but as far as we know the main obstacle would be security (or the SPU attitude towards it). Remove this factor, and Daallo is a pretty realistic goal, whether you walk the reasonably flat 16km from Erigavo to Karin, cycle, or catch a 4x4 heading on to Maydh. From Karin, you should be able to walk to the Scenic Overlook in about 90 minutes. Security concerns aside, a logistical obstacle at present is the lack of accommodation: you wouldn't want to camp at the chilly and potentially damp

Scenic Overlook without suitable gear, so your only alternative would be to try to arrange an informal room in Karin.

🏠 **WHERE TO STAY AND EAT** The only option at the moment, used by a few birding tour groups in 2010, is to **camp** rough at the Scenic Overlook Campsite. This looks to be an absolutely stunning place to overnight, although at an altitude of 2,133m it might be quite chilly after dark, and it is also very exposed to rain and wind. The only facility is a water pump about 100m behind the main clearing, so you will need to bring all your own food, although very basic provisions may be available in Karin. Adventurous hikers carrying their own camping gear could also theoretically walk down the 30km road pass between Karin and Rugay, stopping overnight at Mader Mage – roughly the halfway mark – but security concerns, whether real or perceived, are likely to prove an insurmountable obstacle at the time of writing.

## WHAT TO SEE
**Around the Scenic Overlook** The 6km dirt road between Karin and the Scenic Overlook is the obvious starting point for any exploration of Daallo, passing as it does through an area of thick highland forest dominated by the coniferous *Juniperus procera*. It is presumably the highest altitude stretch of road in the country, crossing the 2,200m contour in at least one place, and the birding can be excellent. Common species include Hemprich's hornbill, African olive pigeon, red-fronted tinkerbird, brown woodland warbler, Abyssinian white-eye, Abyssinian black wheatear, brown-rumped seedeater and cinnamon-breasted rock bunting. The common fowl here is the attractive yellow-throated spurfowl, but check carefully, because this is also the best place in Somaliland to seek out Archer's francolin, a localised regional endemic that sometimes attracts attention at dawn and dusk with its whistled calls.

The Scenic Overlook, set at an altitude of 2,133m, is aptly named indeed, offering as it does a superb view from the edge of the escarpment over tall limestone cliffs to the forested footslopes and – weather permitting – the seashore around Maydh, some 30km away. It is also a great spot to scan for cliff-associated raptors such as Verreaux's eagle, peregrine falcon, common kestrel and the endemic Archer's buzzard – a large and striking bird sometimes treated as a colour form of augur buzzard and easily recognised by its rich chestnut chest and rump. It's worth checking any peregrine falcons carefully, as the closely related and more localised Barbary falcon is also reported to occur here. The water pump and small pool about 100m behind the main clearing is a hive of avian activity: the endemic Warsangli linnet has been recorded, Somali thrush and Somali starling are very common, and there is a steady stream of other woodland birds, ranging from the dapper little rock-thrush to the lovely African paradise flycatcher. There is some debate about the identity of the scops owls that occur here and some reports suggest they might be Arabian scops owls (a species unrecorded elsewhere in Africa), while others affirm they are the more common African scops owl.

**Mount Shimbiris** Situated to the immediate west of the road from Erigavo to Karin, Shimbiris rises to at least 2,416m, although recent surveys suggest a more likely altitude of around 2,450m. Its name literally means 'Abode of Birds', in reference to the avian wealth of the Daallo Forest on its eastern slopes, and it is also known locally as Surad Cad or Shimbir Beris. The mountain is of some historical note as the site of a fort built by the early 20th-century resistance leader Mohammed

An aromatic accompaniment to religious rites since the time of the ancient Egyptians, frankincense will be familiar to most Westerners, at least by name, as one of the three gifts offered by the three wise men to the baby Jesus in his manger. Characterised by a spicy, almost camphoric aroma, it is made from the resin of trees of the genus *Boswellia*, several hardy species of which are associated with rocky slopes on the shores of the Red Sea and Gulf of Aden. The usual method of collection is to make a deep incision, roughly 12–15cm long, into the bark of the tree, which then exudes a milky resin that congeals to form a large yellow tear-shaped scab which is ready to harvest about three months later.

In Pharaonic times, frankincense was burned not only in temples, but also to make *kohl*, the black powder which Egyptian women used as eyeliner. One of the incenses favoured in early Hebrew temples, it is name-checked as far back as the Book of Exodus, and is also mentioned as being sourced from Arabia in the classical writings of Herodotus and Pliny the Elder, among others. Banned by the early Roman church, the fragrant resin was introduced to Europe during the Crusades, and since then it has been burnt at funerals by the Catholic Church, which reputedly still sources most of its supplies from Somaliland and Yemen. Frankincense has also been subject to numerous (mostly spurious) medicinal uses over the millennia: as an antidote to hemlock poisoning, to inhibit vomiting and fevers, and to cure everything from leprosy to gonorrhoea. More recently, medical scientists have observed frankincense to contain an agent that may slow the spread of cancer, and its potential as a cure for this disease is currently being researched.

The coast of what is now Yemen and Somaliland has probably been the main global source of frankincense since the second millennium BC, when a mural depicting sacks shipped from the so-called Land of Punt were painted on the outer walls of Queen Hatshepsut's Temple near Luxor. The lower slope of Daallo forms the most important Somali source of frankincense, which is traditionally traded through Maydh (indeed the local variety, rated by some as the world's finest, is known as *maydi*) and transported to Saudi Arabia, where it is sold as an expensive chewing gum. *Boswellia frereana*, the species that grows in Daallo, often taking root in the most improbable rocky clefts, is abundant in the vicinity of Mader Mage and Rugay, where frankincense production is the mainstay of the local economy. In ancient times, the value of the resin sometimes rivalled that of gold and the finest silk, but today it costs around US$2 per kilogram locally, a price that inflates rapidly as it travels further from its Somali source.

Abdullah Hassan, and unsuccessfully attacked by British troops in 1914 and 1916 prior to the death of the 'Mad Mullah' in 1920. Despite its status as the highest point anywhere in Somalia, Shimbiris is not really a mountain in the conventional sense, but a large hill set along a high escarpment that contains several other peaks topping the 2,200m mark. As such, while we have not heard of any ascents in recent times, it shouldn't represent a daunting physical challenge to determined peak-baggers. Whether it would be permitted to hike there is another matter, and it would certainly be a good idea to ask about landmines or other security threats before making any attempt.

**The Karin–Rugay road** Constructed using the labour of Italian prisoners during World War II and completed in 1952, the **Tabah Pass** follows an old camel caravan track down the Daallo Escarpment from Karin to Rugay – an altitude drop of almost 1,700m in the space of 30 multiple-switchbacked kilometres that takes at least 2½ hours to cover in either direction. It is easily the most spectacular road in Somaliland, offering a succession of superb views across steep forested slopes to the tall limestone cliffs of the upper escarpment and the more distant Gulf of Aden, haze permitting. For dedicated birders, this road is the best place to look out for two of the more elusive Somali endemics, namely Warsangli linnet and Somali golden-winged grosbeak, both of which favour rocky slopes, although the former is often attracted to the berry-like cones of junipers in the wet season.

On the right side of the road as you descend, there are excellent views into the steep-sided Tabah Gorge, often framed by prehistoric-looking dragon's blood trees. About 6.5km out of Karin, the road passes through a short Italian-built **tunnel**, complete with a rock-hewn window looking out over the forest. After another 10km, at an altitude of 1,265m, you reach the relatively substantial village of **Mader Mage**, which has a few shops and is a major centre of frankincense production (see box, page 135). It is another 12km from here to Rugay, from where you can either continue to Maydh or turn back to Erigavo. About halfway between Mader Mage and Rugay, at an altitude of 825m (N 10°48.523, E 47°19.212), the stone embankment supporting the right side of the road is home to at least one pair of Speke's pectinator, a peculiar rock-dwelling rodent endemic to the Somali region.

## MAYDH

After reaching the base of the escarpment base at Rugay, the road from Erigavo straightens out to run more or less directly across the flat coastal plain, emerging after 33km – about an hour's drive – at the venerable port of Maydh (N 11°00.320, E 47°06.588). It's a fascinating stretch of road, passing through a wide riverine valley that seems to support a few perennial pools, and is flanked by heavily eroded slopes pockmarked with caves, and overlooked by the forested main escarpment to the south. *En route*, it passes within metres of some massive prehistoric cairns, as well as the whitewashed tomb of Sheikh Issa, founder of the Dir Issa clan of western Awdal and Djibouti.

Maydh, also transliterated as Mait, doesn't look like much of a place today, comprising as it does only a tiny cluster of perhaps 100 buildings (some in the traditional Swahili style), housing an estimated 2,000 to 3,000 people, a small jetty, and a beach lined with fishing nets and merchant *dhows* from elsewhere in the Gulf of Aden. However, it has probably been an active trade port for at least 1,000 years, quite possibly longer, considering that the nearby mountains are a legendary source of frankincense, an important item of trade for millennia. Sometime before the end of the 13th century, the area's older Galla inhabitants were displaced by Islamic settlers, among them Sheikh Isaq, the founder of Somaliland's dominant clan, whose tomb stands on the beach south of Maydh. The small port is also the mainland springboard for boat trips to Jasiira Maydh, an offshore island that supports seasonally impressive flocks of marine birds.

**PRACTICALITIES** A couple of 4x4s seem to operate daily as public transport between Erigavo and Maydh, but they tend to be very cramped and it is unlikely the police would permit a foreigner to travel on one. Otherwise, the only realistic way to get to Maydh is in a **private 4x4**, a trip that takes between four and five hours along the rough road down the Daallo Escarpment – longer if you make a few stops. There is no formal accommodation in Maydh, but with advance permission (ask at the municipal office in Erigavo) you should be allowed to stay at the small and inexpensive beachfront **government guesthouse**. Failing that, it is usually possible to **camp** or crash in the security of the marine police camp, although you may be expected to pay a small fee. A small restaurant in the centre of town serves basic fish and pasta dishes, and a few shops sell biscuits and soft drinks.

**WHAT TO SEE** As aspirant beachfront idylls go, Maydh has a somewhat austere location, but it is quite scenic all the same, with its mountainous backdrop being particularly pretty in the soft light of early morning and late afternoon. There is little specific to do in the town itself, and local dress codes probably make swimming problematic, but the atmosphere is very relaxed and friendly if you just feel like hanging out. Outside town, several sites of interest are worth investigating and are detailed below.

**Sheikh Isaq's Tomb** Situated on a small seafront rise about 3km south of Maydh, and clearly visible from the small port's jetty, the striking domed and whitewashed tomb of Sheikh Isaq is one of the most important cultural landmarks in the whole of Somaliland. The Isaq (or Isaaq) clan, founded by its namesake in the 12th or 13th century, is the most numerically and politically important clan in Somaliland, with its various subclans accounting for the majority of the population of the country's five largest towns: Hargeisa, Burao, Berbera, Erigavo and Gebiley. Foreigners are usually allowed to look at the exterior, but not to enter the compound, and photography may be forbidden. The tomb attracts pilgrims from all over Somaliland and further afield, particularly on Isaq's birthday, commemorated on the 20th day of the Islamic month of Safar (which will fall between mid-December and mid-January between 2012 and 2015). There is also reason to believe the medieval town of Maydh was centred around the site of the tomb, although at the moment it remains unexcavated.

**Jasiira Maydh** Situated 13km offshore, Jasiira Maydh (also known as Rabshie or Mait Island) is a dramatic, barren granite outcrop that rises steeply from above the waves to a maximum altitude of 125m. Almost 2km long but nowhere more than 300m wide, the island is an important seasonal breeding site for several species of marine bird, and it is thus listed as one of the country's six 'Important Bird Areas', and has also been proposed as a future marine protected area. The breeding season is from June to September, when up to 100,000 birds are sometimes estimated to be present, but there are few birds at other times of the year, when locals from the mainland visit the island regularly to collect guano. Most numerous during the breeding season is brown noddy, with up to 20,000 pairs, while other species recorded frequently include masked booby, brown booby, sooty tern, bridled tern, white-cheeked tern, the localised Socotra cormorant and the spectacular red-billed tropicbird.

To get here from Maydh you can either ask to charter the marine police's motorboat, which costs around US$300–400 per party for the round trip (assuming it is available), or you can cut a deal with one of the local boat owners, which is more likely to cost US$50–60 per group. Either way, it is best to set sail in the early morning, when the sea is relatively calm, and there is little point in visiting between October and May, when the breeding birds are absent.

**Sheikh Issa's Tomb and the Taalla Galla** The most conspicuous artificial landmark between Rugay and Maydh, standing in bold whitewashed contrast to the surrounding hills, some 300m east of the main road, is the Tomb of Sheikh Issa (N 10°58.496, E 47°13.900), which lies about halfway between the two villages. This Dir Somali clan, whose main population base is now in Djibouti, reputedly traces its lineage back to Aqeel bin Abi Talib, a cousin of the Prophet Muhammad, who died in the late 7th century. It is unclear when exactly Sheikh Issa founded the clan that now bears his name, but some sources suggest he was a contemporary of Sheikh Isaq, which would suggest the Maydh area was an important springboard of Islamic infiltration into the Somali interior. There seems to be no problem with non-Islamic foreigners visiting and photographing this tomb.

Between Sheikh Issa's Tomb and Rugay, the road passes through an area studded with dozens of immense *tumuli* (stone burial cairns), the most elaborate of which must stand 5m tall and 10m wide. Different coloured stone is used for different lateral sections, and the cairns are enclosed in a larger circular clearing demarcated by an outer boundary ring of stones. These impressive and enigmatic mounds are known locally as Taalla Galla, literally 'Graves of the Galla' (an archaic name for the Oromo people, now numerically dominant in southern Ethiopia). The cairns are also often referred to by locals as 'Christian graves', which might indicate some link with the ancient Christian Empire of neighbouring Ethiopia (a separate cultural entity to the Galla/Oromo), or might simply be a way of expressing their non-Islamic origin. Either way, these fascinating and evocative structures most likely pre-date the local arrival of Islam, which would mean their construction took place in the 13th century or earlier. Little excavation has taken place, but the few cairns that have been opened contain a small central burial chamber covered by a large flat rock. It has been suggested, perhaps a little fancifully, that the pyramidal shape of the *tumuli* demonstrates a religious or cultural link with Ancient Egypt, which is thought to have traded with the coast of present-day Somaliland.

# 10

# West of Hargeisa

Awdal, the most northwesterly province of Somaliland, takes its name from the Adal (or Awdal) Sultanate that flourished there in the 15th and early 16th centuries. In 2010, its leaders controversially declared the province to be the autonomous state of Awdalland, but for all practical purposes it still functions as part of Somaliland, and there is no specific issue relating to travel there at the time of writing. Indeed, Awdal provides most overland travellers with their introduction to Somaliland, since the two main overland border crossings, Tog Wajaale (for Ethiopia) and Looyada (for Djibouti), both lie within it.

Most new arrivals to Somaliland simply catch the first available transport between the border and Hargeisa. And in reality there isn't a great deal of room to explore further afield, since the province is served by one solitary and largely unmaintained trunk road that runs from Hargeisa to Djibouti, via the provincial capital Borama, passing within 20km of Tog Wajaale *en route*. Nevertheless, in common with the rest of Somaliland, the region is steeped in history and rich in archaeological interest. There are two ancient rock art sites off the main road between Hargeisa and Tog Wajaale; a trio of ruined stone cities in the vicinity of Borama; and most tantalisingly the ancient port of Zeila, now a mere shadow of what it was in its medieval prime, but still worth stopping at on the way to the Djibouti border.

## ROCK ART SITES ON THE BORAMA ROAD

The main – indeed only – road running west from Hargeisa leads after 110km to Borama, a substantial town seldom visited by travellers unless they happen to be heading for Djibouti. This same road provides access to Dhagax Khoure and Dhagax Marodi – important prehistoric rock art sites that have both suffered from recent defacements – as well as to Tog Wajaale, the somewhat uninspiring border town along the only functional overland route between Somaliland and Ethiopia.

Three main settlements can be found along the Borama road. The largest is Gebiley, about 50km from Hargeisa, which is also the site of Dhagax Marodi. Some 18km west of this, tiny Kalabaydh stands at the junction for Tog Wajaale, and another 18km further west brings you to Dilla. Coming from Hargeisa, the road as far as Dilla is surfaced, and most vehicles travel at a comfortable 60–80km/h, not allowing for potential delays at several roadblocks. The tracks leading north to Dhagax Khoure and south to Tog Wajaale, though rough and unsurfaced, are usually navigable in any saloon car.

Although this road isn't much to shout about scenically, there's usually a bit of wildlife around, especially in the early morning. The giant 'Ethiopian' form of leopard tortoise, which can weigh in at over 50kg and is sometimes classified as a local sub-species (*Stigmochelys pardalis somalica*), seems to be very common here,

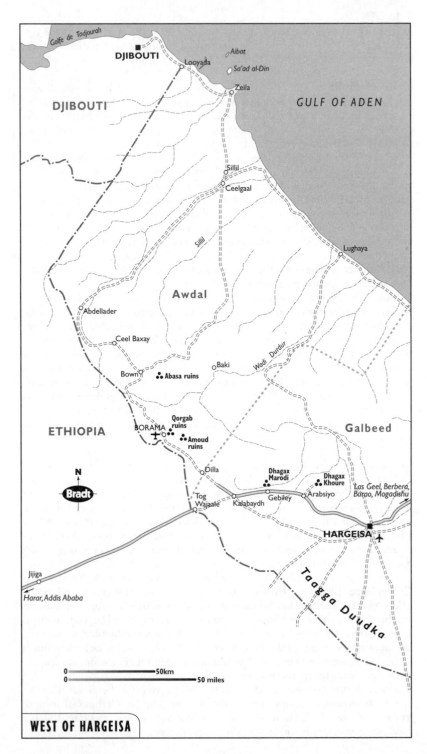

WEST OF HARGEISA

particularly in March and April, during the build-up to the rains. Pairs of dik-dik are also often seen by the roadside, and the varied birdlife includes the likes of little brown bustard, yellow-breasted barbet, Gillett's lark and golden-breasted starling.

**DHAGAX KHOURE**  Situated 45km northwest of Hargeisa amid a chain of spectacular granite outcrops, Dhagax Khoure (also transliterated as Dagah Kuure, Dagax Gure and variations thereof) was the most celebrated rock art site in Somaliland prior to the 2002 discovery of Las Geel. It remains a site of exceptional merit, comprising hundreds of individual bovid, human and other figures spread across at least six different panels on a massive turtleback protuberance. Tragically, however, several of the paintings – which may be more than 5,000 years old – were defaced in early 2011, reputedly as a result of a dispute between two local factions over their curatorship. It remains to be seen whether the damage can be reversed. Although Dhagax Khoure is of great interest to rock art enthusiasts, its overall impact doesn't compare to Las Geel, and it should certainly be the second choice for anybody whose resources only stretch to visiting one Somaliland rock art site.

**Practicalities**  Dhagax Khoure lies about 90 minutes' drive from Hargeisa, allowing for at least three roadblock stops before you reach the junction. It is accessible only by **private vehicle**, and although 4x4 is recommended it's usually possible to get through in an ordinary saloon car, at least in the dry season. It's advisable to travel with a recognised operator, although you could presumably broker a cheaper deal with one of the **taxis** that operate between Hargeisa and Tog Wajaale or Borama, assuming the driver knows the way or that you're prepared to try to direct him. As far as we can ascertain, an SPU escort is technically required to accompany you on a visit Dhagax Khoure, but it seems unlikely that this would be enforced by roadblocks on this side of Hargeisa, since they are already accustomed to travellers without SPU protection heading to the Ethiopian border.

To get to Dhagax Khoure from Hargeisa, follow the surfaced Borama road out past the first roadblock for 27.5km (N 9°39.609, E 43°47.787; if you arrive at the village of Arabsiyo then you've gone 4km too far). Here, you must turn right onto an unclear and unmarked sandy track that runs in a broadly northerly direction for 5km, after which the conspicuous ragged outline of the rocky hills surrounding Dhagax Khoure are visible to the left. Depending on which of several criss-crossing tracks you follow from this point, it's another 12–15km to the car park below the site (N 9°43.695, E 43°51.949). There is no formal entrance gate or signpost to indicate you've arrived, and it may take a few minutes to locate the caretaker, who lives nearby and can show you all the key panels, but will expect a tip (around US$5–10 feels about right).

**What to see**  Two particular panels stand out: the evocatively named **Got Libah** ('House of the Lion'), where a montage of superimposed cows is depicted in several different styles, presumably painted over a period of many years, and the more prosaically titled **Shelter One**, which contains a more stylistically cohesive ensemble of 68 cows and 156 human figures spread over an area of perhaps 10m$^2$. Close to the base of the hill is a mysterious **tomb** of unknown vintage, which can be entered through a narrow crack at the base of a hollow rock. A moderately tall person can actually stand up inside the tomb.

Antiquities aside, Dhagax Khoure lies in a striking landscape of balancing boulders that recalls the Valley of Marvels (near Jijiga, in eastern Ethiopia), and the area is reputedly earmarked for national park status. It certainly seems to hold

10

a fair amount of wildlife, most visibly gerenuk and dik-dik on the plains, and rock hyraxes and gaudy agama lizards in the hills. It may also be that other lesser-known (or just lesser) rock art sites exist in the surrounding area: indeed, one local source mentioned that more than 35 panels are dotted around nearby.

**GEBILEY AND DHAGAX MARODI** The most accessible rock art site in Somaliland, Dhagax Marodi lies within walking distance of the small town of Gebiley, which straddles the road to Borama and Tog Wajaale, 20km west of the Dhagax Khoure turn-off. Despite its name (*marodi* means 'elephant'), the site comprises a single engraving of a cow, perhaps 1.5m tall, on a flat rock face situated less than 3km north of the main road. A photograph taken in the 1990s shows the prehistoric engraving was in pristine condition back then, but unfortunately it has since been defaced by graffiti etched in 2000 and again in 2008 (yes, the dolts responsible thoughtfully dated their handiwork) and is now almost unrecognisable.

**Practicalities** In its favour, Dhagax Marodi can easily be visited in a **private car** in conjunction with Dhagax Khoure (see above), or on foot by hopping off a **shared taxi** between Hargeisa and Tog Wajaale, and then walking the last 3km to the site (assuming that the local police allow it). To get here from the main road, turn north at the main junction in Gebiley (about 50m west of the Asker Hotel) and follow this road for 1km, passing the police station to your left *en route*, until you reach the school. The road forks in front of the school; stick to the right and keep going for another 1km, and then turn right onto the 200m footpath that leads to the engraved rock (N 9°42.882, E 43°38.647).

You'd be unlikely to stay in Gebiley out of choice, but it is an option if you arrive late in the day from the border on public transport. Unfortunately, the once popular Asker Hotel currently functions as a restaurant only, and then not very convincingly, but there is talk of renovating and re-opening the rooms in the near future. Until that happens, the unsignposted **Werrer Hotel**, around the corner from the police station and opposite the Salahu-Diin Institute, is the only option in town, with the solitary merit of affordability (a very basic single room costs US$3). There are a couple of decent local eateries on the main road, and shared taxis to or from Hargeisa, Borama and Tog Wajaale leave from opposite the police station.

# TOG WAJAALE

The only legal overland crossing point from Ethiopia, Tog Wajaale is the name shared by a pair of small, rundown and uninspiring towns that flank the Wajaale River, the shallow *wadi* that delineates Somaliland's most important international border. Dry for most of the year, the river can create havoc when it goes into flood, something that happened most recently in April 2009 following three days of solid rain. An estimated 6,000 head of livestock, weakened by long months of drought, perished in the waters, which also destroyed hundreds of homes, and swept away the road bridge that connected the two towns.

**GETTING THERE AND AWAY** For those coming from Ethiopia, transport as far as Jijiga is covered in *Chapter 11*. Once in Jijiga, a steady stream of buses and minibuses leave from the main bus station, about 1km east of the town centre. The drive to Tog Wajaale, around 50km on a good tarmacked road, takes up to 90 minutes, depending on the age of the engine and the regularity of the roadblocks. Tickets should cost US$1.50–2 per person, but tourists are frequently overcharged and will

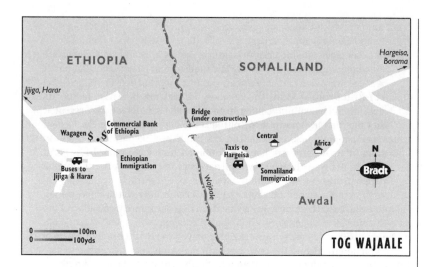

TOG WAJAALE

be expected to pay something to the luggage loaders. In Tog Wajaale, buses from and to Jijiga leave from the small bus station on a back road more or less opposite the banks and immigration offices.

Coming from Hargeisa to Tog Wajaale, you follow the excellent surfaced Borama road for about 70km as far as Kalabaydh, then head south along a criss-crossing network of sandy tracks for another 20km to the border. This last stretch drives well enough in dry weather, but it looks like it could get pretty treacherous after rain. Transport is in **shared taxis** that leave Hargeisa from the taxi park next to Gobinoor Market, downhill from Radio Hargeisa. Those in Tog Wajaale leave from right in front of the immigration office. The ride usually takes up to two hours, and costs around US$6 per person plus maybe US$1 extra for luggage, although overcharging is commonplace. Seating arrangements are two passengers in the front next to the driver, four in the back seat, and if it is a station wagon, three more facing backwards in the boot. If you don't feel like being crammed in, or waiting for the vehicle to fill up, expect to pay around US$40 for a private hire.

**BORDER FORMALITIES** This is a quiet border post by any standards, and the limited formalities are dealt with quickly and in a straightforward manner, assuming that your papers are in order. This essentially means that you need a valid visa stamped in your passport to enter either country. The Ethiopian immigration office is perhaps 100m from the bus station – it's not signposted but is easy to find, sandwiched as it is between the town's only two banks. From here it is a 200m walk to the *wadi* (riverbed) that forms the actual border, and another 100m through the taxi park to the Somaliland border post, with its gleaming new computers and friendly English-speaking officials. Note that the international bridge across the *wadi* was still being rebuilt in mid-2011, so crossing between the countries could be problematic after heavy rain.

**WHAT TO SEE** There isn't much to Tog Wajaale other than its immigration offices, and with luck you'll be in one side and out the other in an hour or so. If you feel like exploring, however, the Ethiopian side of town has two banks and a busy little market, while its Somaliland counterpart is moderately larger, and boasts at least two basic crash pads (the **Africa Hotel**, about 300m past the border, looks

The clay plains around Tog Wajaale are the type locality of Archer's lark (*Heteromirafra archeri*), a 'Critically Endangered' Somali endemic that hasn't been recorded with certainty since it was first collected here in 1922. Several recent attempts to locate this relatively nondescript bird have failed, the most recent being a three-day expedition in 2010, which also reported back that the tiny known range of the lark is now overrun with *Parthenium hysterophorus*, a noxious American invasive. Based on this, there is reason to fear that Archer's lark has the unwanted distinction of being the first bird species in mainland Africa to have become extinct after it became known to science.

All of this assumes, however, that *H. archeri* is indeed a distinct species. An equally credible possibility is that it is a disjunct Somali population of the Sidamo lark *H. sidamoensis*, an Ethiopian endemic whose limited range lies about 600km further southwest. Either way, given that these two 'Critically Endangered' larks are the only species in the genus known from the region, a series of sightings and photographs of what looked to be a *Heteromirafra* lark in the vicinity of Jijiga prompted a Birdlife International expedition to the area in May 2011. This expedition confirmed the presence of a *Heteromirafra* of as yet uncertain species, pending the results of genetic analysis. This has to be cause for optimism: either Archer's lark is alive and well on the Ethiopian side of the border, or it and the Sidamo lark represent a single species that is evidently more widely distributed than previously suspected.

marginally the best bet, should you arrive too late to move on, but the **Central Hotel** might also be worth a try). The Somaliland side of town also has the greater cyberspace presence, in the form of www.wajaale.com, with its eyebrow-convulsing motto, 'City of Wajaale: where the business deals are done'. Otherwise, for those arriving in Somaliland, the riverine scrub lining the *wadi* provides a dramatic introduction to the widespread phenomenon of thorn trees draped with hundreds of disused plastic bags (litter-consciousness here is very low, compared even with Ethiopia).

## BORAMA

The third-largest town in Somaliland, with a population of 300,000, Borama is the capital of Awdal Province. It is set at an altitude of 1,450m amid relatively fertile hills 110km west of Hargeisa and a mere 1km from the international boundary with Ethiopia (note, however, that there is no border crossing here). The few tourists who pass through are mostly making their way between Hargeisa and the port of Zeila or the neighbouring country of Djibouti, and stopping here overnight can feel like an attractive way to break up an arduous trip. The focal point of Borama, as with most Somali towns, is the sprawling **market** area, which is not quite as large as its counterpart in Hargeisa but is still fun to browse.

Referring to Borama as a student town might raise unrealistic expectations about its nightlife. Nevertheless, Amoud University – Somaliland's oldest post-independence institute of higher education, inaugurated in November 1998 and now reputedly ranked among Africa's top 100 universities – is cloistered in the Amoud Valley, 4km east of the town centre, and most of its 1,500 students

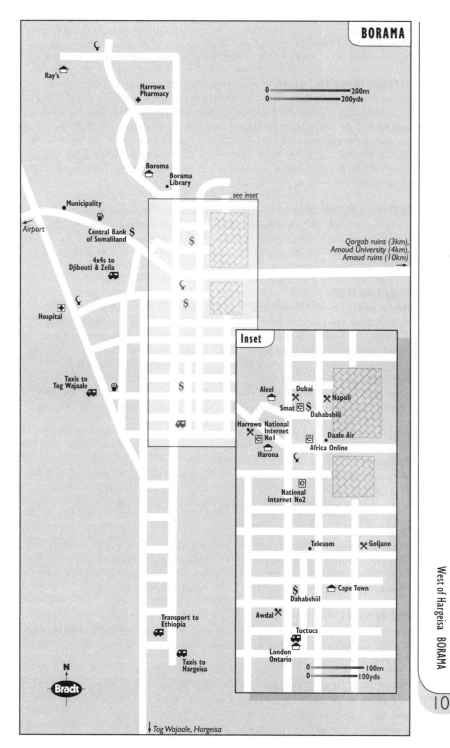

Ray's

Harrowa
Pharmacy

0 —————— 200m
0 —————— 200yds

Boroma

Borama
Library

see inset

Municipality

Airport

Central Bank
of Somaliland $

Qorgab ruins (3km),
Amoud University (4km),
Amoud ruins (10km) →

4x4s to
Djibouti & Zeila

$

Hospital

$

**Inset**

Taxis to
Tog Wajaale

$

Aleel      Dubai
                    ✕ Napoli
    Smat ⓔ $
        Dahabshiil

Harrowo National
✕   Internet
    No1        ⓔ Daalo Air
    ⓔ        Africa Online
Harona      ç

$

National
Internet No2

Telesom      ✕ Goljano

$      ⌂ Cape Town
Dahabshiil

Awdal ✕

Transport to
Ethiopia

Tuctucs

London
Ontario

0 —————— 100m
0 —————— 100yds

N

**Bradt**

Taxis to
Hargeisa

↓ Tog Wajaale, Hargeisa

10

are based in town during term time. Also situated outside of town are the ruined Islamic cities of Qorgab, Amoud and Abasa, relics of an ancient trade route that once connected the port of Zeila to the Ethiopian citadel of Harar via Borama.

**GETTING THERE AND AWAY** The main road from Hargeisa to Borama is tarmacked for the first 80km, as far as Dilla, but the last 30km is unsurfaced and rather rough going. Allowing for roadblocks, expect the trip to take up to two hours in a **private vehicle** and an hour longer by **shared taxi** (US$5 per person). Shared taxis leave Hargeisa from the taxi park next to Gobinoor Market, and leave Borama from the small taxi park near where the tar ends at the southern end of town. There are also direct taxis to Tog Wajaale, leaving from just south of the hospital, while **4x4s** to Zeila and Djibouti depart from the open square south of the Central Bank of Somaliland.

**GETTING AROUND** Borama is a small town and most places of interest lie within ten minutes' **walk** of each other. However, if needed, **tuctucs** can be picked up at a rank next to the London Ontario Hotel. For trips further afield – for instance to the Amoud ruins – you'll need to cut a deal with one of the taxis that normally ply the Hargeisa road.

 **WHERE TO STAY**
## Moderate
**Ray's Hotel** (20 rooms) ✆614370, 350313; m 445 6553; e service@rayshotel.com, rays_hotel@hotmail.com; www.rayshotel.com. Situated on the outskirts of town, around 500m north of the main intersection, this is the smartest & most pleasant hotel in Borama, & the one place where you are likely to meet other foreigners after hours. The rooms are freshly painted & clean, & they all come with en-suite hot shower, TV & telephone. Other facilities include free Wi-Fi, a pleasant garden &, an important factor if the 17.30 curfew is enforced, a restaurant serving a varied selection of international dishes (including chicken, a rarity in Somaliland) in the US$3–6 range. *Sgls (which actually have a dbl bed) US$20, dbls (with twin bed) US$25 & suites US$30.*

## Budget
**London Ontario Hotel** (15 rooms) ✆614469. The very central 3-storey hotel has a variety of large clean rooms, most of which are en suite with a hot shower. *US$5 for a sgl (with dbl bed), US$10 for a dbl (twin bed) or US$22 for a family room with a bath.*

## Shoestring
**Nasimo Hotel** (15 rooms) m 450 5153. This is a clean hotel offering simple rooms with shared showers. *US$4/6/8 sgl/twin/dbl.*
**Boroma Hotel** (27 rooms) ✆613072; m 445 6520; e boromahotel@hotmail.com. This pleasant cheapie, reminiscent of an east African guesthouse, has adequate rooms with nets & shared showers. *US$3/5 sgl/dbl.*

✗ **WHERE TO EAT** The best option is undoubtedly **Ray's Hotel**, although it may not be as convenient for those staying more centrally. Otherwise, the **Goljano Restaurant & Café** is rated as the best of several conspicuous local eateries, and the **Awdal Restaurant** is also worth a try.

**OTHER PRACTICALITIES** Several banks and private moneychangers are dotted around the town centre. There is no shortage of internet cafés in Borama, with at least half a dozen scattered within a block or three of the main intersection. The going rate is around US$1 for 15 minutes.

**Safety** As usual, the situation is ambiguous. Our understanding is that foreigners travelling to Borama technically require SPU protection, even on public transport, but since this is not required if taking a taxi to Tog Wajaale or a 4x4 to Djibouti via Borama, it is questionable whether roadblocks on this side of Hargeisa will make an issue of it. However, if you want to travel without SPU protection it is probably worth playing it safe and asking the Chief of Police in Hargeisa for written permission (see page 90). Once in Borama, exploring the town on foot seems to be permitted during daylight hours, although some hotels may insist you hire an SPU guard to accompany you, and you may be forbidden from leaving the hotel between 17.30 and 07.00.

## WHAT TO SEE
### Ruined towns around Borama
The border area of Awdal is dotted with around a dozen abandoned stone towns, and the main point of archaeological interest around Borama is the trio that lies within a 25km radius of the modern town. Abasa, the best preserved of these three ancient ruins, is also the most remote, situated about 25km north of Borama as the crow flies, and double that distance by road. By contrast, while the Qorgab ruins lie within walking distance of central Borama, and the Amoud ruins are only 10km east of town, neither is likely to convey much to the casual visitor. If you plan on visiting any of these ruins, a local guide will be invaluable, as will a letter of permission from the Tourist Office in Hargeisa.

The precise history and contemporary names of Awdal's ancient settlements is a matter of conjecture since there are few local traditions relating to them, but much can be deduced from the limited excavations that have taken place so far. All three cities are constructed around large central mosques, confirming they post-date the arrival of Islam in the region, and the largest contained upwards of 200 houses with stone walls that originally stood more than 5m tall. Numerous Chinese pottery fragments assignable to the 12th to 15th century Sung and Ming dynasties have been uncovered at these and other more remote sites of a similar type, while other findings demonstrate direct or indirect medieval trade links with India and Mediterranean Europe. Several 15th and 16th-century Egyptian coins have also been uncovered.

All of this strongly suggests that these ruined towns flourished as waypoints along a trade route that connected Zeila to Harar from medieval times until 1655, after which the Adal Sultanate fell into decline and Oromo expansion isolated Harar from the coast. Exactly when the likes of Amoud and Abasa were abandoned is unknown, but the substantial ruins that still remained at these sites until the 1930s are now greatly diminished in size and impact, largely due to locals having removed the old stones for reuse as house-building material.

**Qorgab ruins** Only 3km southeast of the main intersection in Borama, the ruined city of Qorgab (also known as Qoorgaab; N 9°55.722, E 43°11.898) pre-dates its present-day counterpart by three or four centuries. Several interesting discoveries were made during early excavations at the site, among them a rounded copper bar measuring 10cm long and a roughly made oval pottery lamp. Unfortunately, though, there isn't much to see today, and you'd need an archaeologist's eye and artist's imagination to extract much from the surviving house foundations and old rows of stones that presumably once demarcated roads.

In their favour, however, the ruins are very easy to get to from Borama. Follow the Amoud road east from the main intersection for about 500m, then turn right onto a network of rough side roads that slope downwards to a normally dry watercourse on the town's outskirts. Follow the vehicular track that runs through the watercourse, emerging on the south bank alongside a cemetery of stone cairns and metre-high grave markers that we were (somewhat improbably) told are pre-Christian. What little of the ruined city remains, lies on the slopes of Bur Qorgab, the hillock to your right, no more than 500m from the watercourse.

**Amoud ruins** Situated at an altitude of 1,475m, some 10km southeast of Borama, the ruined city of Amoud (also known as Amud; N 9°55.632, E 43°14.969) extends over 10ha of rocky slopes overlooking the Amoud Valley, close to the eponymous watercourse and university. As with other stone towns in Awdal, Amoud appears to have thrived as a trade centre in medieval times, but some sources indicate it might be a lot older than this. The town is also the burial place of several important Somali religious leaders, including its namesake Saint Amud, and it remained an important pilgrimage site well into the 20th century.

Photographs from the 1930s show that the tall stone walls of the city's courtyard houses, complete with triangular niches, were still partially intact at that time, while contemporary excavations unearthed multi-coloured bead jewellery and a wealth of Chinese ceramics. Today, there's barely a wall left standing, just a sprawl of stony mounds where the houses used to be, although you can pick out the shape of several roads and a solitary well. No excavations have been undertaken since the 1930s and very little is known about the people who lived here.

To get some idea of how Amoud looked in its prime, archaeologist GWD Huntingford, who made a tentative study of the site in the 1930s, published the following description entitled *The Town of Amud, Somalia* in Azania XIII:

> The houses are scattered about without any apparent plan; there are no streets and no trace of a surrounding wall. There is a mosque in the southern half of the dwelling area … [with a] rather oddly built mihrab facing the entrance … and immediately to the south … is the cemetery. There are upwards of two hundred houses, all well-built of stone [and] as much as 2.6m in height … The number of rooms ranges from two to four … there is sometimes no sign of an entrance to the inner rooms. This implies that entry was made from the roof, which was doubtless flat and reached by steps now vanished … There are many niches or cupboards in the inner walls.

To get to Amoud, follow the main road out of Borama east along a decent surfaced track that leads after 4km to Amoud University, which comprises a scattering of British colonial and more modern buildings, set in austere grounds flanking a wide (but usually dry) watercourse. From here, a rougher dirt road – just about navigable in a saloon car, at least in dry conditions – crosses the watercourse before ascending to the hilltop ruins.

**Abasa ruins** Abasa (N 10°08.028, E 43°12.998), the most impressive of the ruins around Borama, is accessible by 4x4 only. It's a bone-rattling two-hour drive that entails following the Zeila road northwest, then heading northeast to the village of Bon (or Bown), before taking a rough 15km track to the east.

The ruins here are far better preserved than their counterparts at Amoud, not least because an infestation of exotic cacti has protected the stones from being collected as home-building material. The old city extends over several hectares and the walls of several of the rectangular houses are still partially intact. The main attraction is the old **mosque**, whose handsome arches collapsed as recently as the 1930s. Still standing are several of the original cylindrical and cruciform supporting columns, which stand up to 4m tall.

One of the oldest ports on the east African coast, Zeila (also known as Zayla or Seylac) is set on a narrow sandy mangrove-lined peninsula that protrudes into the shallow island-studded waters of the Gulf of Aden, some 25km southeast of the Djibouti border. Supporting a population of no more than 5,000, the port today is overhung with an aura of sleepy isolation that belies an eventful history stretching back more than 2,000 years. Small and rundown it may be, but the present-day town of Zeila is studded with ruins that date to its medieval heyday as an Islamic mercantile port, including one of the world's oldest mosques. Zeila is also the gateway for boat trips to an offshore archipelago of six small islands, including Sa'ad ad-Din and Aibat, noted for their historic and avian significance. Recently designated as one of Somaliland's two marine national parks, the pristine reefs and islands off Zeila also boast immense potential for snorkelling and diving, and while no suitable facilities for submarine exploration are currently in place, diving trips can be arranged through the dive operation in Berbera (see page 110).

**HISTORY**  It is uncertain what, if any, role was played by Zeila in the earliest recorded maritime trade out of east Africa, as undertaken by the Egyptians during the reign of Queen Hatshepsut approximately 3,500 years ago. However, the port has often been cited, along with Assab in Eritrea, as a probable location for Avalites, a 'small market-town … reached by boats and rafts' described in the *Periplus of the Erythraean Sea*, a unique ancient Greek document that discusses navigational and trading opportunities along the Red Sea and Indian Ocean cAD50 (see page 8).

According to the *Periplus*, 1st century Avalites was inhabited by 'unruly Berbers' who traded locally sourced 'spices, a little ivory, tortoise-shell, and a very little myrrh' for 'flint glass, juice of sour grapes from Diospolis, dressed cloth, wheat, wine and a little tin' imported by Arabian ships. At the time the *Periplus* was written, the Axumite Kingdom (centred on Axum in northern Ethiopia) was entering the most expansive and influential period of its thousand-year existence. It can therefore be assumed not only that the area around Zeila fell within Axumite territory, but also that Avalites, wherever it was located, was one of the empire's key ports.

The presence of what appears to be a ruined Masjid al-Qiblatayn ('Mosque with Two Qiblas') in Zeila has intriguing historical implications. This type of mosque reputedly dates exclusively to a brief transitional period when mosques contained two Qibla niches, one facing Jerusalem and the other Mecca. Locals claim that this is actually the world's second-oldest mosque, a controversial statement that is impossible to verify, but it almost certainly dates to the 7th century. This suggests that Zeila was a very early to convert to Islam, or possibly that it was the ultimate destination for some of the followers of Muhammad, who the Axumite emperor permitted to settle at Negash (Ethiopia) during the prophet's lifetime.

The earliest known mention of Zeila by name is in the *Kitab al-Balden* ('Book of Countries') written in the 9th century AD by geographer al-Yaqubi. The port is also namechecked in al-Masudi's *Muruj al-Dhahab*, penned c935, and almost 50 years later as an important port of embarkation between Ethiopia and Yemen in Ibn Hawqal's *Surat al-'Ard* ('Face of the Earth'). The 13th-century geographer, Ibn Said al-Maghribi, describes Zeila as a large town and important trade centre. By this time, Zeila was the principal port serving Shewa (or Shoa), then the dominant Islamic state in the Ethiopian Highlands (although it would later convert to Christianity). In 1285, the local sheikh Umar Walashma conquered Shewa to consolidate the Sultanate of Ifat, which was based out of Zeila, ruled by the

In November 1854, the explorer Richard Burton spent 'twenty-six quiet, similar, uninteresting days ... of sleep, and pipes, and coffee' in Zeila (which he spelled Zayla), preparing for his pioneering expedition to Harar. He wrote extensively about the port in the first two chapters of his 1856 book *First Footsteps in East Africa*, edited highlights of which are reproduced below.

Zayla [is] about the size of Suez, built for 3,000–4,000 inhabitants, containing a dozen large whitewashed stone houses, and upwards of 200 thatched huts ... The situation is a low and level spit of sand, which high tides make almost an island. There is no harbour: a vessel of 250 tonnes cannot approach within a mile of the landing-place ... The walls, without guns or embrasures, are built, like the houses, of coralline rubble and mud, in places dilapidated. There are five gates ... [and] six mosques, including the Jami, for Friday prayer: these buildings have queer little crenelles on whitewashed walls, and a kind of elevated summer-house to represent the minaret ... Festival prayers are recited near the Saint's Tomb outside the eastern gate... [It] is cooler than Aden, and, the site being open all around, not so unhealthy. Much spare room is enclosed by the town walls: evaporation and nature's scavengers act [as] sewerage ...

It sends caravans northwards to the Danakil, and southwestwards [to Ethiopia]. The exports are valuable – slaves, ivory, hides, honey, antelope horns, clarified butter, and gums: the coast abounds in sponge, coral, and small pearls ... Native craft, large and small ... trade with Berbera, Arabia, and Western India, and are navigated by 'Rajput' or Hindu pilots ... During my residence at Zayla few slaves were imported, owing to the main road having been closed. In former years ... the numbers annually ... varied from 600 to 1,000. The Hajj received as duty one gold '*Kirsh*', or about three-fourths of a dollar, per head.

Provisions at Zayla are cheap ... The general food is mutton, [and] camels' meat, beef, and in winter kid, abound. Fish is rare, and fowls are not commonly eaten ... The people make a sweet cake [from wheat] called *sabaya* ... a favourite dish also is *harisah* – flesh, rice flour, and boiled wheat, all finely pounded and mixed together ... The well is about four miles distant ... all the pits within the walls supply brackish or bitter water, fit only for external use. This is probably the reason why vegetables are unknown ... Flies abound ... Before the monsoon their bite is painful, especially that of the small green species; and there is a red variety ... whose venom, according to the people, causes them to vomit ... The mosquito bites bring on, according to the same authority, deadly fevers ...

[A typical day can] be succinctly depicted. With earliest dawn we arise, thankful to escape from mosquitoes and close air. We repair to the terrace [for] devotions ... At 6am we descend to [a] breakfast ... of sour grain cakes and roast mutton ... we squat on the uncarpeted floor, round a circular stool, eat hard, and never stop to drink ... Then, provided with some sanctified Arabic book, I prepare for the reception of visitors. They come in by dozens – no man having apparently any business to occupy him – doff their slippers at the door, enter wrapped up in their togas, and deposit their spears, point upwards, in the corner ... Generally the assembly is one of the Somal, who talk in their own tongue, laugh, yell, stretch their legs, and lie like cattle upon the floor, smoking the common hookah ... industriously cleaning their teeth with sticks, and eating snuff ... At about 11am, when the fresh water arrives from the wells, the Hajj sends us dinner, mutton stews, of exceeding greasiness, boiled rice, maize cakes, sometimes fish, and generally curds or milk ...

[When] the sun declines ... it is time to ... repair to the terrace for fresh air, or to dress for a walk. Generally our direction is [to] a little mosque of wattle-work: we sit there under the shade, and play a rude form of draughts ... [or] shoot at a mark, throw the javelin, leap, or engage in some gymnastic exercise ... The citizens amuse themselves with the ball ... they are divided into two parties, bachelors and married men; accidents often occur, and no player wears any but the scantiest clothing, otherwise he would retire from the conflict in rags. The victors sing and dance about the town for hours, brandishing their spears, shouting their slogans, boasting of ideal victories ...

We usually find an encampment of Bedouins outside the gate. Their tents are ... low, smoky, and of the rudest construction ... Their huge heads of shock hair, dyed red and dripping with butter, are garnished with a ... long three-pronged comb, a stick, which acts as scratcher ... and sometimes with the ominous ostrich feather, showing that the wearer has 'killed his man'. All wear coarse sandals ... Some of the women would be pretty did they not resemble the men in their scowling, Satanic expression of countenance ... The cantonment is surrounded by asses, camels, and a troop of naked Flibbertigibbets, who dance and jump in astonishment whenever they see me: 'The white man! The white man!' they shriek; 'run away, run away, or we shall be eaten!'

[At] sunset ... the gates are locked and the keys are carried to the Hajj, a vain precaution, when a donkey could clear half a dozen places in the town wall. The call to evening prayer sounds as we enter: none of my companions pray, but ... they have the decency not to appear in public at the hours of devotion. The Somal ... are of a somewhat irreverent turn of mind. When reproached with gambling, and asked why they persist in the forbidden pleasure, they simply answer 'Because we like.' One night ... I was disturbed by ... an elderly lady ... suffering from tooth-ache, and the refrain of her groans was, 'O Allah, may thy teeth ache like mine! O Allah, may thy gums be sore as mine are!' ... The wilder Bedouins will inquire where Allah is to be found...

Our supper, also provided by the hospitable Hajj, is the counterpart of the midday dinner ... [Afterwards] the night breeze and the music of the water come up from the sea [to] alternate with the hyena's laugh, the jackal's cry, and the wild dog's lengthened howl ... At this hour my companions become imaginative and superstitious. One Salimayn [who] read our fortunes in the rosary ... never sent away a questioner with an ill-omened reply, but he also regularly insisted upon the efficacy of sacrifice and almsgiving, which, as they would assuredly be neglected, afforded him an excuse in case of accident ... Then we had a recital of the tales common to Africa, and perhaps to all the world ... [of people who] assume the shapes of lions, hyenas, and leopards ... Individuals having this power were pointed out to me ... at Zayla I was shown a Bedouin ... who notably became a hyena at times, for the purpose of tasting human blood.

Walashma Dynasty, and extended over vast swathes of present-day Somalia and southeast Ethiopia.

The earliest description, indubitably based on his first-hand experience, was penned by Ibn Buttata, who stopped at 'Zeila, the city of the Barbara' in early 1331 *en route* to Kilwa and India, when the Ifat Sultanate was at its peak. Zeila impressed Buttata as a 'large city with a great bazaar' and he noted that it was predominantly inhabited by pastoralists whose 'cattle are camels, and [who] also have sheep which are famed for their fat'. Ibn Buttata also characterised Zeila as, 'the dirtiest, most desolate and smelliest town in the world' and attributed these flaws to 'the quantity of fish and the blood of the camels they butcher in its alleyways'. Buttata was so disgusted at the stench that, despite the rough seas, he spent his only night there aboard his ship.

Ongoing religious tensions and occasional military clashes were a feature of the relationship between Ifat and its Christian neighbours in Ethiopia. Marco Polo, for instance, recounted the story of an Ethiopian bishop who was abducted by an Islamic leader, presumably the Sultan of Ifat at Zeila, while travelling home from Jerusalem, and forcibly circumcised in accordance with Islamic custom before being released back to Ethiopia. However, when not warring with its neighbours, 14th-century Zeila and its cosmopolitan cast of Somali, Afar, Oromo, Arab, Indian and Persian traders prospered by selling frankincense, myrrh, gold, silver, camels, slaves and other goods to passing ships. Religious tensions finally came to a head in 1403, when Emperor Dawit I of Ethiopia invaded Ifat and defeated the Islamic army he described as the 'Enemies of the Lord'. Dawit pursued Sultan Sa'ad ad-Din II to his base in Zeila and had him killed, but the Walashma Dynasty quickly bounced back under the leadership of Sa'ad ad-Din's eldest son Sabr ad-Din II, who is generally credited as the founder of the Adal Sultanate.

Zeila continued to do well during the 15th and 16th centuries, despite being ravaged by the Portuguese in 1517 and again in 1528. The port's subsequent decline is linked largely to an inland power shift, initiated in the 1520s by Ahmed Gragn (who captured almost three-quarters of Ethiopia prior to having his military progress arrested by Portuguese intervention in the 1540s) and completed when Harar was made capital of the Adal Sultanate in 1577. In the late 16th century, trade out of Zeila also suffered as a result of several raids on the town, undertaken by opposing Somali tribes and by the incursion of the Oromo into much of the territory between the port and Harar.

A much-diminished Zeila became a dependency of the Yemeni port of Mocha in 1630, and was nominally incorporated into the Ottoman Empire in 1821, by which time its permanent population had dropped as low as 1,000. The Turks handed it over to the Egyptians in 1874 and, following a series of Anglo-French spats, it was claimed as part of British Somaliland in 1888. Its decline was further exacerbated in the late 19th century by the construction of a railway connecting Addis Ababa and Dire Dawa to the port of Djibouti, only 40km further north as the crow flies. Post-independence, a series of aerial bombardments during the civil war demolished or semi-demolished nearly every standing building in Zeila, and most residents fled to Djibouti or elsewhere. Today, Zeila is a shadow of its former self, and its population of a few thousand eke out a basic living as farmers of fishermen.

**GETTING THERE AND AWAY** A few **4x4s** run daily between Zeila and Hargeisa, usually at night, but be warned that you are looking at a bumpy drive of *at least* 12 hours (it often takes two or three times longer, especially after rains) along a very rough desert track. In Zeila, the place to ask around for transport is the car park between the customs office and the jetty, where vehicles congregate most afternoons before tackling the arduous ride to Hargeisa. From Hargeisa, it's usually

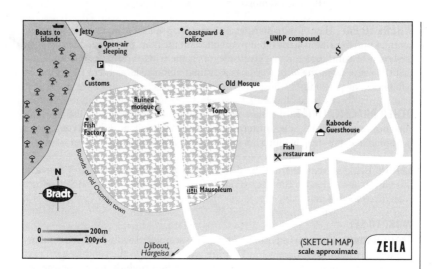

easier to take one of the 4x4s that leave for the Looyada border post from behind Radio Hargeisa (for Djibouti City, see page 155). Either way, expect to pay around US$38 for a cabin seat, US$28 to sit in the boot and less to perch on the roof.

Note that the only place where the journey between Hargeisa and Zeila or Looyada can be broken up reliably is Borama. Elsewhere, an unimposing acacia tree in the middle of the desert with some pieces of cardboard underneath may sometimes function as a bus station, where passengers and merchandise destined for Zeila are unloaded and picked up by a vehicle from that town, but don't count on it.

A tantalising option on paper is to travel along the coast between Zeila and Berbera. In practice, there is little or no public transport headed this way, and the tracks are very rough and unsignposted, but a solid 4x4 should get through in around two days during the dry season although might well be forced to turn back by seasonally flooded rivers after rain. We have also heard of people undertaking this journey on camels, a potentially risky enterprise that will take at last two weeks.

**GETTING AROUND** Zeila is a very small and compact town situated on a land tongue spitting out into the sea, so it's impossible to get lost and you can **walk** everywhere. Easy reference points to use for orientation are the communication towers and the two minarets that dominate the skyline.

**WHERE TO STAY** Prior to the opening of the guesthouse, the only option was to bunk down in the open air on one of the beds at the **customs** area for just US$1. These beds lie under a roof (offering daytime shelter from the baking sun) and remain a good safe bet for those trying to save some money before heading to super-expensive Djibouti.

**⌂Kaboode Guesthouse** (3 rooms) New (it opened at the end of 2010) but already dilapidated, the only guesthouse in Zeila is overpriced compared to accommodation in other regions of Somaliland. After the hellish ride from Hargeisa, however, the bare rooms, each with a couple of beds & a fan, will look like heaven! Other facilities are limited to a shared bucket shower & toilet, a pleasant private courtyard strewn with shells, & a 05.00 wake-up call provided by the mosque right across the street. The owner of the guesthouse is a good source of information about the region. *US$10/20/21 sgl/dbl/trpl.*

**✕ WHERE TO EAT** There is a scattering of small restaurants and eateries in the town centre. One of them, unnamed but pinpointed on the map, prepares and serves the fresh fish of your choice – just go inside, open the fridge and pick one out. Note that the water from the local wells has a distinctly brackish tang, but it's reputedly safe to drink.

**OTHER PRACTICALITIES** There are no moneychangers, but there is a bank where you could try your luck. Shop owners readily accept US dollars and give you change in Somaliland shillings. No internet services were available at the time of writing.

**Safety** Being so remote from the disputed borders with Puntland and Somalia, this part of Somaliland is considered very safe and as far as we know no SPU escort is required to visit it.

## WHAT TO SEE
**Around town** The most important sights are the scarce and badly damaged **remains of the city** from the Ottoman Era. They are concentrated in the southwestern part of town and, although some of them are now used as a rubbish dump, they are an evocative reminder of the more prosperous times this town has known.

There are two old **mosques** in the town centre. The Masjid al-Qiblatayn, the older of the two that possibly dates to Muhammad's lifetime, is almost completely in ruins, with only one of the original two *qiblas* and the floor plan still intact. The other mosque, which is about 200 years old, is still in use. Further on, there is a big **mausoleum** in the southern part of the town and a nondescript tomb situated right in the centre.

Even if you're not planning to go to the islands, you may want to visit the active little **harbour** to absorb the peculiar atmosphere and enjoy the views out over the tidal flood plains, the ocean and the surrounding mangrove forests. By far the best viewpoint over the mangroves is right next to the fish factory on the outskirts of town.

**The Islands** Just off the coast of Zeila is an archipelago of six islands, blessed with sandy beaches, mangrove forests and an incredible underwater world whose limitless, but largely unrealised, potential for snorkelling and diving might gain greater recognition now that the area is set aside as an official marine park (see page 114). The largest and best-known of the islands is the 540ha **Sa'ad ad-Din** (also known as Sada Din or Jasiira Sacaada Diin), named after the Sultan of Ifat who was killed here by the Ethiopian army in 1403. The island is still sometimes visited as a shrine to the martyred sultan and, while it is no longer inhabited, the floor plan of several ruined houses, probably of a similar vintage to Amud and Abasa, can still be discerned. Together with the smaller **Aibat** island (also known as Jasiira Ceebaad), Sa'ad ad-Din is listed as an 'Important Bird Area' for its significant breeding populations of crab plover, white-eyed gull and bridled tern.

The best option for serious **underwater exploration** of the islands is the diving centre in Berbera (see page 110). Otherwise, the owner of the Kaboode Guesthouse, who is also district chief of fisheries, is the most trustworthy (although expensive) person to arrange an outing there, which will coat around US$60. It's best to discuss plans with him as soon as you arrive in town, as he has to obtain permission from the Coast Guard and find a soldier to escort you. Make sure you go at high tide to avoid muddy beaches and be aware that no snorkelling equipment is available unless you bring your own. Alternatively, if you can talk your way past the custom officers, you might try to catch a cheaper ride to the islands with one of the private boat owners at the harbour, but be warned, we have heard they can be a little dodgy.

*Callan Cohen & Mike Mills*

A coastal estuary (N 11°27.459, E 43°18.107) surrounded by mangroves offers excellent birding and a chance to see the mangrove warbler, a species recently split from African reed warbler. To reach the best area, turn north onto a track almost exactly 5km east of Looyada border post, and head towards the coast. As well as the mangrove warbler, which is commonly found in mangroves along with the much larger clamorous reed warbler, other estuarine birds include crab plover, Eurasian spoonbill, Kentish plover and Goliath heron.

Typical mangrove birds can also be seen on the offshore islands (see opposite), and the crab plover is common and tame in the degraded mangrove swamp immediately northwest of Zeila town itself.

## GIRIYAD PLAINS

The vast waterless expanse between Borama and Zeila is known locally as Giriyad or Gegriyaad, literally the 'Plain of Death', in reference to the inevitable fate of anybody stranded there without water for a significant period of time. These empty plains are also home to a fair amount of wildlife, including several species unlikely to be seen elsewhere in the country. It's probably the most reliable part of eastern Africa for the massive Arabian bustard (alongside the even larger but far more widespread Kori bustard), certain smaller and less conspicuous species such as greater hoopoe-lark and Red Sea warbler, and it is also the one place in Somaliland where the Somali ostrich – a distinct blue-legged species restricted to the Horn of Africa – is a regular. Mammals include Soemmerring's gazelle and dorcas gazelle, as well as more widespread Somali species such as Salt's dik-dik, Hamadryas baboon and desert warthog.

## LOOYADA

The main border crossing into Djibouti is all but a one-street town, with an immigration office at its westernmost point. The border closes between 12.00 and 16.00 (so the officials can indulge in some *khat* chewing) and the officers have a reputation for corruption: they may ask you to hand over US$20 to smooth the way, but they don't generally take it hard if you refuse to oblige. That aside, the town is full of small restaurants, there is a Dahabshiil office and filling station, and changing money (a combination of US dollars, Somaliland shillings and Djibouti francs) doesn't pose a problem. You can also buy a Somaliland SIM card for your mobile phone here.

**GETTING THERE AND AWAY** Those on direct transport between Hargeisa and Djibouti will pass straight through Looyada in the same vehicle. Coming to or from Zeila, very infrequent **shared taxis** do the one-hour trip to Looyada, charging US$5 per person, or you can hire a **private taxi** for US$30. Taxis from Looyada to Djibouti City are also rather infrequent and cost the same. Note that if you opt for the shared taxi on either leg, it's best to show the driver your fare rather than just saying 'five', otherwise he may think you are offering him 5,000 Djibouti francs (about US$30) to hire the whole car. From the Djibouti side of the border to Djibouti City, a shared taxi shouldn't set you back more than 300 Djibouti francs (less than US$2).

# Overland Routes to Hargeisa From Addis Ababa

A large proportion of visitors to Somaliland arrive there overland, after starting from the Ethiopian capital Addis Ababa, one of the most important international flight hubs on the African continent. From Addis Ababa, there are daily flights and coaches to Jijiga, the capital of Ethiopia's Somali region, situated a mere 75km from the Somaliland border, and about four or five hours by public transport from Hargeisa. For this reason, this Somaliland guidebook includes an introductory chapter to Addis Ababa and the far east of Ethiopia – not only Jijiga, but also the larger towns of Dire Dawa and Harar, both of which are frequently visited *en route* to Somaliland – drawn from the more extensive coverage in the companion guide, Bradt's *Ethiopia*. This chapter is not intended to be a substitute for that guidebook for travellers exploring Ethiopia more extensively, but we do include enough information for travellers using Addis Ababa as a gateway to Somaliland.

## ADDIS ABABA

The world's third-highest capital city, Addis Ababa ('New Flower'), founded and named by Emperor Menelik II in 1887, lies at a temperate altitude of 2,400m in the central Ethiopian Highlands. One of Africa's largest cities, with a population of 3.5 million, it can be overwhelming on first exposure, with beggars, cripples, taxi drivers and hawkers clamouring for your attention, and con artists and pickpockets doing their utmost to divert it. However, it is also a very vibrant and likeable city, far safer than the likes of Nairobi or Johannesburg, and with a character that is singularly and unmistakably Ethiopian. Further in its favour for those using it as a starting point for a visit to Somaliland, it offers plenty of interesting sightseeing, and it is well worth setting aside a couple of days to explore.

### GETTING THERE AND AWAY

**By air** Plenty of international airlines fly between Europe or North America and Addis Ababa, among them the highly regarded national carrier **Ethiopian Airlines** (` 011 661 6161/661 6666/551 2222; www.flyethiopian.com`), **Egypt Air** (` 011 156 4494; www.egyptair.com`), **Kenya Airways** (` 011 551 3018/9; www.kenya-airways.com`), **KLM** (` 011 552 5495; www.klm.com`), **Lufthansa** (` 011 551 5666; www.lufthansa.com`) and **South African Airways** (` 011 553 7880; www.flysaa.com`).

From Addis Ababa, there are two daily domestic flights to Dire Dawa, one of which usually continues on to Jijiga. These are costly when booked internationally

Overland Routes to Hargeisa from Addis Ababa  ADDIS ABABA

11

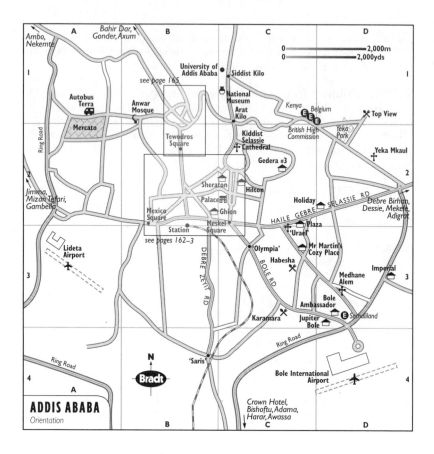

or online (around US$150 one way at the time of writing), but if you're prepared to leave things to the last minute they can be almost half the price when booked in Addis Ababa (around US$48 to Dire Dawa and US$56 to Jijiga one way).

All international and domestic flights land at, or leave from, Bole International Airport, which lies within walking distance of several hotels at the north end of Bole road, only 5km from the city centre. Fixed-fare taxis can be hired in the airport building, and there are also taxis outside. In addition, shared minibuses can whisk you straight from the airport to the Piazza for less than US$1 per head.

**By bus** The best coach services for the far east of Ethiopia are Selam Bus and Sky Bus, both closer in style to a Greyhound-type coach service than a typical African bus. **Selam Bus** [162 D6] (\ *011 554 8800/1; e selam.bus@ethionet.et; www. selambus.com*) has a booking office in front of the central railway station, as well as a theoretical online booking service (we were unable to make it work). The booking office for **Sky Bus** [165 D5] (\ *011 1568080/8585*) is in the popular Itegue Taitu Hotel. Both companies offer a direct daily service in either direction; from Addis Ababa to Dire Dawa (nine hours, US$20), Harar (nine hours, US$20) or Jijiga (12 hours, US$22). All buses leave from Meskel Square at 05.30. Other cheaper bus services cover these routes, leaving from the main Autobus Terra near the Mercato, but they are unreliable and cannot be recommended.

**By rail** The rail service to Dire Dawa and Djibouti was discontinued in 2008. It is unclear when or indeed whether the line will re-open; we'll post any news on our update website http://updates.bradtguides.com/ethiopia.

**GETTING AROUND** Ubiquitous and cheap, **private taxis** cost around US$4 from the Piazza to the city centre or Arat/Siddist Kilo, or US$5–10 from the Piazza to the airport. In addition, an efficient network of cheap **minibuses** services the city from 05.00 to 21.00. A useful minibus route for travellers, described using landmarks favoured by conductors, runs between Bole Airport and the Piazza via Olympia, Meskel Square, the Ambassador Theatre and the post office.

**WHERE TO STAY** Literally hundreds of hotels are scattered around the city, and plenty of choice exists at every level. We list a few established favourites below, but fuller coverage is available in Bradt's guide to Ethiopia.

**Upmarket** Hotels in this range broadly conform to international standards, with facilities such as satellite TV in all rooms, Wi-Fi and a business centre, and they all take Visa.

**Addis Ababa Sheraton** [163 F2] (293 rooms) Taitu St; 011 517 1717; e reservations. addisethiopia@luxurycollection.com; www. sheratonaddis.com. This is the top hotel in Ethiopia, & entering the lavish reception area feels like stepping into a European capital. Rooms & service are immaculate, & facilities include a swimming pool, several restaurants & a business centre. *From US$275 en-suite dbl.*

**Addis Ababa Hilton** [163 H3] (400 rooms) 011 517 0000; e hilton.addis@ethionet.et; www1.hilton.com. Set in large landscaped grounds near the UN headquarters, the long-serving Hilton isn't as plush as the Sheraton, but it remains a popular choice with business travellers. *Rates start at US$250 en-suite dbl.*

**Addis Regency Hotel** (33 rooms) St George Roundabout; 011 155 0000; e info@ addisregency.com; www.addisregencyhotel.com. This highly rated new 4-star hotel is less convenient than others listed in this range, but the facilities are excellent & it's exceptional value. *From US$75 en-suite dbl.*

**Jupiter International Hotel** [163 H4] (144 rooms) 011 552 7333; e jupiter@ ethionet.et; www.jupiterinternationalhotel.com. There are 2 branches of this presentable 4-star hotel, one in the central Kazanchis area, the other on Bole road close to both the airport & the Somaliland Embassy. *From US$90/100 en-suite sgl/dbl.*

## Moderate

**Bole Ambassador Hotel** [158 D3] (52 rooms) Bole road; 011 618 7098/8281; e boleambassadorhotel@ethionet.et; www. boleambassadorhotel.com. This is a very reasonably priced all-suite hotel with excellent facilities. *From US$72 dbl.*

**Ghion Hotel** [163 F5] (190 rooms) Ras Desta Damtew Av; 011 551 3222; e ghion@ ethionet.et; www.ghionhotel.com.et. This long-serving hotel lies in wooded grounds that offer some of the best birdwatching in the city, but are also conveniently central for sampling the city's restaurants & nightlife. Room are a touch rundown but adequate. *From US$70 dbl.*

**Wabe Shebelle Hotel** [162 B5] (72 rooms) Ras Abebe Aregay Av; 011 551 7187; f 011 551 8477; www.wabeshebellehotels.com.et. Another centrally located flagship hotel for a government chain, one represented mostly in the south, the Wabe Shebelle is a decent enough set-up, lacking the lovely gardens of the Ghion. *US$56/74 sgl/dbl.*

**Ras Hotel** [166 C4] (90 rooms) Churchill Av; 011 551 7060; www.ras-hotels.com. With a superb central location, this former government hotel has recently been privatised with most rooms completely refitted & modernised. In spite of the makeover, it doesn't lack for character,

11

**CLIMATE** Contrary to Western myth, much of Ethiopia, including Addis Ababa, is moist, fertile and usually cool for the tropics. The main rainy season runs from June until early October.

**VISA REQUIREMENTS** All visitors require a visa. However, visitors holding passports for the USA, Canada, Mexico, Brazil, New Zealand, Australia, South Africa, China, Japan, Korea, Israel, Russia, the UK and all other European Union countries can buy a one-month single-entry visa upon arrival at Bole International Airport for around US$30. Note that Ethiopian visas *cannot* be bought at overland borders. So, if you plan to return overland from Somaliland to Ethiopia, you will either need a multiple-entry visa (best bought in advance at the Ethiopian Embassy in your home country) or to set aside time to arrange a new single-entry visa in Hargeisa (see box, *Ethiopian visas*, page 91).

**MONEY** The Ethiopian birr is one of the strongest currencies in Africa, with exchange rates in mid-2011 standing at around US$1 = birr 17. Hard currency cash can be exchanged at private foreign-exchange bureaux or at most branches of the Commercial Bank of Ethiopia (CBE) or Dashen Bank, or (most efficient) the branches of the NIB and United Banks in the Hilton Hotel. Visa credit cards are widely accepted at upmarket hotels in Addis Ababa, and can be used to draw local currency at about 30 Dashen Bank ATMs citywide (including one in the Hilton Hotel). It is best not to rely on credit cards outside of Addis Ababa.

**ACCOMMODATION** If you are not too fussy, Ethiopia must have more hotels per capita than any country in Africa, and rooms are very cheap by global standards. Many of these hotels are very basic local places, often clustered around the bus station, and typically asking less than US$5 per room, but

playing host to many a dignitary over the years including former South African President, Nelson Mandela, who stayed here during the 1960s &

now has an entire floor named after him. The patio bar/restaurant is a popular central spot for a rendezvous. *From US$23/26 sgl/dbl.*

## Budget

🏠**Itegue Taitu Hotel** [165 D5] (73 rooms) \011 156 0787; e reservations@taituhotel.com; www.taituhotel.com. Addis Ababa's oldest hotel was constructed in 1907 for the Empress Taitu (wife of Menelik II), only 500m from what was then the main market area & is now the Piazza. Privatised in 1999, it retains much of its original character, & it forms the hub of backpacker activity in Addis Ababa, with a good restaurant, free internet & Wi-Fi, & no discriminatory 'faranji prices'. The best rooms, in the original building, are shabby but very comfortable. *US$10 dbl with shared shower (annex), US$20–35 en-suite dbl; US$50 suite.*

🏠**Holiday Hotel** [158 D2] (25 rooms) Haile Gebre Selassie Rd; \011 661 2181.This stalwart favourite has clean, compact en-suite rooms with satellite TV, friendly helpful staff & a ground-floor restaurant serving good local food. *US$18/20 en-suite sgl/dbl.*

🏠**Hotel Buffet de la Gare** [162 D3] (7 rooms) \011 553 6286–87. This pleasantly timeworn small hotel is tucked away in somewhat neglected green grounds in front of the central railway station. *US$15/20 en-suite sgl/dbl.*

most towns of any substance also have a good choice of smarter hotels offering decent en-suite accommodation starting at around US$15. Genuine upmarket accommodation is rare outside of Addis Ababa and a few main tourist centres.

**FOOD** Coming from elsewhere in Africa, Ethiopia's deliciously spicy food can be a true revelation. The main staple *injera* is a large sour pancake with a foam-rubber texture, usually made from *tef*, a nutty-tasting grain unique to Ethiopia. It is normally eaten by hand with *wat*, a meat or vegetable stew that comes in two varieties: hot red *kai* flavoured with *beriberi* (peppers) or blander *alicha*. The normal dish on fasting days (Wednesday and Friday) is *atkilt bayinetu*, which consists of various dollops of vegetarian *wat* heaped on the *injera*.

**PUBLIC HOLIDAYS** Many shops are closed on these days, as are banks and – crucially for planning purposes – the Somaliland Embassy. The main public holidays are 7 January (Ethiopian Christmas), 19 January (Ethiopian Epiphany), 2 March (Adwa Day), 1 May (International Labour Day), 5 May (Patriots' Victory Day), 28 May (Downfall of the Derg), 11 September (Ethiopian New Year) and 27 September (Meskel). Moveable holidays include the Islamic Eid al-Fitri and Maulid al-Nabi (see *Public holidays*, page 61), as well as Ethiopian Good Friday.

**INTERNET** The state-run Ethionet server has a legal monopoly, which means that all locally hosted email addresses have the same suffix (@ethionet.et). It is generally very slow by international standards, and even by African standards (indeed, internet in Hargeisa is faster). Nevertheless, it is possible to find reliable and cheap internet cafés dotted all around Addis Ababa, and more sparsely distributed in the other towns covered in this chapter.

## Shoestring

🏠**Mr Martin's Cozy Place** [158 C3] (10 rooms) ☎011 663 2611; m 091 088 4585; e coze376@yahoo.com; www.bds-ethiopia.net/cozy-place. This friendly backpacker-oriented hotel is close to the airport & city centre, & the staff are very jacked-up when it comes to travel information for Ethiopia & Somaliland. All rooms share 3 clean bathrooms. *US$10/16/19 sgl/dbl/trpl, or US$23 for a family room with fridge & TV.*

🏠**Baro Hotel** [165 C5] (26 rooms) Muniyem St; ☎011 157 4157/155 9846. This long-serving backpackers' favourite is the shoestring counterpart to the nearby Itegue Taitu. It is safe, & well organised when it comes to practicalities such as changing money, phone calls, internet access, safe luggage storage & 4x4 rental. It is also a good place to hang out if you are looking for a travelling companion to Somaliland. *From US$9/12 sgl/dbl.*

🍴 **WHERE TO EAT AND DRINK** If finding a room in Addis is straightforward, then locating a good meal is even easier. All the hotels listed above serve decent food, and there are plenty of standalone restaurants to choose from, along with a plethora of bars and pastry shops, many of which serve savoury mini-pizzas and spicy hamburgers in addition to coffee, fruit juice, cakes and biscuits. A few established favourites are listed overleaf.

11

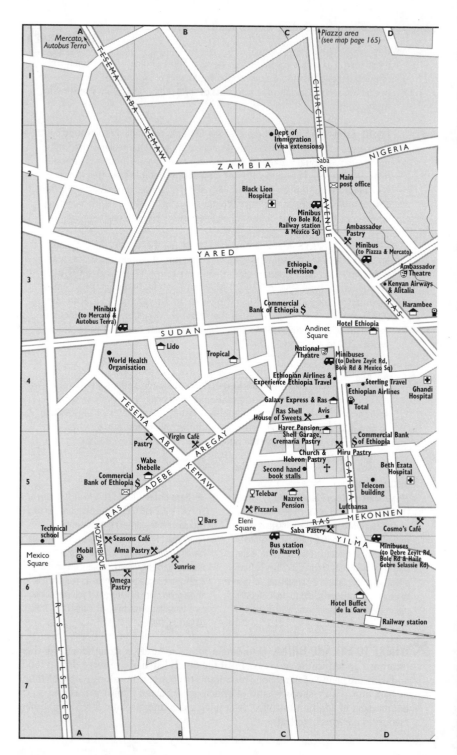

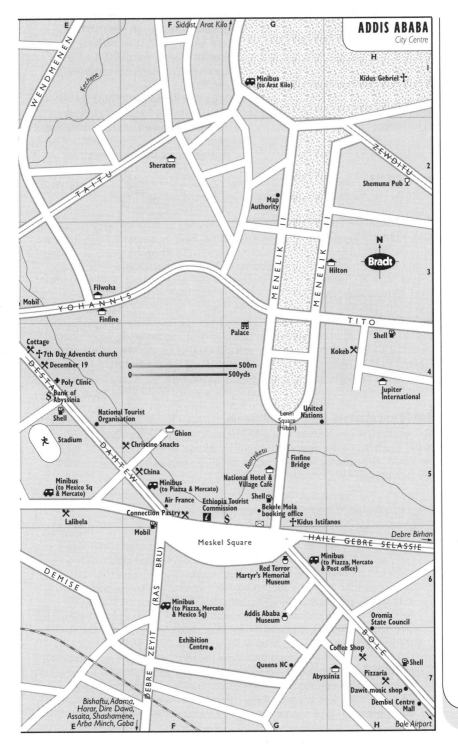

# ADDIS ABABA
## City Centre

Minibus (to Arat Kilo)

Kidus Gebriel ✝

Sheraton

Shemuna Pub ♀

Map Authority

Hilton

**Bradt** N

Filwoha

Mobil

Finfine

Palace

Shell

TITO

Kokeb ✕

Cottage ✕
✝7th Day Adventist church
✕December 19

0 ━━━━━━ 500m
0 ━━━━━━ 500yds

Jupiter International

✚ Poly Clinic

Bank of Abyssinia

Shell

National Tourist Organisation

Ghion

Lenin Square (Hilton)

United Nations

Stadium

✕ Christine Snacks

✕ China

Minibus (to Piazza & Mercato)

Bantiketu

Finfine Bridge

Minibus (to Mexico Sq & Mercato)

Air France

National Hotel & Village Café

Shell

Ethiopia Tourist Commission

Bekele Mola booking office

✕ Lalibela

Connection Pastry ✕

Mobil

✝Kidus Istifanos

Debre Birhan

HAILE GEBRE SELASSIE

Meskel Square

Minibus (to Piazza, Mercato & Post office)

Red Terror Martyr's Memorial Museum

Minibus (to Piazza, Mercato & Mexico Sq)

Addis Ababa Museum

Oromia State Council

Exhibition Centre

Coffee Shop ✕

Shell

Queens NC

Abyssinia

Pizzaria ✕

Dawit music shop

Dembel Centre Mall

Bishoftu, Adama, Harar, Dire Dawa, Assaita, Shashamene, Arba Minch, Goba

Bole Airport

*Overland Routes to Hargeisa from Addis Ababa* **ADDIS ABABA**

11

✕**Castelli's** [165 C5] De Gaulle Sq; ☏011 157 1757/156 3580. Managed by the same Italian family for 50 years, this place specialises in pasta, grills & seafood, with most dishes costing US$6–8.
✕**Cottage Restaurant** [163 E4] Ras Desta Damtew St; ☏011 551 6359. This central Swiss restaurant serves great continental food in the US$4–5 range.

✕**Habesha Restaurant** [158 C3] Off Bole road; ☏011 551 8358. Serves traditional Ethiopian dishes for around US$2–3, & has a beautiful outdoor seating area with live music after 20.00.
✕**Top View Restaurant** [158 D1] ☏011 651 1573/77. Set on the footslopes of the Entoto Mountains, this upmarket restaurant combines a grandstand view of the city centre with excellent Italian-influenced cuisine. Mains from US$5.

**WHAT TO SEE** Addis Ababa is a fascinating city and a few highlights are described briefly below; for more detailed coverage see Bradt's guide to Ethiopia.

## Kiddist Selassie Cathedral [158 C2] Tucked away in a wooded area near Arat Kilo, Kiddist Selassie ('Holy Trinity') Cathedral, built by Emperor Haile Selassie in 1933, is probably the most attractive church in Addis Ababa. It has an Arabic façade, an interior lavishly decorated by ecclesiastical paintings, and is the final resting place of Emperor Haile Selassie, who was interred here on 5 November 2000, 25 years after his death.

## National Museum of Ethiopia [158 C1] On the road connecting Arat Kilo and Siddist Kilo, this superb museum houses several displays on human evolution, including a replica of the 3.5-million-year-old skull of Lucy, discovered in eastern Ethiopia in 1974. Also worth the nominal admission price are several pre-Judaic and pre-Axumite artefacts dating back to the 1st millennium BC, among them a stone statue of a seated female, and a 2m-high throne adorned with engravings of ibex.

## Red Terror Martyrs' Memorial Museum [163 G6] (*www.redterrormartyrs.org*) This worthwhile new museum, next to Meskel Square, is dedicated to the victims of the Red Terror campaign under President Mengistu. Displays include riveting black-and-white photographs dating to the 1975 coup, as well as some chilling relics of the genocidal era that followed.

### THE SOMALILAND EMBASSY IN ADDIS ABABA

Addis Ababa is the site of Somaliland's only proper international embassy [158 D3] (☏ *011 453 4998 or 011 101 0998*; ⏱ *08.30–14.00 Mon–Fri*), which is situated right next to the Namibian Embassy, about 200m from Bole road. To get here from the city centre, walk or catch a shared minibus up Bole road as far as the well-known Saay Cake pastry shop, or rather less celebrated but boldly painted red-and-yellow Assamar Hotel, both of which lie on the left side of the road. The junction to the embassy, clearly signposted, is also on the left, between the pastry shop and the hotel, and the building itself is a few hundred metres along this road, on the right, next to the Namibian Embassy. A visa can usually be issued on the spot, although this may be dependent on the presence of the ambassador, so it is probably safest to plan on an overnight wait, or longer if you arrive in Addis over a weekend or on a public holiday. Two passport photos are required, and the visa costs US$40.

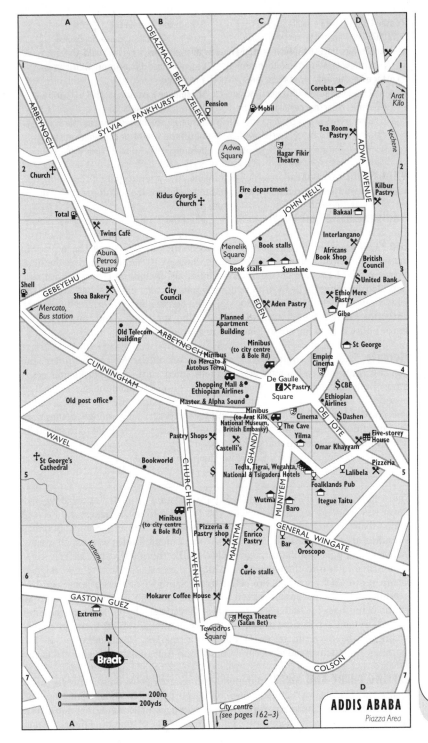

**ADDIS ABABA**

*Piazza Area*

*City centre
(see pages 162–3)*

0 ─── 200m
0 ─── 200yds

**N**

**Bradt**

11

165

**The Piazza**  (see map on page 165) The economic pulse of Addis Ababa prior to the Italian construction of the present-day Mercato in 1938, the Piazza is the most characterful part of the city. Interesting buildings include St George's Cathedral (founded by Menelik in 1896 to commemorate victory over Italy at Adwa), the Itegue Taitu Hotel, the Bank of Abyssinia, the Foalklands Bar (originally a Greek Orthodox church, consecrated c1915), and the sprawling Armenian-style five-storey house next to the Omar Khayyam restaurant.

**Mercato**  [158 A2] Reputedly the largest market on the African continent, the Mercato sprawls across a vast grid of roads lined with stalls, kiosks and small shops. Here, you can buy just about any product known to mankind: the latest local cassettes or CDs; traditional Ethiopian crosses, clothes and other curios; vegetables, spices and pulses; custom-made silver and gold jewellery; and enough *khat* to keep the entire population of Somaliland masticating for a week. Prices are generally negotiable, and be warned that pickpockets are rife.

## DIRE DAWA

The second-largest city in Ethiopia, with a population estimated at 600,000, Dire Dawa was founded in 1902 to service the Franco–Ethiopian railway connecting Addis Ababa to Djibouti. In recent years, it has experienced an economic boom as a result of the secession of Eritrea, and the subsequent border war, which greatly increased the port volume through Djibouti. The (normally dry) Dachata River divides it into two distinct quarters. West of the watercourse, French-designed Kezira, a rare African product of active town planning, consists of a neat grid of tree-lined avenues that emanate from the central square in front of the old railway station (a must-see for students of colonial architecture). The old Muslim quarter of Megala, by contrast, is more organic in shape and mood, with all alleys apparently leading to the colourful bustle of the central market, which is busiest in the morning, and often attended by rural Oromo and Afar traders in traditional garb.

**GETTING THERE AND AWAY** Ethiopian Airlines flies twice daily between Addis Ababa and Dire Dawa (see page 56). The airport, situated about 5km from the city centre, is a large, modern, stinking-hot building with roof fans that don't work because some dolt erected supportive pillars in their line of rotation. **Flights** are met

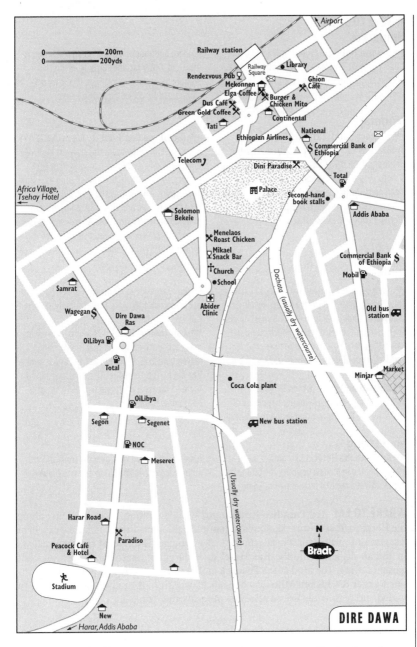

DIRE DAWA

by **charter taxis**, which cost around US$5 to the city centre, as well as by **shared taxis** whose drivers routinely overcharge tourists and aren't very open to negotiation.

The **Sky** and **Selam Bus** both operate daily to Dire Dawa (see page 158). **Minibuses** run back and forth to Harar every ten minutes or so throughout the day, leaving from the old bus station near the market, and taking about one hour in either direction.

**WHERE TO STAY**
## Upmarket
**Samrat Hotel** (58 rooms) ☎025 113 0600; f 025 113 0601. This smart new centrally located hotel is currently Dire Dawa's top hotel. All rooms come with AC, multi-channel satellite TV & modern bathrooms. A good Indian restaurant is attached. Other facilities include an internet station, nightclub & pool. *From US$36 for a standard dbl to US$63 for a luxury suite.*

## Moderate
**Peacock Hotel** (8 rooms) ☎025 111 3968/130 0168; m 091 176 0720. Located next to the stadium, this is one of the best restaurants & cafés in town. The addition of large, faded but clean rooms with queen bed, ceiling fan, TV & en-suite cold shower makes it a great choice. *US$10/15 dbl with shower/bath.*

**Dire Dawa Ras Hotel** (49 rooms) ☎025 111 3255. Recently privatised, this stalwart high-rise is set in a leafy garden with a swimming pool (empty when visited). It was preparing for major renovations when inspected, with old rooms set for a facelift & an additional 39 rooms in a new building under construction. All rooms have fans. *From US$9 for a pokey en-suite sgl with cold shower to US$18 for a suite.*

## Budget
**Tsehay Hotel** (30 rooms) ☎025 111 1023. This friendly place has a huge garden restaurant that serves traditional food, pasta & roast meats. There is a rooftop disco & pub, which might get noisy. *US$6 for a basic room with three-quarter bed & clean en-suite cold shower, US$3.50 with shared facilities.*

**Mekonnen Hotel** (8 rooms) ☎025 111 3348. This long-serving favourite has plenty of character & a historic location facing the railway station. Large, clean rooms with queen bed & fan use cold shared showers. Unfortunately, it's often full. *US$4.50 dbl.*

**Continental Hotel** (24 rooms) One could make too much of the fact that Evelyn Waugh stayed here in its 1930s heyday, but still it's not a bad bet in its price range. All rooms have fans & there's a pleasant courtyard bar. *US$4.50 sgl or US$9 en-suite dbl.*

## Shoestring
**Addis Ababa Hotel** (16 rooms) ☎024 111 3941. Situated in Megala opposite the bridge to Kezira, this is a popular budget haunt. Some rooms have a good view over the *wadi. US$2/3 for an adequate sgl/dbl using a shared shower.*

**WHERE TO EAT** The **Paradiso Restaurant**, set in an atmospheric old house along the Harar road, serves a selection of Italian and Ethiopian dishes, including excellent lasagne and various roast meats, in the US$3–6 range. The **Samrat Hotel** specialises in Indian dishes, while the **Ras Hotel** does decent Western meals in a pleasant garden setting. The food at the **Peacock** and **Tsehay** hotels is also good. The all-in-one **Burger & Chicken Mito**, just one block away from the railway station, serves a varied and reasonably priced selection of meals and drinks.

# HARAR

The world's fourth-holiest Muslim city (after Mecca, Medina and Jerusalem), the walled citadel of Harar is the spiritual heart of Ethiopia's Islamic community. It also has strong historic links to Somaliland, having been connected by trade routes to Zeila and then to Berbera since medieval times. One of the most pleasant cities in Ethiopia, it is lively, friendly and stimulating, with a cultural integrity and aura of lived-in antiquity, complemented by a mild highland climate and fertile surrounds

About 100 traditional Harar houses survive more or less intact, the oldest reputedly built in the 18th century for Emir Yusuf. As viewed from the outside, these houses are unremarkable rectangular blocks occasionally enlivened by an old carved door. But the design of the interiors is totally unique to the town. The ground floor has an open plan and is dominated by a carpet-draped raised area where all social activity takes place. The walls are decorated with small niches and dangling items of crockery, including the famed Harar baskets, some of which are hundreds of years old. Above the main door are grilles from where carpets are hung to indicate there is a daughter of marriageable age in the family. When the carpets come down, newlyweds in Harar take residence in a tiny corner cell, where they spend their first week of wedlock in cramped, isolated revelry, all they might need being passed to them by relatives through a small service window.

renowned for producing high-quality coffee and *khat*. The old walled city retains a strong Islamic character – its 90-odd mosques, many private, are said to form the largest such concentration in the world. By contrast, the new part of town, outside the city walls, is predominantly Christian, although the traditional Oromo are also much in evidence. Despite its prominent role in past Muslim–Christian– Oromo conflicts, Harar today possesses a mood of religious and cultural tolerance, with compulsive *khat*-chewing dominating public life and – surprisingly – a concentration of bars within the old city walls that come close to matching public mosques one-for-one.

**HISTORY** The early days of Harar are shrouded in legend. Its foundation is often attributed to Sultan Abu Bekr Mohammed of the Walashma Dynasty, who relocated here from the Somali port of Zeila in 1520, but Harar is actually much older than this suggests. Harar is mentioned in an early 14th-century manuscript, its oldest mosque was founded in the 12th century, and one local story – more contentiously – claims that it was founded in the 7th century by a contemporary follower of the Prophet Mohammed, who legendarily saw the hill on which it stands as a shining light during his ascent to heaven, and was told by an angel that it was the Mountain of Saints.

In 1525, Ahmed Gragn killed the sultan of Harar, and used the city as the base from which to launch a succession of bloody and destructive raids on the Christian empire of the Ethiopian Highlands. Gragn died in battle in 1543, but the jihad continued, culminating in a 1559 retaliatory attack on Harar led by the Ethiopian emperor Galawdewos, who was killed, and had his head paraded around town on a stake. The tall protective walls that enclose Harar were built in the 1560s to repel attacks from the pagan Oromo, who had taken advantage of the devastating Muslim–Christian conflict to occupy much of southern Ethiopia.

In 1647, Emir Ali Ibn Daud founded a ruling dynasty under which Harar became the most populous and important trade centre in the region. At this time, Muslims only were allowed to enter the walls of Harar, which was the source of more rumour than substance in the Christian world until the arrival of the British explorer Richard Burton, who spent ten anxious days in what he referred to as 'the forbidden city' in 1855. Another famous 19th-century visitor was the French poet Arthur Rimbaud, who moved to Harar in 1880, set himself up as a trader, and was based there until his death in 1891.

Harar's autonomy ended in 1887, when it was captured by the future Emperor Menelik II of Ethiopia. Menelik warded off religious sectarianism by including several members of the old Emir's family in his new administration, which he headed with a Christian governor, Ras Mekonnen (the father of the future Emperor Haile Selassie). Today, Harar plays second fiddle to Dire Dawa commercially, but is still recognised as one of the country's three federal city-states (along with Dire Dawa and Addis Ababa).

**GETTING THERE AND AWAY** Flights from Addis Ababa terminate at Dire Dawa or Jijiga rather than Harar, as do most direct buses to the area, although Sky and Selam Buses (see page 158) both run direct daily services between Addis Ababa and Harar. Dire Dawa and Harar are connected by a regular stream of minibuses taking about one hour in either direction, and there is also plenty of minibus action along the surfaced road between Harar and Jijiga. The bus and minibus station is outside the city walls, close to the Christian Market and the Harar Gate.

## WHERE TO STAY
### Moderate

**Heritage Plaza Hotel** (26 rooms) \025 666 5137; e info@plazahotelharar.com or plaza@ethionet.et; www.plazahotelharar.com. This multi-storey hotel has clean comfortable rooms with a Middle Eastern décor, on-site wells that ensure a constant water supply, & a restaurant offering mains in the US$3–5 range. *US$35/48/53 sgl/dbl/twin.*

**Belayneh Hotel** (22 rooms) \025 666 2030. This popular 4-storey hotel has a convenient location on the fringe of the walled city. The en-suite rooms with hot shower are among the cleanest in town, but suffer from regular water cuts. The rooftop restaurant serves decent local & Western dishes. *US$11/17 sgl/dbl.*

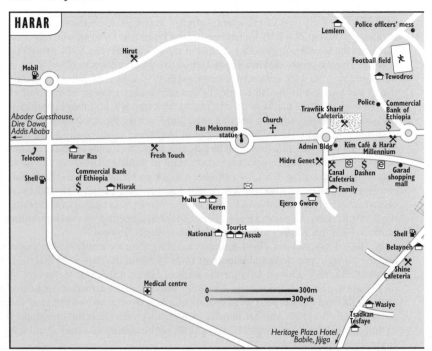

## Budget

🏠 **Tewodros Hotel** (22 rooms) ☎ 025 666 0217. This venerable backpackers' favourite lies just outside the Harar Gate, in an area frequented by hyenas after dark. The ground-floor rooms are dingy so pay extra for a small but clean 1st-floor room, which comes with a three-quarter bed & en-suite cold shower. *US$4.50 (ground floor, shared facilities) or US$9 (1st floor).*

🏠 **Tsadkan Tesfaye Hotel** (24 rooms) ☎ 025 666 1546. This double-storey hotel, a few hundred metres from the bus station along the Jijiga road, is scruffy but decent value. *US$8 en-suite dbl.*

## Shoestring

🏠 **Lemlem Hotel** (13 rooms) ☎ 025 666 1246. This basic lodge near Tewodros Hotel has adequately clean rooms. *US$4 using shared shower, US$4 en suite.*

🏠 **Ejerso Gworo Hotel** (10 rooms) The best of a sordid cluster of hotels in the new part of town near the post office. *US$5 for a large en-suite sgl; US$3/6 sgl/twin with shared shower.*

✖ **WHERE TO EAT AND DRINK** The restaurants at the **Heritage Plaza Hotel** and **Belayneh Hotel** have long, varied menus. The **Fresh Touch Restaurant** along the main road is the current hot spot, featuring pizzas and stir-fry, while the restaurant at the **Tewodros Hotel** has been one of the best in Harar for some years now. The house speciality of roast chicken, which comes with an impressive array of condiments, is popular with both locals and travellers. The pick of the many pastry shops is probably the **Kim Café**, which serves fresh fruit juice, pastries and ice-cream, and also stocks a fair range of imported sweets and biscuits. Harar is well endowed with bars, of which the **Bar Cottage**, with its organic banana-leaf walls, is almost as cosy as the name suggests.

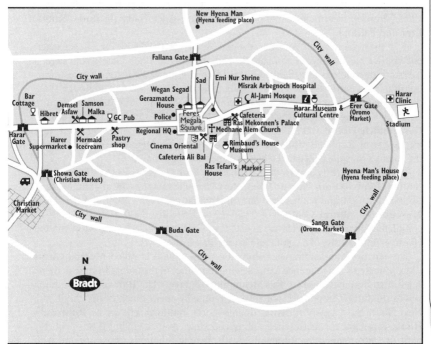

One of Harar's most enduringly popular attractions is its resident hyena men, so-called because they make their living from feeding wild hyenas every night on the outskirts of town. This odd custom probably started in the 1950s, but it is loosely rooted in a much older annual ceremony called Ashura, which takes place on 7 Muhharam (normally 9 July), and dates back to a famine many centuries ago, when the people of Harar decided to feed the hyenas porridge to prevent them from attacking livestock.

A visit to the hyena men is a highlight of Harar. The feeding starts at 19.00, at one of two sites outside the walled city: the shrine of Aw Anser Ahmed (between Erer and Sanga gates) and the Christian slaughterhouse (outside Fallana Gate). The ritual is that the hyena man starts calling the hyenas by name, then, after ten minutes or so, the animals appear from the shadows. Timid at first, the hyenas are soon eating bones passed to them by hand, and the hyena man teases them and even passes them bones from his mouth. It is easiest to arrange to see the hyena men through a guide, which generally costs US$3–6 per person, depending on group size.

**WHAT TO SEE** The old town, known locally as Jugal, extends over 60ha and is enclosed by the 5m-high wall that defined the town's full extent from the 1560s until the Italian occupation of 1936–41. Five traditional gates lie along the 3.5km wall, but the normal first point of entry is the **Harar Gate**, a motor-friendly Haile Selassie-era addition that faces west, opening to the Dire Dawa road. The only pedestrian gate connecting the old and new towns is **Showa Gate**, which adjoins the Christian Market opposite the bus station. The other four gates, running in anticlockwise order from the Showa Gate, are **Buda**, **Sanga**, **Erer** and **Fallana**.

It is most convenient to enter the old town via the Harar or Showa gates, but neither has an impact comparable with arriving at Buda Gate. From here, a labyrinth of cobbled alleys flanked by traditional whitewashed stone houses winds uphill to the central square **Feres Megala** (literally 'Horse Market', although these days *khat* Megala or Peugeot Megala would be more apt), the obvious place to start any walking tour, and the best place to find a guide. Overlooking the square, **Gerazmatch House** was built by Egyptians in the 1870s and later used as a warehouse by Rimbaud, while the **Church of Medhane Alem** was built in 1890 on the site of a mosque constructed by the unpopular Egyptians.

The road that runs east from the square to **Erer Gate** passes the domed 16th-century **Tomb of Emir Nur**, a 19th century Catholic mission, the **al-Jami Mosque** (founded in 1216 and with at least one minaret dating to the 1760s), and the **Harar Museum & Cultural Centre** (⊕ *09.00–12.00 & 14.00–17.00 Mon–Fri*) with its complete replica of an old Harari house. Erer Gate, where Richard Burton entered Harar, is now the site of a colourful Oromo *khat* market.

The narrow lane leading east from the main square is called **Mekina Girgir** ('Machine Road') in reference to the sewing machines of the tailors who work there. A left turn from here leads to **Ras Mekonnen's Palace**, a late 19th-century building where the future Emperor Haile Selassie reputedly spent much of his childhood. Next door, the vaguely Oriental double-storey building known as **Rimbaud's House** is notable for its frescoed ceiling and views over town, but it was probably built in 1908, years after Rimbaud's death. It now functions as a museum, with ground-floor displays about the poet, and a collection of compelling turn-of-the-20th-century photographs of Harar on the first floor.

# JIJIGA

The closest Ethiopian town to Somaliland is Jijiga, which lies 106km east of Harar and 75km west of the border post at Tog Wajaale along a new (and, at the time of writing, excellent) surfaced road. Jijiga has existed by that name at least since 1842, when the explorer WC Barker mentioned it as a stopover along the caravan route between Zeila and Harar. By the time Swayne passed through in 1893, it comprised a stockaded fort with a garrison of 25 men next to a group of wells. Today, it is the capital of Ethiopia's Somali region, and is one the country's fastest-growing towns, with a population estimated at 120,000. Despite this, it is a rather underwhelming place with little going for it other than the vast sprawling market, a few blocks south of the main road, which forms an important trade hub between Ethiopia and Somaliland.

More impressive than Jijiga itself is the drive there from Harar, which passes through the so-called Valley of Marvels, east of the small town of Babile. This scenic valley is renowned for its gravity-defying balancing rock formations, especially Dakata Rock, which appears to be just one puff away from collapse. The rock lies close to the Jijiga road, about 7km past Babile, and if you want to check it out, you can ask any bus travelling from Harar to Jijiga to drop you at the tiny village of Dakata, and ask directions from there. Inhabited by colourful Oromo pastoralists, the Dakata area also hosts a fair bit of wildlife, most visibly warthog and Hamadryas baboon, but various antelope and the occasional lion and hyena are also seen.

**GETTING THERE AND AWAY** If you are interested in Jijiga purely as a springboard to visit Somaliland, Ethiopian Airlines **flies** there daily from Addis Ababa (see page 156). Alternatively, **Selam** and **Sky Bus** (see page 158) both operate direct services from Addis Ababa to Jijiga, passing through but not stopping at Harar. More locally,

---

## ETHIOPIAN CUSTOMS SCAMS

All visitors crossing between Jijiga and Somaliland will be stopped at the Ethiopian customs checkpoint a couple of kilometres before the border. Here, male passengers of all nationalities will be patted down thoroughly (whatever it is they are looking for, women are evidently ill equipped to carry it) and foreigners of both genders will be asked to produce their passports to have their immigration stamps and visas checked. Assuming your passport is in order, and you respond to the officers questions politely, that will almost certainly be the end of it. However, we have heard of travellers being harassed about carrying electronic equipment or foreign currency that wasn't registered upon arrival in Ethiopia, and having to bribe their way out of the situation. Happily, this is far from being an everyday occurrence, but it would make sense to tuck away any electronic gear (camera, iPod, laptop) deep in your luggage or daypack, and to carry a relatively small sum of cash in your pockets. If you do run into problems, being polite but firm is the best approach for making the problem go away, as in reality these rules are very seldom enforced.

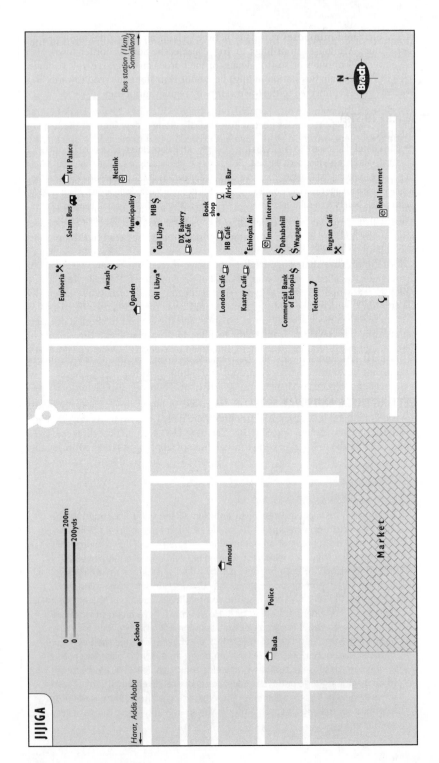

JIJIGA

Harar, Addis Ababa

Bus station (1km), Somaliland

School

Bada

Police

Amoud

Market

Euphoria

Awash $

Ogaden

Oil Libya

London Café

Kaatey Café

Commercial Bank of Ethiopia $

Telecom

KH Palace

Selam Bus

Municipality

Netlink

Oil Libya

MIB $

DX Bakery & Café

Book shop

HB Café

Ethiopia Air

Africa Bar

Imam Internet

Dehabshiil $

Wagagen $

Rugsan Café

Real Internet

200m
200yds

Bradt

N

174

plenty of shared **minibuses** run daily between Harar and Jijiga, taking less than three hours. Minibuses from Jijiga to Tog Wajaale, the Somali border town, also leave every 30 minutes or so (for details of the border crossing, see *Tog Wajaale*, page 142). The main bus station in Jijiga lies about 1km along the road towards Tog Wajaale, and is connected to the town centre by regular minibuses.

## WHERE TO STAY
### Budget

**Bada Hotel** (40 rooms) `025 775 2841`. This family-run place has long been the best hotel in Jijiga, offering comfortable accommodation in large clean rooms with a proper double bed, TV & en-suite hot shower with a 24-hr water supply. The brothers who own it are also a good source of up-to-date information about the border crossing into Somaliland. Good value. *US$15 en-suite dbl.*

**KH Palace Hotel** (25 rooms) This isn't as nice as the similarly priced Bada Hotel, but it has the advantage of also being the terminus for the Selam Bus to & from Addis Ababa, which parks in the adjoining open lot & has its booking office directly opposite. Adequate value. *US$15 en-suite dbl.*

### Shoestring

**Ogaden Hotel** (15 rooms) `025 775 4990`. Situated on the main road through town, this offers a choice of rooms with a three-quarter bed.

A decent restaurant & bar is attached. *US$5 using shared showers or US$8 en suite.*

## WHERE TO EAT
Indisputably the best eatery in town, the affordable **Euphoria Restaurant** has traditional décor, indoor and outdoor seating, a good selection of fish, meat and vegetarian dishes, and a varied bar. There are also plenty of decent snack bars, of which the **DX Bakery & Café** stands out for its breakfast selection, while the remarkably well-stocked **Rugsan Café** wouldn't look out of place in Addis Ababa.

# Appendix I

## LANGUAGE

### SOMALI

Pronunciation of Somali words is generally quite straightforward, but there are a few quirks worth noting:

- Certain consonants are absent entirely from the Somali language, namely f, p, v and z. Many words derived from other languages, such as English or Italian, substitute the p or v with a b – for example pasta becomes baasto.
- Some consonants are pronounced very differently to how they would be in English. X is a more emphatic variation of h, hence the interchangeable spelling of words such as libah/Libaax (lion), while q is pronounced like a more throaty k.
- C is not a true consonant but an h-like vowel modifier used, for instance, in the Somali spelling of place names such as Burao (Burco) and Erigavo (Ceerigaabo).
- Double vowels are widely and rather inconsistently used to denote a more lingering pronunciation than a single vowel. For instance 'oo' is pronounced more like the 'oa' in boat than the 'oo' in boot, whole 'ee' sounds more like the 'ai' in bait than the 'ee' in beet. For other vowels, 'aa' is pronounced like the 'a' in bath, 'ii' like the 'ee' in beet, and 'uu' like the 'oo' in boot.

The introduction to a few Somali words and phrases below should suffice for most short-term visitors. However, those spending longer in the country should get hold of Nicholas Awde's affordable and compact *Somali–English English–Somali Dictionary & Phrasebook* (Hippocrene Books, 1999, 7th printing 2009), while more serious students of the language are pointed to Martin Orwin's highly praised *Colloquial Somali: A Complete Language Course* (Routledge, 1995), which includes detailed audio material.

### Some Somali words and phrases
*Expanded from a vocabulary list compiled by Josephine Heger*

#### Greetings and other courtesies

| | | | |
|---|---|---|---|
| Hello | Hayya (or Nabad) | I am fine | Waa nabad |
| Good morning | Subax wanaagsan | (lit. It is peace.) | |
| Good afternoon | Galab wanaagsan | How are you? | Ma fiicantahay? |
| Good evening | Caweys wanaagsan | (lit. Are you well?) | |
| Good night | Habeen wanaagsan | I am fine | Haa, waan |
| Peace be with you | Assalaamu | (lit. Yes, I am well) | fiicanahay |
| (Islamic greeting) | calaykum | What is your name? | Magacaa? |
| … and peace be | Calaykum | My name is … | Macaygu waa … |
| with you (response | assalaam | | |
| to above) | | | |
| How are you? | Is ka warran! | | |
| (lit. Give news | | | |
| about yourself!) | | | |

## Travel

| | | | |
|---|---|---|---|
| I am going to … | … baan tagayaa | taxi | tagsi |
| Are you going to … ? | … ma tagaysaa? | bicycle | baaskeel |
| I want to go to … | Waxaan rabaa inaan tago … | boat | doonni |
| | | car | gaadhi |
| I would like … | Waxaan doonayaa … | town centre | faras magaale |
| shop | dukaan | road | jid |
| price | sicir | cheap | jubani |
| market | suuq | single room | qol singal ah |
| university | jamaacad | double room | qol laba nafar |
| hotel | hudheel | bathroom | baad |
| guesthouse | guri martiyeed | bed | sariir |
| bus | bas | lock (on door) | handaraab |
| house | guri | key | fure |
| bus stop/station | bas istob/istayshin | | |

## Other words

| | | | |
|---|---|---|---|
| yes | haa | now | imminka |
| no | maya | tomorrow | berri(to) |
| and | iyo | yesterday | shalay(to)/xalay(to) |
| or | ama | closed | xidhan |
| but | laakin | open | furan |
| right | midig | toilets | baytalmayo |
| left | bidix | I | aniga |
| big | weyn | you | adiga |
| small | yar | we | annaga |
| stop | joogso | this | kan |
| pen | qalin(ka) | that | kaas |
| money | lacag(ta) | here | halkan |
| I don't have … | … ma hayo | there | halkaas |
| Another time | Mar kale | help | hayaay |
| Leave me alone! | I dah! | where? | xaggee? |
| Excuse me | Raali ahow | who? | kuma? |
| I am sorry | Waan ka xumahay | when? | goorma? |
| Thanks | Mahadsanid | very | aad |
| Please ... | Fadlan ... | I don't understand | maan fahmin |
| Goodbye | Nabadgelyo | no problem | dhib malaha |
| Stop here (for me) | Halkan ii jooji | | |

## Food

| | | | |
|---|---|---|---|
| breakfast | quraac | onions | basal |
| lunch | qado | tomatoes | tomaando |
| dinner | casho | French bread | roodhi |
| glass/cup | bakeeri/koob | Somali bread | mofo |
| plate | saxan | sugar | sonkor |
| bananas | muus | flour | daqiiq |
| orange | liin macaan | pasta | baasto |
| lime | liin dhanaan | rice | bariis |
| apple | tufaax | samosa | sambuse |
| potato | badhaadho | biscuit | biskit |

| | | | |
|---|---|---|---|
| water | *biyo* | chicken | *digaag* |
| egg | *beed* | fish | *kalluun* |
| pepper | *basbaas* | lamb | *wan* |
| salt | *cusbo* | coffee (with milk) | *bun (caano leh)* |
| chilli pepper | *basbaas* | milk | *caano* |
| spice | *xawaash* | tea | *shaah* |
| sugar | *sonkor* | fruit juice | *casiir* |
| meat | *hilib* | traditional savoury | *soor* |
| beef | *hilib lo'aad* | porridge | |

## Counting

| | | | |
|---|---|---|---|
| 0 | *eber* | 20 | *labaatan* |
| 1 | *kow* | 30 | *soddon* |
| 2 | *laba* | 40 | *afartan* |
| 3 | *saddex* | 50 | *konton* |
| 4 | *afar* | 60 | *lixdan* |
| 5 | *shan* | 70 | *todobataan* |
| 6 | *lix* | 80 | *siddeetan* |
| 7 | *tododa* | 90 | *sahaashan* |
| 8 | *siddeed* | 100 | *boqol* |
| 9 | *sagaal* | 200 | *laba boqol* |
| 10 | *toban* | 1,000 | *kun* |
| 11 | *kow iyo toban* | 1,000,000 | *malyuun* |
| 12 | *laba iyo toban* | | |

## Days of the week

| | | | |
|---|---|---|---|
| Monday | *isniin* | Saturday | *sabti* |
| Tuesday | *salaasa* | Sunday | *axad* |
| Wednesday | *arbaca* | | |
| Thursday | *khamiis* | | |
| Friday | *jimce* | | |

# Appendix 2

## FURTHER READING

Somaliland is not well served by the publishing world, and the limited literature that is widely available is mostly quite specialised and focused on the recent political turmoil in the Somali region as a whole. The list below includes all those books I consulted during the course of researching this guide that might be of interest to the general reader.

### HISTORY AND CULTURE

Abraham, Kinfe *Somali Calling* EIPDD, 2002. Detailed overview of the collapse of the Somali state, with good chapters on Somaliland and Puntland.

Bradbury, Mark *Becoming Somaliland* James Currey, 2008. Probably the most useful starting point to the modern history of Somaliland (and to a lesser extent Somalia), and particularly strong on developments since it declared unilateral independence from Somali in 1991. If you only buy one background work, this should probably be it.

Lewis, Ioan *A Modern History of the Somali* James Currey, 1965, revised, updated & expanded 4th edition 2002. The best one-volume history of the Somali region in print, this excellent introduction to Somalia and Somaliland, as well as Somali parts of Ethiopia and Kenya, is stylistically accessible, well organised, and of manageable length.

Lewis, Ioan *Saints and Somalis: Popular Islam in a Clan-Based Society* Red Sea Press, 1998. A fascinating collection of essays exploring the unique nature of Islam in Somaliland, and providing an excellent background to the saints and clan founders credited with establishing the religion in the Somali interior.

Lewis, Ioan *Understanding Somalia & Somaliland*, Hurst & Company, 2008. Covers similar ground to the same author's *Modern History*, but less formal in style, more concise (the main body of text is just 100 pages) and with greater emphasis on post-1991 developments. Another useful starting point.

Pankhurst, Richard *The Ethiopian Borderlands* Red Sea Press, 1997. Subtitled 'Essays in Regional History from Ancient Times to the End of the 18th Century', this fascinating book sees Pankhurst, the most prolific writer on Ethiopian historical matters, provide a historical overview to those parts of the Horn of Africa that are generally ignored in mainstream texts. It probably includes the most thorough coverage available of the ancient Somali coast and its trade links to Ethiopia,

Reader, John *Africa: A Biography of the Continent* Hamish Hamilton, 1997. This award-winning book, available as a Penguin paperback, provides a compulsively readable introduction to Africa's past, from the formation of the continent to post-independence politics – the ideal starting point for anybody seeking to place their Somaliland experience in a broader African context.

WSP International *Rebuilding Somaliland: Issues & Possibilities* Red Sea Press, 2005. A selection of essays covering similar ground to Bradbury's book listed above, but somewhat more theoretical in its approach, and more likely to interest specialised academics and aid workers than general readers.

### NATURAL HISTORY

Ash, JS & Miskell, JE *Birds of Somalia* Pica Press, 1998. This superb large-format book, a bird atlas rather than a field guide, is the most detailed modern reference to the Somali avifauna, with detailed distribution maps and descriptions of all species recorded in the region, as well as illustrations of a few national and regional endemics. It also contains a useful overview of the region's geology and vegetation. It has been out of print for a few years, but secondhand copies can still be bought through online retailers such as Amazon or eBay, at steep but not (as yet) forbidding prices.

Awale, Ahmed Ibriham *Environment in Crisis: Selected Essays with Focus on Somali Environment* Ponte Invisible 2010. Includes a dozen or so essays on various environmental issues in Somaliland, printed in the original Somali but also translated into English.

Kingdon, Jonathan *The Kingdon Field Guide to African Mammals* Academic Press, 1997, 2nd edition 2003. The most detailed, thorough and up to date of several titles covering the mammals of Africa, this superb book transcends all expectations of a standard field guide. The author, a highly respected biologist, supplements detailed descriptions and good illustrations of all the continent's large mammals with an ecological overview of each species. An essential purchase for anybody with a serious interest in mammal identification – or their natural history.

Redman, N, Stevenson, T & Fanshawe, J *Birds of the Horn of Africa* Helm Field Guides, 2009, 2nd edition 2011. This is the only complete field guide to the Horn of Africa, covering Ethiopia, Eritrea and Djibouti as well as Somalia/Somaliland, and it is truly excellent – a 'must buy' for any visitor with a reasonably serious interest in birds, ideally but not necessarily supplemented by the atlas described above. Make sure you get the second edition, which will include tweaked distribution maps based on range extensions noted by three ornithological visits to Somaliland in 2010.

## MAPS

*International Travel Map to Somalia & Djibouti* ITMB, 2008. The scale and accuracy of this 1:1,700,000 map may leave something to be desired, but as just about the only commercial option in print, it is definitely worth locating.

# Index

Page numbers in **bold** indicate major entries; those in *italic* indicate maps